ROYAL HISTORICAL SOCIETY

STUDIES IN HISTORY

*New Series*

# THE CULTURE OF COMMERCE IN ENGLAND
## 1660–1720

# THE CULTURE OF COMMERCE
# IN ENGLAND
# 1660–1720

*Natasha Glaisyer*

THE ROYAL HISTORICAL SOCIETY
THE BOYDELL PRESS

First published 2006

A Royal Historical Society publication
Published by The Boydell Press
an imprint of Boydell & Brewer Ltd
PO Box 9, Woodbridge, Suffolk IP12 3DF, UK
and of Boydell & Brewer Inc.
668 Mt Hope Avenue, Rochester, NY 14620, USA
website: www.boydellandbrewer.com

ISBN 0 86193 281 1

ISSN 0269-2244

A CIP catalogue record for this book is available
from the British Library

This book is printed on acid-free paper

Printed in Great Britain by
MPG Books Ltd, Bodmin, Cornwall

# Contents

# List of Figures

FOR MY PARENTS

Publication of this volume was aided by a generous grant from the Scouloudi Foundation, in association with the Institute of Historical Research

# Acknowledgements

This book began as a Cambridge PhD thesis which developed out of my undergraduate interests at the University of Canterbury, Christchurch, New Zealand. The thesis was supervised by Mark Goldie and I am extremely grateful to him for all his advice and support throughout the project.

The thesis was undertaken with the very generous financial support of various bodies. My thanks go to the Cambridge Commonwealth Trust for their award of a Prince of Wales Scholarship, the New Zealand Vice-Chancellors' Committee for a William Georgetti Scholarship and the Committee of Vice-Chancellors and Principals of the Universities of the United Kingdom Overseas Research Students Awards Scheme for an award. Grants for specific expenses were also awarded by the Cambridge Historical Society and the managers of the Ellen McArthur Fund. My thanks also go to the Arts and Humanities Research Board for a Research Leave Award which allowed me to complete the book. Publication of the book has been made possible by means of a grant from the Scouloudi Foundation.

I am also very thankful for support from Darwin College, Cambridge, where I was a graduate student, from Peterhouse, Cambridge, where I completed the thesis and began post-doctoral work and from the Department of History and Centre for Eighteenth Century Studies at the University of York, where I finished the book.

I am grateful to the many libraries and archives that have provided assistance with this project and I would like particularly to thank the staff of the Cambridge University Library and the University of York Library. For their invaluable comments I am indebted to Keith Wrightson and Julian Hoppit, my examiners; David Eastwood, Christine Linehan and John Morrill at the Royal Historical Society; the anonymous readers of the manuscript; and members of seminar audiences in Oxford, Cambridge, Reading and London. I would also like to thank Glenn Burgess, Milly Cockayne, Mark Jenner, Matthew Kempshall, Rina Knoeff, Kate Retford, Alex Shepard, Heather Shore, Craig Taylor, Matt Townend, Sarah Waters and Jonathan White for their invaluable suggestions, help and encouragement. Parts of chapter 1 of the book appeared in another form as 'Merchants at the Royal Exchange, 1660–1720', in A. Saunders (ed.), *The Royal Exchange*, London 1997. I am grateful to the London Topographical Society for permission to re-use it here.

This book is dedicated to my parents with thanks for their unstinting love and support.

Natasha Glaisyer

# Abbreviations

| | |
|---|---|
| BH | *Business History* |
| BL | British Library |
| BM | *British Mercury* |
| CIHT | John Houghton, *A Collection for Improvement of Husbandry and Trade* |
| CLRO | Corporation of London Record Office |
| EcHR | *Economic History Review* |
| ECS | *Eighteenth-Century Studies* |
| EHR | *English Historical Review* |
| GL | Guildhall Library |
| HJ | *Historical Journal* |
| HR | *Historical Research* |
| JBS | *Journal of British Studies* |
| JEcH | *Journal of Economic History* |
| JIH | *Journal of Interdisciplinary History* |
| LG | *London Gazette* |
| LJ | *London Journal* |
| LMA | London Metropolitan Archives |
| MCA | Mercers' Company Archives |
| NC | *New-castle Courant* |
| NM | *Northampton Mercury* |
| NottM | *Nottingham Mercury* |
| NRRS | *Notes and Records of the Royal Society of London* |
| ODNB | H. C. G. Matthew and B. Harrison (eds), *Oxford Dictionary of National Biography*, Oxford 2004 |
| P&P | *Past and Present* |
| Pepys | Samuel Pepys, *The diary of Samuel Pepys*, ed. R. Latham and W. Mathews, London 1970–84 |
| PT | *Philosophical Transactions* |
| RHMC | *Revue d'histoire moderne et contemporaine* |
| SH | *Social History* |
| TNA | The National Archives |
| TRHS | *Transactions of the Royal Historical Society* |
| WC | *Weekly Courant* (Nottingham) |
| WPM | *Worcester Post-Man* |
| YM | *York Mercury* |

# Introduction

In late seventeenth- and early eighteenth-century England many people engaged with the culture of commerce. In this book we will see visitors to London enjoying the spectacle of merchants trading in the quadrangle at the Royal Exchange from balconies built for the purpose, we will see readers struggling to come to grips with mercantile arithmetic, preachers standing before merchants hoping for a job in the Levant, and readers in the north of England learning about the stock market from their local newspaper. This is a book about the packaging and portrayal of commerce, and of commercial knowledge, to an audience that included but went beyond merchants. It concerns the late seventeenth and early eighteenth centuries when England experienced rapid commercial development and the beginning of a financial revolution. It is to outlining these changes that we turn first.

## Commercial and financial revolutions

In the last four decades of the late seventeenth century England experienced, in Ralph Davis's words, a 'revolution in trade'.[1] Although England's traditional export – woollen cloth – still dominated the export market at the end of the seventeenth century, there were dramatic developments in the re-export trade in the last decades of the century. Tobacco, sugar, calicoes and other goods were imported in increasing quantities into England and then re-exported to continental Europe. By the turn of the century the re-export trade was worth almost a third of the total trade in exports.[2] This expansion of the re-export market was accompanied by a much higher rate of new investment in commerce than in industry, which allowed, according to Davis, 'the English merchant class . . . to grow rich, to accumulate capital, on middlemen's profits and on the growing shipping industry'.[3] Richard Grassby's finding that there was an increase in real terms in the personal fortunes of members of the London business community at the end of the seventeenth century, especially amongst the richest members, confirms this conclusion.[4] The eighteenth century witnessed the continuation of these trends, and the expansion of the colonial export market, to such an extent

---

[1]  R. Davis, 'English foreign trade, 1660–1700', *EcHR* 2nd ser. vii (1954–5), 162.
[2]  Ibid. table 1, p. 151.
[3]  Ibid. 163.
[4]  R. Grassby, 'The personal wealth of the business community in seventeenth-century England', *EcHR* 2nd ser. xxiii (1970), 226, 230.

that David Hancock claims that the 'export and re-export sector was the most expansive area of Britain's economy and opened up opportunities that were obvious to merchants in the empire'.[5] Although developments in provincial trade should not be underestimated, undoubtedly London's pre-eminent role in the English economy developed unchallenged at least until the third quarter of the eighteenth century.[6]

Alongside these developments in overseas trade and intimately related to them, England witnessed what P. G. M. Dickson has termed a 'financial revolution'.[7] Although Dickson's chronology has been questioned, his central thesis that the financial burden of waging wars effected this transformation has remained unchallenged, and his account forms the foundation upon which most studies in this area have been constructed.[8] England was at war in over half the years from 1688 to 1783. The economic demands of these wars did not go unnoticed by contemporaries; the political arithmetician Charles Davenant observed in 1695: 'the whole Art of War is in a manner reduced to Money'.[9] Military costs dominated public spending and led to the development of public borrowing and the formation of the Bank of England in 1694, heralding the beginning of 'modern finance' which enabled England to pay for wars which cost far more than the income raised from taxes.[10] The national debt was only one side of the story of England's development as a fiscal-military state; the other was an effective tax system. In John Brewer's words, 'the state's ability to borrow was contingent upon the belief among its

---

5   D. Hancock, Citizens of the world: London merchants and the integration of the British Atlantic community, 1735–1785, Cambridge 1995, 29. See also N. F. R. Crafts, British economic growth during the industrial revolution, Oxford 1985; R. Davis 'English foreign trade, 1700–1774', EcHR 2nd ser. xv (1962–3), 285–303; P. Deane and W. A. Cole, British economic growth, 1688–1959: trends and structure, 2nd edn, Cambridge 1967; and J. M. Price, 'What did merchants do? Reflections on British overseas trade, 1660–1790', JEcH xlix (1989), 277–8.

6   On the provinces see, for example, P. G. E. Clemens, 'The rise of Liverpool, 1665–1750', EcHR 2nd ser. xxix (1976), 211–25; D. H. Sacks, The widening gate: Bristol and the Atlantic economy, 1450–1700, Berkeley 1991; and J. E. Williams, 'Whitehaven in the eighteenth century', EcHR 2nd ser. viii (1955–6), 393–404. On London see A. L. Beier and R. Finlay (eds), The making of the metropolis: London, 1500–1700, London 1986; C. J. French, ' "Crowded with traders and a great commerce": London's domination of English overseas trade, 1700–1775', LJ xvii (1992), 27–35; E. A. Wrigley, 'A simple model of London's importance in changing English society and economy, 1650–1750', P&P xxxvii (1967), 44–70; and N. Zahedieh, 'London and the colonial consumer in the late seventeenth century', EcHR 2nd ser. xlvii (1994), 239–61.

7   P. G. M. Dickson, The financial revolution in England: a study in the development of public credit, 1688–1756, London 1967.

8   Henry Roseveare questions the 'abrupt commencement of Dickson's account': The financial revolution, 1660–1760, London 1991, p. vi.

9   [Charles Davenant], An essay upon ways and means of supplying the war, London 1695, 27.

10  R. Ashton, The crown and the money market, 1603–1640, Oxford 1960, 187; Dickson, Financial revolution, 9.

creditors that it had the capacity and determination to meet its payments'.[11] Patrick O'Brien and Philip Hunt in their study of the fiscal state in England over three centuries point towards the multi-faceted nature of these developments which began in the late seventeenth century: 'the transition from a fiscal regime largely dependent on taxes supplemented with Crown estate and other income to a regime armed with the political support, the administrative capacity and fiscal base required to accumulate and service a perpetual debt deserves to be called a financial revolution'.[12] Although the transformation of the financial environment throughout the country continued well into the eighteenth century, substantial change can be observed in the period up to the South Sea Bubble in 1720.[13] During the War of the Spanish Succession, the years 1702–13, when military expenditure was considerable, just over 30 per cent of government expenditure was financed by public loans, and by 1720 less than one tenth of the government debt was unfunded.[14] The trade in the stock of the government's major creditors – the South Sea Company, the East India Company and the Bank of England – was accompanied by investment in other shares, and by 1720 a fully developed stock market, which operated principally in the alleys and coffee-houses around the Royal Exchange, had emerged.[15]

An important repercussion of the financial revolution was the emergence in London of a group of 'moneyed men', many of whom both invested in government securities and were contracted by the government to pay and provision troops.[16] Although craftsmen and civil servants and others did take advantage of the investment opportunities, Dickson found that the majority of investors were merchants and financiers.[17] Among them was a 'group of capitalists of international outlook and connections, and of mixed origins' who were in positions of 'considerable power'.[18]

---

11 J. Brewer, *The sinews of power: war, money and the English state, 1688–1783*, Cambridge, Mass. 1990, 88. For an account of taxation in the late seventeenth and early eighteenth centuries which places developments in their social and political contexts see C. Brooks, 'Taxation, finance and public opinion, 1688–1714', unpubl. PhD thesis, Cambridge 1970, and 'Public finance and political stability: the administration of the land tax, 1688–1720', *HJ* xvii (1974), 281–300.

12 P. O'Brien and P. A. Hunt, 'The rise of a fiscal state in England, 1485–1815', *HR* lxvi (1993), 134.

13 On the provincial dimensions of some of these developments see B. L. Anderson, 'Provincial aspects of the financial revolution of the eighteenth century', *BH* xi (1969), 11–22.

14 Dickson, *Financial revolution*, 10; Brewer, *Sinews of power*, fig. 4.9, 121; B. G. Carruthers, *City of capital: politics and markets in the English financial revolution*, Princeton 1996, fig. 3.3, 81; O'Brien and Hunt, 'Fiscal state', graphs 1 and 2.

15 Dickson, *Financial revolution*, ch. xx; J. Francis, *Chronicles and characters of the Stock Exchange*, London 1849; W. R. Scott, *The constitution and finance of English, Scottish and Irish joint-stock companies to 1720*, Cambridge 1910–12.

16 Brewer, *Sinews of power*, 208.

17 Dickson, *Financial revolution*, 302.

18 Ibid. 265.

Although not a member of this echelon of investors, Samuel Jeake, a merchant from Rye, was amongst those from the provinces who took advantage of the new investment opportunities 'to venture & try to advance my Income'. In 1694, having been 'animated by the Example of the Londoners', he purchased tickets in the Million Adventure and went on to invest in the East India Company, the Bank of England, the Lustring Company and various annuities.[19] Similarly, Peter Briggins, a London hop and honey merchant, keenly observed the changing prices of various stocks at the beginning of the eighteenth century, as regular entries in his diary reveal.[20] These diaries tell the story of an investment culture that the company ledgers, upon which other studies are based, can hide.[21] Indeed, analysis of this type of source suggests that perhaps we should be slightly less confident in the financial revolution's contribution to the formation of a class of moneyed men, and also consider investigating the large number of proxy investments that were being conducted. As Susan Whyman observes in her study of the Verney family: 'when private records are overlaid upon corporate documents, investments by women and provincials emerge . . . [w]ives, cousins, and housekeepers indirectly used new forms of non-landed assets to pay for clothes, maids, and sheer survival'.[22]

A number of other economic developments of this period, some integral to the financial and commercial revolutions, should not be overlooked. Changes on the international economic scene, for example, were signalled by the financial market of London's increasingly close integration with the markets in Amsterdam and Paris in the years up to 1720.[23] The production of business newspapers, although usually omitted in conventional accounts of the history of seventeenth- and eighteenth-century periodical publication, took off in this period, partly in response to the demands for information

[19] Samuel Jeake, *An astrological diary of the seventeenth century: Samuel Jeake of Rye, 1652–1699*, ed. M. Hunter and A. Gregory, Oxford 1988, 232, 233. On the Million Adventure see Scott, *Constitution and finance*, iii. 275–87.

[20] Peter Briggins diary, 1706–8, London, LMA, ACC 1017/2.

[21] K. G. Davies, 'Joint-stock investment in the later seventeenth century', *EcHR* 2nd ser. iv (1952), 296–300; Dickson, *Financial revolution*, 253–337; D. Hancock, ' "Domestic bubbling": eighteenth-century London merchants and individual investment in the funds', *EcHR* 2nd ser. xlvii (1994), 679–702. Admittedly, Dickson does acknowledge that the 'structure of ownership of securities as formally recorded in the stock ledgers of the monied companies and the receipt books and annuity rolls of the Exchequer might be held to be largely a fiction': *Financial revolution*, 251.

[22] S. E. Whyman, 'Land and trade revisited: the case of John Verney, London merchant and baronet, 1660–1720', *LJ* xxii (1997), 25. See also her *Sociability and power in late-Stuart England: the cultural worlds of the Verneys, 1660–1720*, Oxford 1999, 75–6.

[23] L. Neal, 'The integration and efficiency of the London and Amsterdam stock markets in the eighteenth century', *JEcH* xlvii (1987), 97–115; E. S. Schubert, 'Innovations, debts, and bubbles: international integration of financial markets in western Europe, 1688–1720', *JEcH* xlviii (1988), 299–306. See also J. Sperling, 'The international payments mechanism in the seventeenth and eighteenth centuries', *EcHR* 2nd ser. xiv (1961–2), 446–68.

which resulted from and fuelled the commercial and financial revolutions.[24]
To the newspapers that had been produced since early in the seventeenth
century – the bills of entry and commodity price currents – were added, in the
1690s, other specialist serial publications, that listed international exchange
rates and stock prices. Other less specialist newspapers, like John Houghton's
*A Collection for Improvement of Husbandry and Trade* (1692–1703), and the
Sun Fire Office's *British Mercury* (1710–15), presented the same sorts of information to a far wider audience. Texts instructing on becoming a merchant,
and providing commercial information, although already an established
genre by the Restoration, were published in increasing numbers during the
late seventeenth and early eighteenth centuries. The prominence of
commercial publications in this period must also, however, be considered in
the context of contemporary developments in print culture; this period
witnessed an expansion of the reading public, new sites for reading, such as
coffee-houses (and not just in London), and the growth of publishing and
marketing of books.[25]

Other spin-offs from the revolutions were more speculative and were
closely aligned to the emergence of the stock market. The expansion and
increasing sophistication of marine, fire and life insurance, for example, is
exemplified by the establishment of the Sun Fire Office in 1710 and the
Royal Exchange Assurance in 1720.[26] Scholars, like Geoffrey Clark, are
beginning to give a 'cultural twist' to their approaches to the history of insurance in this period.[27] Amongst other speculative projects that were pursued
in this period were lotteries. The 1690s witnessed their rapid take-off, one of

---

[24] J. J. McCusker, 'European bills of entry and marine lists: early commercial publications
and the origins of the business press, I: Introduction', and 'British bills of entry, II: British
marine lists and continental counterparts', *Harvard Library Bulletin* xxxi (1983), 209–55,
316–39; 'The business press in England before 1775', *The Library* 6th ser. viii (1986),
205–31; and 'The early history of "Lloyd's List"', *HR* lxiv (1991), 427–3; J. J. McCusker and
C. Gravesteijn, *The beginnings of commercial and financial journalism: the commodity price
currents, exchange rate currents, and money currents of early modern Europe*, Amsterdam 1991;
L. Neal, 'The rise of a financial press: London and Amsterdam, 1681–1810', *BH* xxx
(1988), 163–78; J. M. Price, 'Notes on some London price-currents, 1667–1715', *EcHR*
2nd ser. vii (1954–5), 240–50.

[25] L. E. Klein, 'Coffee-house civility, 1660–1714: an aspect of post-courtly culture in
England', *Huntington Library Quarterly* lix (1997), 31–51; S. C. A. Pincus, ' "Coffee politicians does create": coffee-houses and Restoration political culture', *Journal of Modern
History* lxvii (1995), 807–34; I. Rivers, 'Introduction', in I. Rivers (ed.), *Books and their
readers in eighteenth-century England*, Leicester 1982.

[26] H. A. L. Cockerell and E. Green, *The British insurance business, 1547–1970: an introduc-
tion and guide to historical records in the United Kingdom*, London 1976; P. G. M. Dickson, *The
Sun Insurance Office, 1710–1960: the history of two and a half centuries of British insurance*,
London 1960; H. E. Raynes, *A history of British insurance*, rev. edn, London 1950; B. E.
Supple, *The Royal Exchange Assurance: a history of British insurance, 1720–1970*, Cambridge
1970.

[27] G. Clark, *Betting on lives: the culture of life insurance in England, 1695–1775*, Manchester
1999.

the most prominent being the Million Adventure in which Jeake invested; a number of these lotteries were organised to raise revenue for the government.[28] Money was not the only prize in many of these schemes, as goods were often sold by lottery.[29] Moreover, developments in credit instruments, in particular the increased usage of inland bills of exchange, were accompanied by changes in associated legal practices.[30] Paper credit became more prevalent and the forms it took more diverse; by the end of the period, private bankers' notes circulated alongside the various Bank of England sealed bills and running-cash notes, as well as lottery tickets and exchequer bills.[31] Such was the enthusiasm generated by these opportunities for 'adventure', especially towards the end of the seventeenth century, that the historian, Christine Macleod, observes the presence of 'a fever of speculation'.[32]

Other economic developments and episodes of this period also need to be outlined here, in particular the problems with the coinage, which came to a head in the 1690s with the recoinage project, as well as the crises surrounding public credit. Precipitated in part by the favourable bullion price of silver compared to the mint price, making the conversion of coin to bullion attractive, and the clipping of the hammered (rather than milled) coins, the recoinage crisis provoked a debate centred on the issue of whether the value of coins was intrinsic, as John Locke argued, or extrinsic, as William Lowndes argued.[33] Richard Temple's response to Locke in 1696 provided a terse summary of both positions:

> That the intrinsick value of Silver is the true Instrument and Measure of Commerce, is partly True and partly False; for the Mony of every Country, and not the Ounce of Silver, or the intrinsick value, is the Instrument and Measure of Commerce there, according to its Denomination, and the Standard of

---

[28] J. Ashton, *A history of English lotteries: now for the first time written*, London 1893, chs iii, iv; C. L'Estrange Ewen, *Lotteries and sweepstakes*, London 1932; R. D. Richards, 'The lottery in the history of English government finance', *Economic History* iii (1934–7), 57–76. On the history of state lotteries for revenue raising see J. Raven, 'The abolition of the English state lotteries', *HJ* xxxiv (1991), 371–89.

[29] An advertisement for a sale of Indian goods by lottery, for example, appears in *CIHT*, 5 Oct. 1694.

[30] J. K. Horsefield, *British monetary experiments, 1650–1710*, Cambridge, Mass. 1960, pp. xii–xiii; J. S. Rogers, *The early history of the law of bills and notes: a study of the origins of Anglo-Amercian commercial law*, Cambridge 1995, ch. v; R. B. Westerfield, *Middlemen in English business: particularly between 1660 and 1760*, New Haven 1915, 389–91.

[31] A. Feavearyear, *The pound sterling: a history of English money*, Oxford 1963, 159.

[32] C. Macleod, 'The 1690s patents boom: invention or stock-jobbing?', *EcHR* 2nd ser. xxxix (1986), 560.

[33] J. O. Appleby, *Economic thought and ideology in seventeenth-century England*, Princeton 1978, ch. viii; Horsefield, *Monetary experiments*, pt 2; M.-H. Li, *The great recoinage of 1696 to 1699*, London 1963; J. Thompson, *Models of value: eighteenth-century political economy and the novel*, Durham, NC 1996, 47–65.

the Coin of each Nation is very different, and does often vary according to Time, Place, and Circumstances.[34]

Of course, this was not a crisis that was only played out in the pages of pamphlets. In May 1696 John Evelyn recorded in his diary the material disruption caused by the recoinage: 'Mony still continuing exceedingly scarcse, so as none was either payed or received, but all on Trust, the mint not supplying sufficient for common necessities'.[35] Furthermore, the deflation subsequent to the recoinage was among a number of factors, including extensive short-term borrowing by the government, that in the late 1690s contributed 'to a crisis of confidence in public credit'.[36]

At other points in this period there were difficulties with public credit which at times led to problems with the ready acceptance and smooth circulation of paper credit. In the middle of 1718, for example, a memoir was prepared for the king which reported on the difficulties with the circulation of paper money:

> That, though paper credit, such as Bank notes, Exchequer bills, and the Government securities for the sixty-five millions . . . do pass in the City of London and will pass while the kingdom is in peace, yet real specie is necessary for the service of the country, where none of these things will be received, either by country gentlemen or the country people, who wish the destruction of the Government, and will therefore never take their paper in payments.[37]

Disruptions to credit were also witnessed in 1720, with the collapse of the market in the shares of the South Sea Company, known as the South Sea Bubble. As the author of *Considerations on the present state of the nation* (1720) wrote: 'no one at this time knows whom to trust for a Remittance of Money, or Goods'.[38] This collapse stimulated extensive contemporary comment from writers, engravers and even the makers of playing-cards.[39]

The sixty-year period which this book considers has been deliberately chosen to pivot around the financial developments which were particularly concentrated in the 1690s, and were epitomised by the formation of the Bank of England in 1694. The boundary dates, 1660 and 1720, are, however, controversial markers of economic change, and caution against treating the narrative of the economic and financial revolutions as an unproblematic

34 Sir Richard Temple, *Some short remarks upon Mr Lock's book*, London 1696, 4.

35 John Evelyn, *The diary of John Evelyn*, ed. E. S. De Beer, Oxford 1955, v. 242.

36 Brewer, *Sinews of power*, 154.

37 Memoir, 17 May 1718, in HMC, *Calendar of the Stuart papers belonging to His Majesty the King, preserved at Windsor Castle*, London 1902–23, vi (1916), 445.

38 *Considerations on the present state of the nation*, London 1720, 18.

39 On the South Sea Bubble see, for example, J. Carswell, *The South Sea Bubble*, London 1960; D. Dabydeen, *Hogarth, Walpole and commercial Britain*, London 1987; and J. T. Klein, 'Satirists and South-Sea baubles in the age of hope and golden mountains', *Southern Review* xiv (1981), 143–54.

backdrop in a cultural-economic history. The Restoration is characterised by some historians, like Charles Wilson, as a critical turning point in the economic history of the century – 'the occasion for economic as well as political renewal' – and yet it is not mentioned in other economic history surveys of the century.[40] The significance of the South Sea Bubble in 1720, which marks the end of this study, is also disputed. Although described by Brewer as the 'one and only occasion on which the whole web of public finance threatened to unravel', and by John Carswell as standing between two epochs, the impact of the bubble on those uninvolved in public finance, and of the Bubble Act on the development of joint-stock companies, has been argued by Julian Hoppit and Ron Harris respectively, to have been minimal.[41] This book in no way sets out to investigate the quantitative and institutional dimensions of the commercial and financial revolutions in England in the late seventeenth and early eighteenth centuries. However, these economic developments are an essential context for this book.

## New directions in economic history

The 'future health' of economic history, argued Donald Coleman in 1987, depends upon 'the breaking down of barriers separating history, economic history, and economics'.[42] The Tillys' call to 'de-economize economic history and re-economize social history', has perhaps begun to be answered, for early modern England at least, in works such as Craig Muldrew's study of credit relations which might be thought of as part of a social history of the market.[43] Certainly a more sophisticated and sensitive pairing of social and economic histories is welcome, but part of the process of de-economising economic history, as scholars have recognised, must involve a closer relationship with literary, cultural and intellectual histories, as well as attempts to cross disciplinary boundaries.

---

[40] C. Wilson, *England's apprenticeship, 1603–1763*, 2nd edn, Harlow 1984, 160, and ch. viii. Donald Coleman provides a useful review of three surveys of early modern economic history in which he notes these contrary treatments of the period: 'Early modern economic history', *EcHR* 2nd ser. xxv (1972), 694.

[41] Brewer, *Sinews of power*, 125; Carswell, *South Sea Bubble*, 272; J. Hoppit, 'Financial crises in eighteenth-century England', *EcHR* 2nd ser. xxxix (1986), 39–58; *Risk and failure in English business, 1700–1800*, Cambridge 1987, 132; and 'The myths of the South Sea Bubble', *TRHS* xii (2002), 141–65; R. Harris, 'The Bubble Act: its passage and its effects on business organization', *JEcH* liv (1994), 610–27.

[42] D. C. Coleman, *History and the economic past: an account of the rise and decline of economic history in Britain*, Oxford 1987, 142.

[43] C. Tilly, L. A. Tilly and R. Tilly, 'European economic and social history in the 1990s', *Journal of European Economic History* xx (1991), 647; C. Muldrew, 'Interpreting the market: the ethics of credit and community relations in early modern England', *SH* xviii (1993), 164, and *The economy of obligation: the culture of credit and social relations in early modern England*, Basingstoke 1998.

Such calls to open up the field of economic history have been particularly encouraged, and interpreted as coming in the wake of the 'new economic history'.[44] Developed in the late 1960s, and typified in the work of Robert Fogel and Douglass North, 'new economic history' reflected perhaps the closest relationship that has existed between economic history and economics in the twentieth century.[45] Coleman laments that with the trend towards quantification of aggregates resulting from this relationship, the 'past has become history without a human face'.[46] If historiographical trends can be partly explained by a rejection of some of what has come before, then it is in response to other sorts of studies as well that new directions are being explored. Until recently, at least for the historical period concentrated on in this book, such topics as the institutional development of bodies like the East India Company and the Bank of England, accounts of contemporary theories of bullion and specie, quantitative analysis of imports, exports and taxes, the economic impact of the navigation acts, and the Scottish dependence on North Sea herring, have received most attention. It must be recognised that it is also in response to these sorts of studies that new directions are being explored.[47]

The trend towards broadening the agenda of economic history, however, cannot be heralded as a completely new departure for the subject. Indeed, economic historians working in the late nineteenth and early twentieth centuries maintained, according to R. M. Hartwell, a

sense of reality about the interdependence of social processes. Economic phenomena, they argued, were obviously so interrelated with other social phenomena that an economics which assumed away other social facts was of little use in explaining economic change . . . [they] clearly recognized the necessity

---

44 B. Supple, 'Old problems and new directions', *JIH* xii (1981), 199–205; P. Temin, 'The future of the new economic history', *JIH* xii (1981), 179–97. For a brief summary of the criticisms levelled at new economic history see D. Cannadine, 'Economic history', in his *The pleasures of the past*, New York 1989, 151.

45 However, as Cipolla discusses, new economic history was the result of an American approach and, although influential in Britain, the attempts of economic historians working in Europe to resolve economic history's relationship with its parent disciplines involved 'loosening their ties with economics': *Between history and economics: an introduction to economic history*, trans. C. Woodall, first published 1988, Oxford 1991, 75. For studies of the practice of economic history in the twentieth century and in particular its ambivalent relationships with history and economics see also Coleman, *History and the economic past*; A. Kadish, *Historians, economists, and economic history*, London 1989; and G. M. Koot, *English historical economics, 1870–1926: the rise of economic history and neomercantilism*, Cambridge 1987, and 'Historians and economists: the study of economic history in Britain ca. 1920–1950', *History of Political Economy* xxv (1993), 641–75.

46 D. C. Coleman, 'History, economic history and the numbers game', *HJ* xxviii (1995), 641. At least one new economic historian has, however, attempted 'to construct a broader analytical approach to history': D. C. North, 'Beyond the new economic history', *JEcH* xxxiv (1974), 3.

47 Tilly, Tilly and Tilly, 'European economic and social history', 645–71.

of incorporating religion, custom, law, politics and other forces which influ-ence behavior into any explanations of economic change.[48]

In answering calls to 'de-economize economic history' by challenging disci-plinary boundaries, scholars have provided reassurance that the discipline need not be in crisis, as it was observed to have been during the late 1980s.[49] Business history 'has not only offered one of the more hopeful avenues of recovery for economic history but', Coleman argues, it 'has also stimulated efforts to bridge the gap between economic history and other sorts of history'.[50] As Martin Daunton, for example, says of his own work on housing in Victorian cities, any 'attempt to separate economic, social, and political history would have produced an incomplete picture'.[51]

Early modernists have already gone some way towards considering these sorts of interdependencies, as will be seen in what follows later in this chapter. At this point, it is worth noting some of the buoyant fields in which scholars are opening up early modern English economic history. Students of the history of consumption have considered economic history in its broadest sense. Many have been stimulated by the seminal work of Neil McKendrick, John Brewer and J. H. Plumb, whose thesis, which situates the birth of consumer society in the late eighteenth century, has been challenged by a number of scholars who now favour accounts in which significant develop-ments are assigned to earlier periods.[52] These recent studies of the history of consumption in Britain, America and parts of Europe have shifted attention away from considering the history of production from the perspective of supply to examining instead the demand for a whole variety of goods, from books to ceramics, from luxury foods to fabrics, and the meanings attached to them and the contexts in which they were consumed. Much of this work pursues interdisciplinary approaches to consider consumption in relation to social hierarchies, gender and aesthetics, among other factors, and can be seen as part of the project to widen the scope of economic history and to explore interdependencies between fields that are usually treated sepa-

---

[48] R. M. Hartwell, 'Good old economic history', *JEcH* xxxiii (1973), 36–7. A prominent example of this type of historian, not discussed by Hartwell, is Eileen Power, a medievalist whose study of economic history was influenced by sociology and anthropology in the inter-war period: M. Berg, *A woman in history: Eileen Power, 1889–1940*, Cambridge 1996, 159–63.

[49] Cipolla, *Between history and economics*, 74. Also relevant here is Martin Daunton's comment that 'the subject is, institutionally at least, in retreat': 'What is economic history . . .?', in J. Gardiner (ed.), *What is history today . . .?*, Basingstoke 1988, 37. Compare to A. K. Cairncross's remark that there is 'some unease and disquiet about the state of the subject': 'In praise of economic history', *EcHR*, 2nd ser. xlii (1989), 183.

[50] Coleman, 'Numbers game', 644.

[51] Daunton, 'What is economic history . . .?', 38.

[52] N. McKendrick, J. Brewer and J. H. Plumb, *The birth of a consumer society: the commer-cialization of eighteenth-century society*, London 1982.

rately.[53] Undoubtedly, the consumption of such luxuries did not occur without comment and was a prominent issue in the luxury debates, which scholars are approaching in ways that also serve to place economic history in wider contexts.[54] Furthermore, recent work in the field of British imperial history reflects a growing awareness of the interdependence of society, politics, culture, science and economics.[55]

Revisionist analysis of the industrial revolution is another striking example of the impact of attempting to bridge the gap between economic history and others sorts of history. Among the prerequisites for the rehabilitation of the notion of an industrial revolution, argue Maxine Berg and Pat Hudson, is the recognition 'that the economic, social, and cultural foundations of an industrial capitalist order rest on much more than conventional measures of industrial or economic performance'.[56] It is within this literature on the industrial revolution, in particular, that scholars have demonstrated that an appreciation of culture, in whatever guise, as part of an approach to economic history, can result in the repositioning of subjects in wider contexts, and the re-evaluation, rejuvenation and reappraisal of whole debates.[57] Economic historians working in many other fields are also turning to various notions of culture as conceptual tools to employ in their studies. In reference to a debate about twentieth-century Japanese and American business practices, for example, Peter Temin advocates, 'greater attention to culture by both economists and historians in the practice of economic history'.[58]

---

53 M. Berg and H. Clifford (eds), *Consumers and luxury: consumer culture in Europe, 1650–1850*, Manchester 1999; A. Bermingham and J. Brewer (eds), *The consumption of culture, 1600–1800: image, object, text*, London 1995; J. Brewer and R. Porter (eds), *Consumption and the world of goods*, London 1993; C. Mukerji, *From graven images: patterns of modern materialism*, New York 1983; C. Shammas, *The pre-industrial consumer in England and America*, Oxford 1990; L. Weatherill, *Consumer behaviour and material culture in Britain, 1660–1760*, London 1988. For reviews see P. Glennie, 'Consumption within historical studies', in D. Miller (ed.), *Acknowledging consumption: a review of new studies*, London 1995, 164–203, and S. Pennell, 'Consumption and consumerism in early modern England', *HJ* xlii (1999), 549–64.

54 C. J. Berry, *The idea of luxury: a conceptual and historical investigation*, Cambridge 1994; J. Sekora, *Luxury: the concept in western thought, Eden to Smollett*, Baltimore 1977.

55 N. Glaisyer, 'Networking: trade and exchange in the eighteenth-century British empire', *HJ* xlvii (2004), 451–76.

56 M. Berg and P. Hudson, 'Rehabilitating the industrial revolution', *EcHR*, 2nd ser. xlv (1992), 44.

57 'One of the strengths of this new interpretation of industrialization is the attention it pays to the social or cultural context of what has traditionally been seen as simply an economic process. Indeed, a focus on cultural change was a point of departure for this new interpretation, for it was through an attempt to explain some of the social anomalies of the traditional Industrial Revolution that scholars realized that industrialization was a process with a much longer and more complex history': J. Smail, 'Manufacturer or artisan? The relationship between economic and cultural change in the early stages of the eighteenth-century industrialization', *Journal of Social History* xxv (1992), 791.

58 P. Temin, 'Is it kosher to talk about culture?', *JEcH* lvii (1997), 267.

Although conceptions of culture are currently reinvigorating various histor-ical fields, it must be noted that the exploration of the relationships between economics and culture is, of course, not without precedent, most notably in the writings of Max Weber.[59]

## The culture of commerce

This book builds upon these projects to reintegrate economic history with history more generally by adopting a cultural approach. The goal is to consider the ways in which commerce was presented and packaged in late seventeenth- and early eighteenth-century England. It aims to look at how the merchant, the trading nation and indeed the trading world were repre-sented visually and in words. Many of these representations were complimen-tary but the book also explores derogatory portrayals and examines tensions between the two. The book also aims to look at how commercial knowledge, whether prices or accounting know-how, circulated, was packaged and consumed. Close attention is paid to the forms the culture of commerce took partly through a sensitivity to genre (whether sermons, ephemera or news-papers, for example) and also in attempts to examine the contexts in which sources were produced and used.

The book is structured around four case studies (introduced in more detail below) which all address topics crucial to the history of the culture of commerce in late seventeenth- and early eighteenth-century England. The first deals with the Royal Exchange, both as a place where merchants gath-ered and negotiated their personal credit, and as an icon of London and the nation's trade. The second examines sermons preached before the Levant Company, and especially the ways in which commerce and merchants were portrayed by those who wished to impress this mercantile audience. The third considers manuals and guides to trading skills and information, and suggests that these manuals, which contained contrary portraits of merchants, were read in various contexts, and not only by merchants. The fourth and final case study is of newspapers and explores the ways in which commercial information (particularly of a numerical kind) circulated and was presented to metropolitan and provincial readers from the middle of the period onwards. Each of these case studies forms a single chapter and can be seen as a contribution to the history of the culture of commerce in this period in its own right.

These studies draw on a very wide range of primary materials from, for example, engravings and woodcuts of the Royal Exchange, produced both as

---

[59] M. Weber, *The Protestant ethic and the spirit of capitalism*, London 1930. On this point more generally see H. A. Innis, 'On the economic significance of culture', *JEcH*, supple-ment iv (1944), 80–97, and T. C. Cochran, 'Cultural factors in economic growth', *JEcH* xx (1960), 515–30.

collectables and as frontispieces to London guide-books, to the clerk of the East India Company's petty cash book. Amongst the printed materials considered are pocket-sized manuals which purported to instruct merchants in bookkeeping and more than 500 issues of a periodical published in the 1690s which listed the price of both bank stock and wheat. Letters written to the editor of the periodical, as well as the minutes of the committee in charge of the management of the Royal Exchange, and letters written home by preachers working for the Levant Company in Smyrna, reveal the range and richness of manuscript material relevant to the questions discussed in this book. This is a deliberately eclectic range of sources, and as will be seen in the chapters that follow it demands attention to be paid to a number of different disciplines.

This book also addresses themes and topics which must be considered within the context of some substantial historiographical debates, and it is to briefly introducing them that we now turn.

## Some debates

Scholars studying early modern England have been particularly interested in the social mobility of merchants and images of merchants; in considering both of these topics the gentleman has provided the point of comparison. Discussion has also revolved around issues of credit, both the private credit of merchants, in terms of reputation and financial capacity, as well as the public credit that flourished and floundered in the new financial world. Historians of science, in particular, have explored the attempts made by contemporaries to chart and understand trade through, for example, the Royal Society's history of trades programme, as well as political arithmetic. These debates and literatures are discussed below and provide points of entry for the arguments which follow in the case studies.

In her study of eighteenth-century British nationalism, Linda Colley remarks that 'a cult of commerce became an increasingly important part of being British'.[60] Associations between concepts of commerce and trade, and images of the nation were not new developments of the eighteenth century for they had been current since the Elizabethan period, as Richard Helgerson shows.[61] It might be argued that one way scholars have attempted to unpack images of the commercial nation has been to consider the ways in which merchants and traders have been represented. For the early modern period, such questions are often framed in terms of the relationship between the ideal of the gentleman and the ideal of the merchant, and are intimately bound up with the social mobility of the merchant. To take the latter first. Could (and

---

[60] L. Colley, *Britons: forging the nation, 1707–1837*, London 1992, 56.
[61] R. Helgerson, *Forms of nationhood: the Elizabethan writing of England*, Chicago 1992, 171–81.

did) merchants become gentlemen and vice versa? Both R. G. Lang's study of aldermen in Jacobean London, and Nicholas Rogers's study of aldermen in mid eighteenth-century London, suggest that merchants in both these periods were firmly tied to the City.[62] Contrary to these portraits, Richard Grassby in an article published in the late 1970s which unusually charts the twin directions of social mobility – the movements of gentry sons into trade, and traders' acquisition of land – characterises the relationship between land and trade in the seventeenth century as a 'dynamic social equilibrium'.[63] Grassby has continued to defend this view against the leading contribution to the debate: the controversial thesis of Jeanne and Lawrence Stone that landed society was not permeated by large numbers of merchants in the early modern period.[64] Grassby argues, in his study of what he calls the seventeenth-century business community, that '[s]imilar and complementary ambitions and needs allowed both merchants and gentry to compromise, co-operate and harmonize their family and regional interests'. Although he cautions against exaggerating the degree of mobility, he asserts that the 'movement between town and country was so continuous that the distinctions of social terminology became blurred'.[65] Most relevant to the time period considered in this book, however, is Henry Horwitz's study of Augustan businessmen. Based on samples of aldermen and non-citizens, Horwitz concludes that for 'those successful businessmen who aimed to put their families upon the map, it was the routes followed by their predecessors – marriage to landed men for their daughters, establishment on the land for their sons – that remained the most travelled ones in the later seventeenth and early eighteenth centuries'.[66]

This debate has not only focused on the incidence of trading apprentice-

[62] R. G. Lang, 'Social origins and social aspirations of Jacobean London merchants', EcHR 2nd ser. xxvii (1974), 28–47; N. Rogers, 'Money, land and lineage: the big bourgeoisie of Hanoverian London', SH iv (1979), 437–54. For a critique of Rogers see D. T. Andrew, 'Aldermen and big bourgeoisie of London reconsidered', SH vi (1981), 359–64, and Rogers's response 'A reply to Donna Andrew', SH vi (1981), 365–9.

[63] R. Grassby, 'Social mobility and business enterprise in seventeenth-century England', in D. Pennington and K. Thomas (eds), Puritans and revolutionaries: essays in seventeenth-century history presented to Christopher Hill, Oxford 1978, 380, and The English gentleman in trade: the life and works of Sir Dudley North, 1641–1691, Oxford 1994.

[64] L. Stone and J. C. F. Stone, An open elite? England, 1540–1880, Oxford 1984. Peter Earle's analysis of inventories from the Augustan Court of Orphans supports the findings of the Stones: The making of the English middle class: business, society and family life in London, 1660–1730, London 1989, 157. For a summary of the criticisms of their thesis see J. V. Beckett, 'Social mobility and English landed society', Social History Society Newsletter xii (1987), 3–5, and S. Halliday, 'Social mobility, demographic change and the landed elite of County Durham, 1610–1819: an open or shut case?', Northern History xxx (1994), 50–1.

[65] R. Grassby, The business community of seventeenth-century England, Cambridge 1995, 386–7.

[66] H. Horwitz, ' "The mess of the middle class" revisited: the case of the "big bourgeoisie" of Augustan London', Continuity and Change ii (1987), 286–7.

ships among gentry sons, the purchase of land by merchants and the significance of marriage partners as indicators of the relationship between landowners and traders. Also disputed are the values and the role of the cultures of the various groups involved. Focusing upon the gentleman engaged in commerce P. J. Cain and A. G. Hopkins present, contentiously, the thesis that not only non-industrial wealth, but what might be called the culture of 'gentlemanly capitalism', was crucial to the history of industrialisation and overseas expansion after 1688: 'The City began as, and remained, an extended network of personal contacts based on mutual trust and concepts of honour which were closer to the culture of the country house circuit or the London club than they were to the more impersonal world inhabited by industrialists.'[67]

Like Grassby, and Cain and Hopkins, Susan Whyman highlights the connections between the gentleman and the merchant in her analysis of the Verney family, in particular the life of John Verney, who after thirty-four years as a merchant unexpectedly inherited a baronetcy and family estate. Whyman thinks that his 'experience suggests that boundaries between London and the shires were more fluid than has been imagined'.[68] She charts a family whose attitudes to trade and merchants warmed in the decades after the Restoration; the family enthusiastically took advantage of the new investment opportunities of the 1690s, and yet retained ambivalent attitudes to money.

Looking at the other side of the coin – the middling sort's involvement with the elite – the Stones argue for an extensive 'cultural mimicry of the elite by the middling sort', and the development of 'an aristocratic bourgeoisie'.[69] Margaret Hunt and Michael Mascuch, however, challenge the prevalence and centrality of the middling sort's adherence to this sort of conception of emulation. Hunt detects in the eighteenth century 'the presence of a deep ambivalence among trading people toward upper-class mores – as middling people defined them, at any rate'.[70] Mascuch, using a sample of

---

67 P. J. Cain and A. G. Hopkins, 'Gentlemanly capitalism and British expansion overseas, I: The old colonial system, 1688–1850', *EcHR* 2nd ser. xxxix (1986), 507. For an extended statement of their argument see their *British imperialism: innovation and expansion, 1688–1914*, London 1993. For a recent summary of the criticisms of their thesis, especially in relation to the long eighteenth century, see H. V. Bowen, *Elites, enterprise and the making of the British overseas empire, 1688–1775*, Basingstoke 1996, 16–21, and more generally, Berg and Hudson, 'Industrial revolution', 43. Dror Wahrman usefully juxtaposes these two sides of the coin, 'the gentlemanly capitalist and the independent bourgeois', as he calls them, and their culture in the eighteenth century: 'National society, communal culture: an argument about the recent historiography of eighteenth-century Britain', *SH* xvii (1992), 53–4.

68 Whyman, *Sociability and power*, 84.

69 Stone and Stone, *Open elite?* 409, 411. They also argue (p. 410) that 'the great strength of the English landed elite was its success in psychologically co-opting those below them into the status hierarchy of gentility'.

70 M. R. Hunt, *The middling sort: commerce, gender, and the family in England, 1680–1780*,

early modern autobiographies, argues that individuals were more concerned about security than improvement, and indeed that there was little opportunity for upward mobility.[71]

The interface between merchants and gentlemen in the early modern period, then, is highly complex, and its exploration is problematic. Although this book does not directly address the social mobility of merchants and gentlemen, a survey of this highly contentious debate is fruitful for the studies that follow. It suggests that we need to be circumspect about employing the notion of a strict division between merchants and gentlemen, whether or not we want to go as far as agreeing with Grassby's characterisation of the relations between merchants and gentlemen as a 'dynamic social equilibrium'. Examining the movement of gentlemen into trade, and merchants to landed estates, and the interchange between and overlap of their values, are only some of the ways to explore the relationship between merchants and gentlemen and indeed the nature of the boundaries that could separate them. To attempt to distinguish between practice and prescription, or perception, can be problematic, and so it is profitable to consider these debates about mobility alongside those which are more closely focused upon the image of the merchant in society. Indeed, many scholars have been particularly concerned with the extent to which writers gave the merchant gentle status in the early modern period.

John McVeagh places images of the merchant within the context of depictions of commerce generally; he argues that the treatment of commerce varied across genres. In the second half of the seventeenth century playwrights exploited the comic potential of commerce rather than characterising the 'menacing aspects of those such as vulgar tradesmen'. Poetry of this period 'is much more exploratory and fine in its response to the changing pressures of life, and so is prose, and muddies often enough a seemingly clear statement with subtle counter-suggestions usually too elusive for drama'. It is in these genres that McVeagh charts the development of appeals to the national interest in defence of commerce and suggests the influence of the ideas of Francis Bacon. For Edmund Waller, John Dryden and John Evelyn, the merchant was 'appreciated . . . as the agent of material felicity', by Thomas Sprat as 'the aristocratic ambassador', and in the first half of the eighteenth century, the merchant was characterised by Daniel Defoe as a 'civilizing pioneer, [and] as inheritor of the earth'.[72] Enlarging on the conclu-

---

Berkeley 1996, 3. Among other historians who have critically examined the role of emulation see, for example, Weatherill, *Consumer behaviour*, 194–6.

[71] M. Mascuch, 'Continuity and change in a patronage society: the social mobility of British autobiographers, 1600–1750', *Journal of Historical Sociology* vii (1994), 177–97, and 'Social mobility and middling self-identity: the ethos of British autobiographers, 1600–1750', *SH* xx (1995), 45–61.

[72] J. McVeagh, *Tradefull merchants: the portrayal of the capitalist in literature*, London 1981, 31, 37, 55. On other satirical portrayals of merchants see also J. Viner, 'Satire and economics in the Augustan age of satire', in H. K. Miller, E. Rothstein and G. S. Rousseau

sions reached by John McVeagh, Neil McKendrick claims that writers judged merchants not on their own 'skills and achievements' but against a gentlemanly ideal.[73] Even for writers like Defoe who, according to McKendrick, 'goes further towards the formulation of a business ideal than any other writer' the merchant is ultimately subordinate to the gentleman.[74] Writing about traders in popular Elizabethan writing, Laura Stevenson too finds that merchants were judged against aristocratic ideals. She shows that merchants and traders were praised in aristocratic terms; they were acclaimed for 'being "magnanimous", "courtly", "chivalric", vassals of the king' rather than for 'their "diligence", "thrift", or financial talents'.[75] Unlike McKendrick, however, Stevenson argues that by the early eighteenth century the paradox had been worked out and 'merchants and "complete tradesmen"' were discussed 'in terms of bourgeois values and gentlemen in terms of aristocratic values'.[76]

Others have claimed, like McKendrick, that the merchant in the late seventeenth and early eighteenth centuries was judged against aristocratic ideals, but unlike McKendrick, they argue that the merchant was not found wanting. Peter Borsay, for example, uses three writers from across the period to demonstrate a warming of attitudes towards trade, and in particular, its increasingly gentle status. According to Edward Chamberlayne in 1669, 'Tradesmen in all Ages and Nations have been reputed ignoble'. Thirty years later, Guy Miège contrasted former times when 'Trading . . . rendered a Gentleman ignoble', with the end of the century when 'an ignoble Person makes himself by Merchandizing as good as a Gentleman; and many Gentlemen born . . . take upon them this Profession, without any prejudice or blemish to their Birth'. In the Complete tradesman (1726) Defoe commemorated the compatibility of trade and commerce: 'Trade is so far . . . from being inconsistent with a Gentleman, that in short trade in England makes Gentlemen, and has peopled this nation with Gentlemen.'[77]

---

(eds), *The Augustan milieu: essays presented to Louis A. Landa*, Oxford 1970, 77–101, and John Loftis, *Comedy and society from Congreve to Fielding*, Stanford 1959. On the appeal to the national interest in texts beyond the narrowly literary see J. A. W. Gunn, *Politics and the public interest in the seventeenth century*, London 1969, and A. O. Hirschman, *The passions and the interests: political arguments for capitalism before its triumph*, Princeton 1977.

[73] N. McKendrick, '"Gentleman and players" revisited: the gentlemanly ideal, the business ideal and the professional ideal in English literary culture', in N. McKendrick and R. B. Outhwaite (eds), *Business life and public policy: essays in honour of D. C. Coleman*, Cambridge 1986, 98–136, 135.

[74] Ibid. 118.

[75] L. C. Stevenson, *Praise and paradox: merchants and craftsmen in Elizabethan popular literature*, Cambridge 1984, 6.

[76] Ibid. 7. See also pp. 156, 196–7.

[77] P. Borsay, *The English urban renaissance: culture and society in the provincial town, 1660–1770*, Oxford 1989, 229; [Edward Chamberlayne] *Angliæ notitia*, London 1669, 478; [Guy Miège], *The new state of England*, 3rd edn, London 1699, pt II, 151; [Daniel Defoe], *The complete English tradesman*, London 1726, 376. For a similar discussion see Earle, *English*

With such a spectrum of opinion amongst historians concerning the status of merchants, and the sets of values against which they were judged, it is tempting to concur with Grassby's view that 'evidence is so prolific and contradictory that it is possible to construct almost any hypothesis about the respectability of trade by selecting individual examples'.[78] The methodological issue of evidence selection can be problematic, and it is certainly called into question if, as in some of the studies mentioned above, scholars rely on as few as three writers to demonstrate a trend which they claim to have taken place over almost twice as many decades. However, just because scholars have claimed that the merchant was depicted in such apparently different ways in the late seventeenth and early eighteenth centuries does not mean that generalisations cannot be made at all. As scholars have probed the mutability of the image of the gentleman, perhaps it is profitable to examine the mutability of the merchant. Moreover, if the ideal against which merchants were often measured – that is the gentleman – was not fixed then we should not expect the merchant to be static either.[79] By carefully situating images in their broader contexts it may be possible to begin to understand the contradictory portrayals of merchants.

Some studies have done exactly this. In her study of the image of the eighteenth-century English merchant, Lisa Harteker claims that some writers in eighteenth-century England endorsed an image of the merchant who served the nation while others criticised merchants for their covetousness and self-interest.[80] Harteker argues that foreign merchants, in particular, were considered by some to be noble, and indeed that there was a category of gentleman that accommodated the merchant.[81] Such tensions are highlighted in the chapters that follow. Merchants at the Royal Exchange in London, for example, were praised for their national endeavours but criticised for deceitfulness. Similarly, Lawrence Klein, in his work on English commercial advice literature, has found disparities between the various identities of the 'commercial self' constructed in many how-to manuals published in the late seventeenth and early eighteenth centuries. He notes that some authors appealed to an image of the merchant as intelligent, diligent, cautious and industrious, evoking 'a world of Weberian commercial vocation', while others 'held out the promise of a kind of gentility'.[82] Indeed,

---

*middle class*, 8. For a study of images of eighteenth-century merchants see D. Donald, ' "Mr Deputy Dumpling and family": satirical images of the city merchant in eighteenth-century England', *Burlington Magazine* cxxxi (1989), 755–63.

[78] Grassby, *Business community*, 29.

[79] P. J. Corfield, 'The rivals: landed and other gentlemen', in N. B. Harte and R. E. Quinault (eds), *Land and society in Britain, 1700–1914*, Manchester 1996, 1–33.

[80] L. M. Harteker, 'Steward of the kingdom's stock: merchants, trade, and discourse in eighteenth-century England', unpubl. PhD thesis, Chicago 1996, i, ch. i.

[81] Ibid. ii, ch. v.

[82] L. E. Klein, 'Politeness for plebes: consumption and social identity in early eighteenth-century England', in Bermingham and Brewer, *Consumption of culture*, 369. In his study of

in the discussion of manuals advising on mercantile writing and conversation, discussed in chapter 4, the style advocated was often closely related to that recommended for polite and gentle communication.

This book tackles the relationship between the gentleman and the merchant, however, largely by considering how commerce was portrayed and packaged. According to Jean Gailhard, for example, part of the 'compleat' gentleman's education when travelling in foreign countries should include becoming acquainted with 'the settlement of Trade, wherein it consists, how many people live by it, and the several East-Indies, Turky, Spanish Companies of Merchants'.[83] Writers of manuals which purported to offer instruction in the skills of a merchant, including accounting methods, and some periodical writers, claimed to address the gentleman amongst their audience. Mastering the techniques commerce entailed, like double-entry bookkeeping, was characterised as a diversion for gentlemen, or something that they needed to know in order to protect themselves from being cheated by their employees. However, although much scholarship has been preoccupied largely with the relationship between the merchant and the gentleman, in this book I also explore how commerce was packaged for a much wider audience. Many of these manuals, for example, also claimed to offer instruction to other groups, such as students in writing schools, women retailers, as well as to gentlemen and merchants, as did newspapers such as the John Houghton's *A Collection for Improvement of Husbandry and Trade* (1692–1703) and the Sun Fire Office's *British Mercury* (1710–15).

The new financial worlds of stock market investment addressed in these particular periodicals were both explained and defended. Defending those who invested in the stock market, and the market itself, involved some difficult challenges. As charted above, public credit with the circulation of bank notes, among other credit instruments, flourished, especially from the end of the seventeenth century onwards. John Pocock, in an account that builds on Dickson's narrative of the financial revolution, charts the course of a debate over real and mobile property which was concerned with the ways in 'which property might determine the relations of personality to government'.[84] The debate was invigorated in the 1690s with the financial revolution and the establishment of the Bank of England and public credit in 1694. These changes were interpreted in the context of civic humanism and were seen to establish a group of people – the government's creditors – who had a

eighteenth-century German business handbooks, Daniel Rabuzzi found a tension between 'rational asceticism and celebratory avarice, between, one might say, the bookkeeper and the buccaneer': 'Eighteenth-century commercial mentalities as reflected and projected in business handbooks', *ECS* xxix (1995–6), 182.

83 J[ean] Gailhard, *The compleat gentleman*, London 1678, second part, 25.

84 J. G. A. Pocock, *Virtue, commerce, and history: essays on political thought and history, chiefly in the eighteenth century*, Cambridge 1985, 109. See also his *The Machiavellian moment: Florentine political thought and the Atlantic republican tradition*, Princeton 1975.

relationship with their government which was potentially corrupt. To over-simplify the situation somewhat, these developments brought new players onto the stage previously occupied only by the gentleman and the merchant. Projectors and stockjobbers emerged alongside investors. Although not without their defenders, these figures were often maligned by contemporary writers for their underhand methods and for the impact their activities were alleged to have upon trade.[85]

The financial revolution, with its attendant stock market, widened opportunities for the ownership of property based on credit, rather than land or goods. Surveying Charles Davenant's writings, Pocock suggests that with these developments, 'men must constantly translate their evaluations of the public good into actions of investment and speculation, so that political behavior is based upon opinion concerning a future rather than memory of a past'.[86] The destabilising effects of investments and speculations were extensive, turning the 'counters' of language 'into marketable commodities' and threatening that 'all men, and all sublunary things, will now become things of paper'.[87] To quote Davenant's words in his *Discourses on the publick revenues* (1698): 'Of all Beings that have Existence only in the Minds of Men, nothing is more fantastical and nice than Credit; 'tis never to be forc'd; it hangs upon Opinion; it depends upon our Passions of Hope and Fear'.[88] Colin Nicholson, in innovative readings of *Gulliver's Travels*, *The Beggar's Opera* and *The Dunciad*, draws on Pocock to explore the 'ways in which the languages and logic of political and economic activity merge and interact with those of imaginative production'.[89] For Nicholson, 'the stability of the ego is itself compromised when what was once a classically derived and coherent moral structure based on *terra firma* is called into question by new forms of capital liquidity increasingly held and passed in paper pledges of credit that were by definition and practice uncertain and socially unstable'.[90]

Some contemporaries attacked the new financial instruments, not only because they seemed flimsy and insubstantial but also because they were seen to draw money and energy out of trade, and left it vulnerable to being taken over by competitors. For example, the projector of one of the land bank schemes in the 1690s, John Briscoe, put the following words into the mouth of a merchant in a dialogue:

[85] H. V. Bowen, ' "The pests of human society": stockbrokers, jobbers and speculators in mid-eighteenth-century Britain', *History* lxxviii (1993), 38–53; Brooks, 'Taxation, finance and public opinion', ch. vii.

[86] Pocock, *Machiavellian moment*, 440.

[87] Ibid. 441, 452.

[88] [Charles Davenant], *Discourses on the publick revenues*, London 1698, pt I, 38.

[89] C. Nicholson, *Writing and the rise of finance: capital satires in the early eighteenth century*, Cambridge 1994, p. xii.

[90] Ibid. 89.

we are tamely resigning up our Trade to others who are industriously prosecuting their Business, and to whom doubtless it is no small Diversion, to see us (who are a trading People) pursuing Butterflies, and busying our selves with Lotteries, while they are studiously employ'd in minding their Business, and are taking our Trade . . . out of our Hands.[91]

Like this writer, many who attacked the world credit created distinguished it from trade which was apparently easier to defend. Others, however not only defended the stock market, but educated their readers about it and sought to promote it to them.

As well as the new threats from the supposed slipperiness of credit, and the undermining ways of stockjobbers, defenders of commerce also dealt with well-established themes. Not a new question, but one not all agreed the answer to, was still being asked in this period: could wealthy traders lead a pious life? As will be seen, those who preached before the Levant Company in the late seventeenth and early eighteenth centuries, on the whole, argued that it could. Other aspects of commerce, though, were less controversial. For example, for all engaged in trade much importance was attached to the maintenance of their credit, in terms of its connected meanings of reputation and ability to pay debts. Craig Muldrew has charted the nature and ubiquity of the financial obligations that linked members of early modern society.[92]

Knowledge of another trader's financial trustworthiness was part of a range of commercial information including the quantities of goods imported and exported at the port of London, international exchange rates and stock prices that might help to make a merchant successful. The circulation of knowledge, whether orally, in manuscript, or in print in a wide variety of fields has attracted much attention in the last twenty years. Evidence of the vibrancy of early modern English oral cultures, and the importance of the circulation of manuscripts challenges the thesis that print became overwhelmingly important.[93] Many have characterised information – in these various forms – as circulating around networks of individuals.[94] The Royal Exchange served as one hub in such a network.

Scholars not only have been concerned with how information moved

---

91 J[ohn] Briscoe, *An explanatory dialogue of a late treatise, intituled,* 'A discourse on the late funds of the Million-Act, Lottery-Act, and Bank of England', London 1694, 34–5.

92 Muldrew, *Economy of obligation*. See also Hunt, *Middling sort*. On eighteenth-century credit see J. Hoppit, 'The use and abuse of credit in eighteenth-century England', in McKendrick and Outhwaite, *Business life and public policy*, 64–78, and 'Attitudes to credit in Britain, 1680–1790', *HJ* xxxiii (1990), 305–22.

93 H. Love, *Scribal publication in seventeenth-century England*, Oxford 1993; A. Fox, *Oral and literate culture in England, 1500–1700*, Oxford 2000.

94 Goldgar, *Impolite learning: conduct and community in the republic of letters, 1680–1750*, New Haven 1995; R. Iliffe, 'Author-mongering: the "editor" between producer and consumer', in Bermingham and Brewer, *Consumption of culture*, 166–92. On international scientific networks (that in many cases overlapped with trading networks) see Glaisyer, 'Networking'.

about (and this book adds to this topic) but also with knowledge-making practices. As a merchant's credit might determine his financial status so the standing of a natural philosopher might determine whether others were prepared to trust their testimony.[95] Scholars have made much of the similarities between the practices of knowledge-making in natural philosophy and in commerce. The challenges presented by the doubts raised by the slipperiness of credit were widespread. In Simon Schaffer's words: 'Bubbles, projects, new philosophies and new systems of credit urgently raised the problem of judgement of matters of fact. . . . In the country and the city, at the Exchange and at the Royal Society, before early eighteenth century Britons came to accept or reject a claim, they judged whether it deserved investigation or investment.'[96] Investigations of the status of knowledge and how printed materials in particular might establish authority have been addressed in the context of the overlapping practices and values of the worlds of commerce and natural philosophy.[97]

There were other connections between the natural philosophical and the commercial. The world of trade was a subject of investigation for many working in natural philosophy in the late seventeenth and early eighteenth centuries. The processes of understanding, charting and explaining the new commercial worlds were built partly on the foundation of the Royal Society's history of trades programme. Members of the Royal Society, and others, undertook to write the histories of trades in which they endeavoured to catalogue and describe various handicrafts and trades, such as glass manufacture, mining and brewing.[98] A number of the projects to chart and explain commerce, as will be seen in what follows, must be placed in the context of

---

[95] S. Shapin, A social history of truth: civility and science in seventeenth-century England, Chicago 1994; M. Poovey, A history of the modern fact: problems of knowledge in the sciences of wealth and society, Chicago 1998.

[96] S. Schaffer, 'A social history of plausibility: country, city and calculation in Augustan Britain', in A. Wilson (ed.), Rethinking social history: English society, 1570–1920, and its interpretation, Manchester 1993, 129.

[97] Idem, 'Defoe's natural philosophy and the worlds of credit', in J. Christie and S. Shuttleworth (eds), Nature transfigured: science and literature, 1700–1900, Manchester 1989, 13–44; A. Johns, The nature of the book: print and knowledge in the making, Chicago 1998.

[98] W. E. Houghton, 'The history of trades: its relation to seventeenth-century thought', in P. P. Wiener and A. Noland (eds), Roots of scientific thought: a cultural perspective, New York 1957, 354–81; M. Hunter, Science and society in Restoration England, Cambridge 1981, repr. Aldershot 1992, and Establishing the new science: the experience of the early Royal Society, Woodbridge 1989; R. Lennard, 'English agriculture under Charles II: the evidence of the Royal Society's "enquiries" ', EcHR 1st ser. iv (1932–4), 23–45; K. H. Ochs, 'The Royal Society of London's history of trades programme: an early episode in applied science', NRRS xxxix (1985), 129–58; L. Stewart, The rise of public science: rhetoric, technology, and natural philosophy in Newtonian Britain, 1660–1750, Cambridge 1992; M. Stubbs, 'John Beale, philosophical gardener of Herefordshire, II: The improvement of agriculture and trade in the Royal Society (1663–1683)', Annals of Science xlvi (1989), 323–63; C. Webster, The great instauration: science, medicine and reform, 1626–1660, London 1975.

these Baconian programmes. Related to such attempts to chart and under-stand commerce was political arithmetic – the study of revenue, land, popu-lation, as well as tax revenues, using quantitative techniques and associated with Gregory King, Charles Davenant and Sir William Petty.[99] As will be seen later in this book, compiling commercial data on, say, annual figures of imports and exports, was recommended by newspaper writers both to provin-cial and metropolitan readers as the proper pursuits for the gentleman 'polit-ical arithmetician'.

## The scope of this book

This book is structured around four case studies which serve to focus a wide range of source materials, approaches, literatures and subject matters. The case studies have been deliberately chosen to incorporate a range of media, from newspapers to sermons, from ready reckoners to elaborate volumes, from engravings to marginalia. These case studies allow the packaging of commerce in a range of situations to be examined, from the context of the quadrangle of the Royal Exchange in London where thousands of traders gathered twice a day, to the final pages of newspapers produced in provincial towns on which the price of Bank stock may or may not have been squeezed in. These studies illuminate a wide range of issues, from the difficulties (or in some cases the ease) with which wealth and piety could be reconciled, to the strategies newspaper writers employed to help readers observe stock market fluctuations, from the reading techniques employed by readers of mercantile manuals to the ways in which the trading world could be captured in a picture.

Each case study is the subject of a chapter. A building, the Royal Exchange, where London's commercial community gathered in this period, is the subject of chapter 1. In the heart of a printing and bookselling area, and surrounded by shops which sold luxury goods and provided legal services for traders, the Exchange was the site of a variety of activities. Principally it was a site for merchants and traders to solicit business, strike bargains and obtain the latest commercial information. However, it was also host to information gathering and dissemination more generally, and was a place where various political activities took place and political associations were forged. It attracted visitors who were encouraged to spectate on the merchants from the balconies above the quadrangle. The chapter looks at notions of credit, and using records contained in the state papers, commercial manuals and court records, I argue that the credit of individual merchants was established,

---

[99] J. Hoppit, 'Political arithmetic in eighteenth-century England', *EcHR* 2nd ser. xlix (1996), 526–40; P. Buck, 'People who counted: political arithmetic in the eighteenth century', *Isis* lxxiii (1982), 28–45.

negotiated, lost and saved at the Exchange. The credit of the Exchange itself is also explored through administrative records, travel accounts, guide-books and poems, and is related to conceptions of London as a trading city, and the country as a commercial nation. As a symbol of trade, particularly in visual representations of the quadrangle, the Exchange was understood by many contemporaries to contain the international trading world. Merchants, and commerce itself, were not always positively portrayed and the chapter also examines the 'vices', as well as the 'vanities', associated with the Exchange.

Chapter 2 is concerned with attitudes to money and trade, and the construction of a merchant identity in sermons preached before a largely mercantile audience. In this period the Levant Company, which held a monopoly to trade with Turkey, appointed chaplains to minister to the factories there. Part of the appointment procedure involved candidates preaching trial sermons, and many of those delivered by successful candidates were published by order of the Company. A Levant Company chaplaincy was a desirable post and often a position held near the beginning of a successful clerical career and so it is unsurprising that preachers presented positive portrayals of trade and merchants; what is interesting, however, is how these images were constructed. As in religious writings in other periods, many of these preachers explored the compatibility of trade and money with piety. More distinctly, however, I argue that these preachers emphasised the special duties and responsibilities of merchants as God's stewards.

The third chapter establishes the importance of commercial stationery, periodicals and didactic literature in this period. Concentrating on the didactic literature, attempts are made to situate texts advising on merchanting in the contexts within which they were read, both by making inferences from the texts and employing the evidence for ownership and reading practices which survives. Many of the texts were written by accounting teachers, accountants and writing masters, and were designed to be used in the schoolroom. Significant numbers of texts have been found in merchants' libraries, and a number were indeed written by merchants. However, it can also be suggested that there were other groups of readers, in particular those who were supposedly reading for 'diversion'. Amongst these, in particular, were gentlemen, for whom knowledge of accounting was considered essential. Some evidence also suggests that these books may have been read as a way of taking an 'imaginary journey' into the world of commerce. Three of these texts included a vocabulary of commercial terms for their readers and it is argued in this chapter that such vocabularies can be usefully situated in various contexts including the natural philosophical programmes for improvement and contemporary notions about writing and conversation.

The final chapter looks at newspapers: John Houghton's 1690s serial publication *A Collection for Improvement of Husbandry and Trade* (1691–1703), which reported stock prices and commodity prices, and promoted the joint-stock enterprises as part of a Baconian-inspired programme; the Sun Fire Office's *British Mercury* (1710–15) which reported foreign news as well as numerical commercial information to thousands of readers; and provincial newspapers which increasingly reported on the stock market, as well as local markets. The chapter looks not only at how newspapers presented numerical information to readers but also in some cases how it was defended and explained to them. Where possible, attempts have been made to show how information was gathered for the pages of the papers, how current is was and who might have been reading it.

Finally, a brief conclusion draws together the themes raised in the preceeding case studies.

# 1

# 'The Glory of the World in a Moment':
# the Royal Exchange

The Royal Exchange, between Cornhill and Threadneedle Street in the heart of the City, was the most important single gathering place for merchants in early modern London. Twice a day thousands of traders, and others, met in the quadrangle to negotiate deals, to find out who was credit-worthy and who was not and to hear the latest news. The Exchange is a good place to start a study of the culture of commerce, not least because no other trading place in England was of comparable importance (although compari-sons were attempted). More than this though, the Exchange was widely cele-brated as a symbol of London's, and indeed the nation's, role in international trade. The quadrangle where the merchants gathered and the shops above, stocked with luxury imports, were seen to represent 'the glory of the world'. Although extensively praised, the Exchange was not without its detractors and tensions between the representations are examined in what follows.

This chapter is divided into five sections. In the first the Exchange is described as a busy trading space, where shoppers bought luxury goods and merchants negotiated deals. The Exchange was also one hub in early modern information networks and this is also established in this section. Discussion in the second section considers the importance of an individual's credit in the early modern period, and argues that the Exchange was a crucial arena for the establishment and negotiation of merchant reputation. An exploration of the ways in which depictions of the Exchange collapsed the trading world into single textual and visual images is undertaken in the third section. Not all representations of the Exchange celebrated it as the centre of the commercial world; some commentators concentrated on the Exchange's 'vices' rather than its 'vanities', and these anxieties about the negative aspects of the Exchange are considered in the fourth section. The chapter ends by consid-ering the wider resonances of the Exchange: its impact on, and role in the reputation and image of the city and the nation, and to a lesser extent, the crown.

## 'The talk upon the Change':
## trade and information at the Royal Exchange

Like other bourses in medieval and early modern Europe, the Royal Exchange, completed in the late sixteenth century, was built ostensibly as a site where merchants could gather.[1] In the late seventeenth and early eighteenth centuries the Exchange was at the commercial heart of London; as the Common Council declared in this period 'the Affairs of Commerce and Negotiation are much advanced by the publick Meeting of such as frequent the Royal Exchange'.[2] 'Merchants, Tradesmen, Factors and Brokers, and the Servants of Merchants and Tradesmen' came together in the enclosed court-yard in the middle of the day, and in the early evening, at hours regulated by the City authorities, known as 'Exchange time'.[3] Attempts were made throughout this period to regulate these hours. Such was the importance of making merchants available to attend the Exchange at the appropriate hours that on a number of occasions London's Court of Aldermen proposed to schedule their own meetings to finish before the beginning of the noon Exchange, and recommended that the East India and Levant Companies, among other metropolitan mercantile bodies, do the same.[4] In the early 1740s it was estimated that more than 8,500 people might gather at a 'full Assembly' in the enclosed courtyard.[5] Even in 1669 the area was thought to be too small; the body in charge of the Exchange, the Gresham Committee, rejected the gift of a large statue of Charles II on horseback to stand in the

[1]  J. Imray, 'The origins of the Royal Exchange', in A. Saunders (ed.), *The Royal Exchange*, London 1997, 20–35. On bourses in Europe more generally see F. Braudel, *The wheels of commerce*, trans. S. Roberts, London 1982, 97–112. Until the collection of essays edited by Ann Saunders was published in 1997 the standard histories of the Exchange were narrowly focused on the architectural and institutional history of the building: S. Angell, *An historical sketch of the Royal Exchange*, London 1838; A. E. W. Mason, *The Royal Exchange: a note on the bicentenary of the Royal Exchange Assurance*, London 1920; E. A. de M. Rudolf, 'Some notes on the building of the second Royal Exchange', *Home Counties Magazine* vi (1904), 293–98; A. Stratton, 'The Royal Exchange, London, II: The second and third buildings', *Architectural Review* xlii (1917), 44–50; J. G. White, *History of the three Royal Exchanges, the Gresham Lectures, and Gresham almshouses*, London 1896. Ann Saunders's collection of essays suggests a far more wide-ranging approach to the Exchange's history.
[2]  *Comune Concil' tent' in Camera Guihald' Civitat' London* [An order appointing hours for meeting in the Royal Exchange], London 1703.
[3]  *Commune Concilium tentum in Camera Guild-Hall Civitatis London die Sabbati, vicesimo primo die Februarii, Annoque Domini, 1673* [An act for the regulation of the brokers upon the Royal Exchange], London 1673; Turner Mayor, *Martis vicesimo sexto die Januarii, 1668. Annóque Regni Regis Caroli Secundi, Dei Grat', Angliæ, &c. vicesimo* [Order respecting the hours of meeting of the citizens, merchants and traders, frequenting the Burse or Royal Exchange, 26 Jan. 1668], London 1668; *Comune Concil' tent'* . . . [An order appointing hours for meeting]. For more details on the opening hours of the Exchange see N. Glaisyer, 'Merchants at the Royal Exchange, 1660–1720', in Saunders, *Royal Exchange*, 198.
[4]  CLRO, London, Rep. 82, 1676–7, fo. 91r; Rep. 108, 1703–4, p. 76.
[5]  John Wood, *A description of the Exchange of Bristol*, Bath 1743, 37.

quadrangle because it would 'take up too much of that roome, which is too little already to conteyne the Concourse of M[er]chants'.[6] The committee also feared that it would 'hinder persons from finding one another soe readily as when the Quadrangle is left free'.[7] Indeed, to make meeting easier the quadrangle was divided into areas called walks, each associated with a commodity or a trading region.

Surrounding the quadrangle on the ground floor were shops, out of which a number of scriveners and notaries conducted their businesses alongside stationers, booksellers, engravers, periwig makers, watchmakers, tobacconists, picture and cabinet sellers.[8] With the exception of the insurance office, access to the shops was not directly from the quadrangle but from the outside of the building.[9] On the upper floor, in the rows of shops known as pawns, fancy goods such as lace, linen, silk, hosiery, buttons and baubles were for sale.[10] During the time that Pepys kept his diary he, or his wife, bought a whisk, gloves, stockings, a muff and a christening bowl from shops at the Exchange. He was given a watch made there, and his wife, to Pepys's disapproval, spent 25s. at the Exchange on 'a pair of pendances for her eares'.[11] Visitors to London also frequented the shops, such as the Leeds antiquary Ralph Thoresby (1658–1725), who in 1678 went to the Exchange, among other places, 'to buy pictures and tokens for relations'.[12] Women made up a substantial proportion of those who shopped at the Exchange, as a list of those indebted to the Exchange shopkeeper, Robert Antrobus, in 1688 reveals. He stocked a wide range of fabric goods including lace, linen, cambric, gauze and crape. The stock and the lease of the shop, the drawers, cupboards, sign and glass (these last four were valued at £80), were estimated to be worth a total of almost £340 in the inventory drawn up after his death. Most of his customers were probably women as among the almost 250 people listed in the categories of good debts, or doubtful and desperate debts there were only a handful of men.[13]

The centre of the city moved west during the period, and although the statistician John Graunt noted that 'did not the Royal Exchange, and London-Bridg stay the Trade, it would remove much faster', the Exchange's popularity as a place to shop declined.[14] In the mid-1680s, and the late 1690s,

---

6   The Gresham Committee was made up of representatives of the Mercers' Company and the City authorities.

7   MCA, London, Gresham repertory, 1626–69, p. 367.

8   Gresham repertories covering the period 1660–1720, passim.

9   Gresham repertory, 1669–76, p. 67. There may also have been access to the quadrangle from another shop leased by a Mr Cowper.

10   Ehver Kynd [Henry Duke], *Londons-nonsuch*, London 1668, sigs C2r–D1r.

11   *Pepys*, i. 299; ii. 80; iv. 290; vii. 39; viii. 548; vi. 101; v. 196.

12   Ralph Thoresby, *The diary of Ralph Thoresby*, ed. J. Hunter, London 1830, i. 12.

13   'An inventory of other Goods of the said Robert Antrobus at his late shop on the Royal Exchange London', TNA, PROB 4/12879, item 2.

14   John Graunt, *Natural and political observations*, 2nd edn, London 1662, 52.

decisions were taken by the Gresham Committee to shut up rows of shops on the upper floor.[15] In 1724 Daniel Defoe lamented that where once had been a great trade in 'Millenary Goods, Fine Laces, &c' were now empty shops, and by 1739 the trade had decayed to the point where William Maitland, the historian of London, was prompted to describe the upper part of the Exchange as being 'like a Wilderness'.[16] Many of the shops were replaced by warehouses, such as those rented by the East India Company (who already rented the cellars for storing pepper) which they used for storing tea.[17] Others were replaced by offices, most prominently those rented by the Royal Exchange Assurance Company in the second decade of the eighteenth century.[18]

In *The exact dealer* (1688), compiled 'chiefly for the advantage of Traders' by John Hill, the Exchange was pictured as a bustling place in the frontispiece and described in the main text as 'the proper place of bargaining' for 'the Goods that are Imported from other Countries'.[19] Part of such bargaining might have involved soliciting for trade. Nathaniel Harley, writing from Aleppo in 1696, reproached his brother Edward: 'How many jaunts do you take to the Exchange and thence to Coffee Houses, and even to ransack the Court itself to find me principals?'[20] Visiting the Exchange was a regular part of many merchants' routines. Some traders were to be found so regularly on the Exchange that they used the walk they frequented as an address. The sale of a brass wire works in Winchester Yard in 1710, for example, was to be handled by three traders who advertised in the *London Gazette* that they could be found at the East-Country walk during Exchange time.[21] Viscount Conway was advised in 1678 that a bill of exchange he received was drawn on 'John Cromyn merc[hant], who is dayly at Exchange time on the Irish walke' and a declaration amongst the state papers was signed by a group of merchants, who could, they wrote, all be found on the New England walk.[22] The Quaker, Peter Briggins, a hop and honey merchant who occasionally traded in other commodities, and invested in stocks, went to the Exchange as many as six times a week in the early eighteenth century. Most of his diary entries over an eighteen-month period, written while Briggins was in his early forties, do not mention the purposes of his trips to the Exchange. On a

15 Gresham repertory, 1678–1722, pp. 109, 330, 498.

16 Daniel Defoe, *A tour thro' the whole island of Great Britain*, London 1724, ii. 121; William Maitland, *The history of London from its foundation by the Romans, to the present time*, London 1739, 467.

17 Gresham repertory, 1678–1722, pp. 335, 580.

18 Ibid. pp. 550, 552; Supple, *Royal Exchange Assurance*, 19, 34.

19 J[ohn] H[ill], *The exact dealer*, London 1688, 4, 12.

20 Nathaniel Harley to Edward Harley, 3 Apr. 1696, in HMC, *Thirteenth report: the manuscripts of his grace the duke of Portland*, London 1891–1931, ii. 246.

21 LG, 22 June 1710.

22 'R. Mildmay to Viscount Conway', 10 Apr. 1678, TNA, SP 63/338 fo. 286r; 'Questions to be asked the New England men', 18 Apr. 1676, TNA, CO 1/36, fo. 83r.

few occasions, however, he did make a record: he went to meet a Captain Bowrey in November 1707, and someone else about wax in September the following year, as well as at other times to visit the insurance office, and to strike a bargain over some tobacco.[23] Briggins is probably representative of a merchant on the periphery of the commercial community at the Exchange, as he did not attend every day like the Turkey merchant John Verney, nor did he depend on it as a place for trading.[24] It is reasonable to conjecture that Briggins went to the Exchange largely to keep abreast of the course of trade generally, to meet people and very occasionally to take advantage of opportunities to engage in foreign trade and invest in stocks.

Although over the period the Exchange attracted decreasing numbers of shoppers, there is little evidence to suggest that the size of the Exchange's trading community had declined by the beginning of the eighteenth century. Indeed, the Exchange and neighbouring alleys were the focal point for the speculative activities that flourished in England from the 1690s onwards. The importance of Exchange Alley and the coffee-houses in the area in such developments has been well established but the Exchange itself was also home to such ventures. In 1695 in the Outropers Office on the west side of the building, for example, the subscription books to the Bank on the Tickets of the Million Adventure were opened.[25] The brokers supposedly left the Exchange quadrangle for the alley in 1698; the exact circumstances of this are unclear but it followed a series of attacks on, and denunciations of, trading in stocks and subsequently an act in 1697 to 'restrain the number and ill practice of brokers and stock jobbers'.[26] By the beginning of the eighteenth century the City authorities were repeatedly regulating against their trading in Exchange Alley because

by the daily Resort and Standing of Brokers and Stock-Jobbers in the . . . Alley, not only the Common Passage to and from the Royal-Exchange is greatly obstructed, but Incouragement is given by the tumultuary Concourse of People attending the said Brokers, to Pick-Pockets, Shop-Lifters, and other Idle and Disorderly People to mix among them.[27]

23 Peter Briggins diary, 1706–8, ACC 1017/2, fo. 36; facing fo. 60; facing fo. 40; facing fo. 44. In the 1890s two other volumes of this diary were extant. Briggins and his diaries are discussed in E. Howard, *The Eliot papers*, Gloucester 1893–4, i. 25–70.

24 Briggins struck many of his deals in Southwark. On Verney see Whyman, *Sociability and power*, 62, 73.

25 *CIHT*, 22 Mar. 1695. On the Outropers Office see M. Harris, 'Exchanging information: print and business at the Royal Exchange in the late seventeenth century', in Saunders, *Royal Exchange*, 197. On the Million Adventure see Scott, *Constitution and finance*, iii. 275–87.

26 8 and 9 William III, c. 32; Carswell, *South Sea Bubble*, 15–16; S. W. Dowling, *The Exchanges of London*, London 1929, 6; C. Duguid, *The Stock Exchange*, rev. E. D. Kissan, 5th edn, London 1926, 110; Francis, *Chronicles*, 24; E. V. Morgan and W. A. Thomas, *The Stock Exchange: its history and functions*, London 1962, 26–7; Scott, *Constitution and finance*, i. 358.

27 Levett Mayor, *Jovis Decimo die Octobris, 1700. Annoq; Regni Regis Willielmi Tertii Angliæ, &c.* [Order that none of the Exchange brokers do for the future agitate any business in open

All the evidence suggests that such attempts were unsuccessful, and that Exchange Alley, the neighbouring coffee-houses and probably the Exchange itself, remained the focus of the developing stock market.

It was not only financial profit that was sought after in the courtyard of the Exchange. Alison Olson has shown that Virginia merchants were 'politicised' there. 'A merchant who might have thought political lobbying a waste of time, if not, indeed, quite improper, might be persuaded to sign a petition circulated by a respected fellow merchant.'[28] Others also went to the Exchange to solicit support for their cause, such as French Protestants protesting in 1713 against the Treaty of Utrecht.[29] Evidence in the state papers suggests that in 1670 opponents of the Conventicle Act attempted to gain a following at the Exchange: 'Col[onel] King . . . is the great Advocate for the Meeters, and is daily upon the Exchange, I will not say to promote sedition alone, but rebellion and Treason.'[30] For satirists such endeavours were part and parcel of the 'Amusements Serious and Comical' to be witnessed at the Exchange: 'I have a pressing Occasion for some Seeds of Sedition, Jacobite Rue, and Whig Herb of Grace', exclaimed Tom Brown's narrator as he stood in the Exchange quadrangle.[31] It was one of the places where royal proclamations were read out and public punishments were conducted. The Exchange was also a venue for the symbolic marking of major incidents in the political arena, whether it was the displaying of scatalogical pictures, celebratory bonfires in the streets around the building or the burning of the Solemn League and Covenant or later a book attacking the French king's treatment of Protestants.[32]

Political points could be made at the Exchange not only by burning books but also by distributing them freely. In a letter dated 21 May 1680, Secretary of State Leoline Jenkins was informed that 'greate quantatyes of that Libell Entituled A letter to a person of hon[ou]r concerning the black box hath been this day Scattered and taken up upon the Royall Exchange, and . . . theer is an Inten[ti]on spedelye to disperse them throughout the Kingdome'.[33] Less

---

Alley, 10 Oct. 1700], London 1700. See also, Comune Concil' tent' . . . [An order appointing hours for meeting]; Dickson, Financial revolution, 518.

[28] A. G. Olson, 'The Virginia merchants of London: a study in eighteenth-century interest-group politics', William and Mary Quarterly 3rd ser. xl (1983), 367.

[29] Braudel, Wheels, 107.

[30] Sir J. Robinson to Sir JosephWilliamson, 18 May 1670, SP 29/275, fo. 204r.

[31] [Tom] Brown, Amusements serious and comical, London 1700, 31–2. My thanks to Milly Cockayne for bringing my attention to this parody of the Exchange.

[32] Pepys, i. 45; John Verney to Edmund Verney, 2 Sept. 1675, in HMC, Seventh report, London 1879, 465; Stephen Charlton to Sir R. Leveson, 25 May 1661, in HMC, Fifth report, London 1876, 171; Evelyn, Diary, iv. 510.

[33] [?] to Sir L. Jenkins, 21 May 1680, SP 29/143, part 2, fo. 28r. This pamphlet, by Robert Ferguson (d. 1714), was published during the exclusion crisis and argued that Monmouth was the legitimate son of Charles II: A letter to a person of honour concerning the black box, London 1680. Roger Morrice noted that 'On 10 June 1689 many copies of King James's

controversial works, such as catalogues for book auctions, were also distributed for free at the bookshops at the Exchange.[34] In fact, geographically the Exchange was in the heart of the publishing district, and as well as the booksellers and printsellers who had shops in the building, there were many others based in the vicinity.[35] Some booksellers catered specifically to the commercial interests of the Exchange's clientele. Robert Horne, and later his son Thomas, had a shop at the south entrance to the Exchange continuously from the Restoration until 1711.[36] They stocked, as will be discussed in more detail in chapter 3, perhaps the widest range of reference books for merchants in London and also an extensive selection of stationery for commercial purposes. The Exchange was also a hub of pamphlet and newspaper distribution, much of which was undertaken by female hawkers.[37] Such hawking practices competed with the booksellers' trade at the Exchange and on at least one occasion 'Mr Horne' was amongst the tenants of shops at the Exchange who approached the Gresham Committee 'desireing' their 'favour ... to take some measures for removeing the great annoyance by Hawkers of papers and other idle persons that resort and continue in bodys on the Southside of the said Exchange'.[38]

The Exchange was central to early modern information networks, and not only because of its pivotal position in the distribution of printed materials.[39] John Hill noted in 1688 that it was the place for 'getting knowledge of what Commodities are brought in, and to be sold; as also Intelligence of the Prices, and whether the Rate rises or falls'.[40] Merchants could receive letters there, and in the quadrangle were posted an enormous variety of notices and advertisements: details about subscription demands for the Bank of England, arrangements concerning lottery tickets, orders issued by the Court of

*Declaration* were scattered in the streets around the Royal Exchange at 1am': Dr Williams's Library, London, Roger Morrice's entring book, vol. Q, p. 573. I am grateful to Mark Goldie for this reference.

34  J. Bullord, *Bibliopoli littleburiani pars quinta, & ultima*, London 1697.

35  On publishing in and around the exchange see L. Worms, 'The book trade at the Royal Exchange', in Saunders, *Royal Exchange*, 209–26.

36  H. R. Plomer, *A dictionary of the booksellers and printers who were at work in England, Scotland and Ireland from 1641 to 1667*, London 1907, 101, and *A dictionary of the printers and booksellers who were at work in England, Scotland and Ireland from 1668 to 1725*, ed. A. Esdaile, Oxford 1922, 161.

37  GL, London, MS 4069/2, Cornhill ward, 1652–1733, fos 281r, 287v, 290v, 470v; CLRO, Rep. 111, 1706–7, p. 62. C. Blagden, *The Stationers' Company: a history, 1403–1959*, London 1960, 164; Harris, 'Exchanging information', 195; M. Hunt, 'Hawkers, bawlers, and mercuries: women and the London press in the Early Enlightenment', in M. Hunt, M. Jacob, P. Mack and R. Perry, *Women and the Enlightenment*, New York 1984, 46. See also *The case of Robert Crosfeild* [London 1696], 2.

38  Gresham repertory, 1678–1722, p. 456.

39  Harris, 'Exchanging information'; R. Cust, 'News and politics in early seventeenth-century England', *P&P* cxii (1986), 70.

40  H[ill], *Exact dealer*, 4, 12.

Aldermen, advertisements for tenders to supply materials for building naval vessels and notices asking parties interested in particular seized ships to attend the High Court of Admiralty.[41] Indeed the originals of the last survive, and at times, for example during the first Anglo-Dutch war, there are large bundles: over fifty 'monitions' were displayed at the Exchange in June 1665 alone.[42] Likewise the Sun Fire Office advertised their fire insurance company at the Exchange; they made arrangements with the Exchange keepers for their printed proposals to be displayed in frames at the Exchange in their first year of operation, 1710.[43] Advertising at the Exchange could also take other forms: in 1713 the firemen employed by the Sun Fire Office were ordered to appear 'in their new Cloaths' about one o'clock at the Exchange on one day in July as a way to promote the company.[44]

The Gresham Committee put up their own advertisements in the quadrangle, some of which were accommodated specifically for the international patrons. In July 1705 papers were to be put on the Exchange to give notice that the north warehouse could be leased, and, in 1687, it was proposed that 'a table' be 'fixed in Severall parts of the Exchange and other remarkable places' with details of the Gresham lectures 'fairly written in most of the Languages now Extant in Europ whereby Strangers may reap the benefitt of the Founders gift who are now wholy Ignorant of the Same'.[45] The duties of the Exchange keepers were also displayed on the north and south sides of the Exchange: they were instructed to 'sweepe the Exchange every weeke day', to ring the bell that marked Exchange time, to keep the benches, roof and the gutters clean, and to 'keepe all Footboys, Beggars, and idle p[er]sons out of the Exchange'.[46]

Tom Brown's interlocutor at the Exchange wished to know 'why they stain'd such stately Pillars with so many Dirty Papers'. On being told 'they were Advertisements' he asked 'Why . . . don't they put them into the Post-Boy? Can't the Folks in this Country read it?'[47] The Exchange's role as a

---

[41] James Claypoole to John Curtis, 17 Aug. 1681, in James Claypoole, *James Claypoole's letter book: London and Philadelphia, 1681–1684*, ed. M. Balderston, San Marino 1967, 51; *A preamble to the books for taking a subscription of ten hundred thousand pounds for the use of the Bank of England*, London 1713, 2; treasury minute book, 11 May 1731, TNA, T 29/27, p. 21; Fryer Mayor, *Martis xxxi die Januarii, 1720* [Order of the Court of Aldermen in reference to persons acting as brokers within the City of London without having been legally admitted to do so], London 1720; admiralty journal, 8 May 1677 and Samuel Pepys to Sir Robert Robinson, 28 July 1676, in J. R. Tanner (ed.), *A descriptive catalogue of the naval manuscripts in the Pepysian Library at Magdalene College, Cambridge*, London 1903–23, iv. 419; iii, pp. x, 237.

[42] TNA, HCA 31/1; HCA 31/24.

[43] GL, MS 11931/1, Sun Fire Office copy book of orders, 1710–15, fo. 22r .

[44] Ibid. fo. 106r.

[45] Gresham repertory, 1678–1722, pp. 404, 164. These lectures were established as part of the benefaction of Thomas Gresham, founder of the Exchange.

[46] Ibid. p. 294.

[47] Brown, *Amusements*, 32.

site for advertising did in fact overlap and complement the newspapers'. Some notices were placed both at the Exchange and in the papers and, as Michael Harris has charted, the Exchange accommodated various offices of intelligence from which advertising sheets were produced in this period.[48] The petty cash books kept by the secretary to the East India Company from the early eighteenth century indicate that the cost of displaying a notice at the Exchange was usually 2s. 6d. which compared favourably with the cost of a newspaper advertisement. From March 1706 to April 1709 the East India Company paid the Exchange keepers or the Mercers' Company beadle for over thirty notices concerning elections, annuities, sales and meetings to be hung at the Exchange while at the same time also making extensive use of newspaper advertising.[49] At times even the Gresham Committee advertised in newspapers, as in December 1714 when advertisements were placed in the *London Gazette* to announce the availability of shops for lease.[50]

As well as the notices and advertisements on display there is substantial evidence to suggest the significance of the Exchange as a site for the oral interchange of news. Indeed, in Harold Love's opinion, it partially filled the gap left by the decline in the mid-seventeenth century of St Paul's Walk as a centre for the exchange of news.[51] In the Restoration period Pepys, for example, went frequently to hear 'The talk upon the Change', and, according to Jean Gailhard in his conduct manual, the Exchange, as well as Westminster Hall and the Court, were the places a 'Country Gentleman' coming to the city should visit to 'get a superficial knowledge of things most important to the Nation'.[52] It was not just commercial and financial news that was discussed at, in the words of one contemporary, 'the great Exchange of all Discourses', but also more general, and especially foreign, news.[53] Various government officials were frequently sent news which had been heard on the Exchange. In the early 1660s, for example, Secretary of State Williamson learned that 'the Dutch have given commission to buy upp all the Brimstone . . . to make powder' from a correspondent who had been 'informed by

48 Notice was to be given 'to Artificers of the sev[er]all trades that must bee used in the rebuilding of the Royall Exchainge' at the temporary Exchange at Gresham College and the 'same notice to be inserted in next gazette': Gresham repertory, 1669–76, p. 286. In 1720 the Gresham lectures were to be advertised both in the *Daily Courant* and the *Daily Post* as well as on boards to be put up at the Exchange and Gresham College in English and Latin 'to oblige the lecturers to a better performance of their duty': Gresham repertory, 1678–1722, pp. 558–9; Harris, 'Exchanging information', 196.

49 BL, India Office Records, H/MISC/17, pp. 109, 113, 119, 123, 127, 131, 135, 149, 151, 161.

50 Gresham repertory, 1678–1722, p. 482; *LG*, 4 Dec. 1714.

51 Love, *Scribal publication*, 194.

52 *Pepys*, v. 181; Gailhard, *Compleat gentleman*, second part, 25–6. The importance of Westminster Hall as a place for the oral interchange of news, particularly in the late seventeenth century, is highlighted in Roger Morrice's entring book: M. Goldie, 'Roger Morrice and his entring book', *History Today*, Nov. 2001, 44.

53 *Hickelty pickelty*, London 1708, 10.

severall Merchants upon the Exchange'.[54] Information was seen by the Treasury to be crucial to the government's attempt to secure public credit in 1710 and it was proposed to Robert Harley that the Royal Exchange should be the focus of the Treasury's attempts to obtain what was required. The proposal recommended that an Assistant Secretary to the Lord Commissioners of the Treasury be appointed to gain the 'soonest intelligence . . . of any contrivances or practices on foot concerning any of the principal stocks in the City, and consider how their fall may be prevented or the public credit secured from any mischiefs by it', as well as 'to take all occasions and opportunities of enquiring into other matters that may be of service to the Government'. To carry out these duties it was designed that the 'Assistant should frequent the Royal Exchange at the usual Exchange hours, and have some known place to be at, where any persons may come to him that are willing to communicate any means or methods for improving the Government's revenues, raising proper funds, or for advancement of the public credit, or any other service for the Government'.[55] Other branches of government also sought advice from the merchants on the Exchange; in the mid 1670s, for example, the Committee of Trade and Plantations asked the 'Merchants of the Exchange as are acquainted with the Trade of Newfound Land' to attend a meeting to give their opinion on developing the fishery there.[56]

Indeed, for those producing all sorts of periodical publications in this period the Exchange was where much news was gathered, as Michael Harris has described.[57] Most important for the themes of this book, the price of stocks and the currency exchange rates established at the Exchange were also reproduced in several commercial and financial newspapers published, and sold, in the area around the building.[58]

Such was the status of the Exchange, the supposed reliability of the news and the expertise of the merchants assembled there that the Exchange itself, semantically at least, was the mouthpiece of the merchants. Reports in the state papers of what was heard on the Exchange employed various formulations: 'The Exchange says that . . .', 'The whole Exchange was not a little joyed at the news of . . .', 'Some sputtering is upon the Exchange this daye . . .', 'They speake upon the Exchange of . . .' and for Pepys, writing about an issue concerning fishing, 'the Exchange here hath been very clamorous'.[59]

54 Charles Porter to Williamson, 9 Apr. 1663, SP 29/71, fo. 141r.
55 'The Treasury and the City: a proposal to create an assistant (financial) secretary, 1710', in H. Roseveare, *The Treasury, 1660–1870: the foundations of control*, London 1973, 174–5.
56 Minutes of the Committee of Trade and Plantations, 25 Feb. 1675, CO 391/1, fo. 5r; Order in Council, 5 May 1675, CO 389/3, fos 1r–4v.
57 Harris, 'Exchanging information', 192.
58 McCusker and Gravesteijn, *Journalism*, ch. xxv. See also chapter 4 below.
59 Henry Muddiman to Mr Watts, 5 Mar. 1666, SP 29/150, fo. 24r; [H. Muddiman] to George Powell, 12 Dec. 1666, SP 29/181 fo.127r; James Hickes to Williamson, 27 Aug. 1668, SP 29/245 fo. 106r; R[obert] Yard to Williamson, 17 June 1671, SP 29/291 fo.10v; Samuel Pepys to Sir Roger Strickland, 18 Mar. 1675, in Tanner, *Descriptive catalogue*, iii. 16.

The Exchange offered its authority to information in more explicit ways as well. A published account of the surviving crew of a shipwreck was 'Attested by the Captain's own Hand, and two others, and very well known by most Merchants upon the Royal Exchange', and one Samuel Wilson wrote to Lord Arlington that what he knew of Acadie in Nova Scotia he 'cann prove by the testimony of sundry merchants who walke the Change daily'.[60] The merchants on the Exchange were, as Michael Harris argued in his study of newspapers, 'a generalised reference point for the validation of reports on a wide range of issues'.[61]

If the merchants on the Exchange, and perhaps the Exchange itself, might have been able to lend credibility to information it was a capacity that was at times toyed with. Misinformation that became in some sense 'public' on the Exchange created problems. Lord Hatton, for example, writing from the Channel Islands in 1672, complained to Lord Arlington that a false report concerning the sale of the islands to the French king had been received from England, which 'had been sent hither as a public discourse on the Exchange'.[62] Some 'false reports' were deliberately made at the Exchange. Two accounts survive of an incident in April 1691 in which a man rode past the Exchange and cried out untruthfully that the siege of Mons had been relieved. This deliberate attempt to spread misinformation was 'a contrivance of some betters, that had wagers about it' and perhaps most vividly reveals the significance of the Exchange as the nucleus of various information networks.[63] As one writer jested, 'It is the general Mint of all famous Lies'.[64]

As news, prices and expertise might be endorsed and questioned on the Exchange so too was the knowledge of individuals' reputations. In the early modern period personal reputation had to be protected at all costs as it partially determined financial success. It is to the negotiations of such reputations at the Exchange that we now turn.

---

60 *A sad and deplorable, but true account of the dreadful hardships, and sufferings of Capt. John Dean, and his company*, London 1711, title page. I am indebted to M. Harris, 'Shipwrecks in print; representations of maritime disaster in the late seventeenth century', in R. Myers and M. Harris (eds), *Journeys through the market: travel, travellers and the book trade*, Newcastle, Del. 1999, 41, for this reference. 'Samuel Wilsons information to the Lord Arlington', 1672, CO 1/29, fo. 21r.

61 Harris, 'Shipwrecks in print', 42.

62 Lord Hatton to Lord [Arlington], 27 Mar. 1672, SP 47/1, item 4.

63 Richard Lapthorne to Richard Coffin, 4 Apr. 1691, HMC, *Fifth report*, 381; Newsletter, London, 2 Apr. 1691, HMC, *Twelfth report, appendix VII, the manuscripts of S. H. Fleming, Esq., of Rydal Hall*, London 1890, 324. The Corporation made attempts to prevent such 'an Evil Practice upon the Publick Exchange, and elsewhere in the City': *Jovis Primo die Dec.embr' 1692; Annoque Regni Regis & Regine, Willielmi & Mariæ, Angl'*, London 1692. On such wagers see also Clark, *Betting on lives*, 21.

64 *Hickelty pickelty*, 10.

# 'He that hath lost his credit is dead to the world': negotiating reputation at the Royal Exchange

In seventeenth- and eighteenth-century England credit transactions, as Craig Muldrew has demonstrated, were ubiquitous. Individuals were bound together across the social hierarchy by their promises to pay later. An individual's reputation, to a large extent, determined whether others were prepared to trust him, or her, to fulfil financial obligations.[65] The term credit in its multiple meanings encapsulates this scenario: it referred to payments to be made later, one's capacity to pay later, and one's reputation. It is important not to separate these meanings because an individual's reputation, to a large extent, determined whether others were prepared to trust him, or her, to pay later.[66] For all members of this society, credit was an asset to be protected, as the proverb cautioned: 'He that hath lost his credit is dead to the world.'[67]

Defoe argued that credit, in the sense of a tradesman's capacity to pay later, was a 'blessing', 'the choicest ware he deals in', and 'the life and soul of his trade'.[68] However, approving views of personal credit were not without opponents in the eighteenth century, as Julian Hoppit has shown.[69] Less controversial was Defoe's claim that a tradesman relied on an untarnished reputation to achieve success to a greater extent than other individuals:

> there is a particular nicety in the credit of a tradesman, which does not reach in other cases: a man is slander'd in his character, or reputation, and 'tis injurious; and if it comes in the way of a marriage, or of a preferment, or post, it may disappoint and ruin him; but if this happens to a tradesman, he is immediately and unavoidably blasted, and undone.[70]

Richard Grassby, in his study of the seventeenth-century business community, substantiates this picture, and argues that the 'importance of honour and reputation cannot be overestimated'.[71] For merchants, a good reputation was an essential asset, not only because trust was required in credit transactions, but because every stage of buying and selling goods involved trust. Merchants in the seventeenth-century colonial trade, for example, actively organised their business to reduce the risks inherent in a commercial environment

---

[65] Muldrew, Economy of obligation; Hoppit, 'Use and abuse', and 'Attitudes to credit'.
[66] Daniel Defoe employs all three meanings of the term credit in a discussion entitled 'Tradesmen ruining one another by Rumour and Clamour, by Scandal and Reproach': Complete English tradesman, 225–6. See also the entries under the headings 'credit', and 'repute or reputation' in Glossographia angliana nova, London 1707.
[67] J[ohn] R[ay], A collection of English proverbs, Cambridge 1670, 6.
[68] [Defoe], Complete English tradesman, 225.
[69] Hoppit, 'Attitudes to credit', 312–16.
[70] [Defoe], Complete English tradesman, 226. Similarly, in The Spectator, the trader's credit 'is to him what Honour, Reputation, Fame, or Glory is to other sort of Men': The Spectator, 14 Oct. 1712.
[71] Grassby, Business community, 299.

which operated on trust.[72] For merchants in London the Exchange was a crucial site where traders' reputations were discussed, lost, saved, defended and attacked.

Samuel Pepys was pleased to record in his diary in 1664 that he began 'to be known' on the Exchange having gone there for several years.[73] Being recognised and, more important, being well esteemed on the Exchange were signs of a good reputation, and probably the most significant for those in London trading circles. For the government, a person's standing on the Exchange could carry a lot of weight. In January 1667 the king wrote to the Council of Barbados concerning the replacement of Lord Willoughby, who had been the island's governor. He was to be replaced by his brother 'whose faire Reputation and generall Esteeme is such, that with one voice and Consent upon the Exchange Hee was wished for his Brothers Successor . . . by the joinet Petition, of the Planters, Merchants, and Masters of Ship, trading and relating to our Island of Barbadas, and other our Charibee Islands'.[74] Similarly, defences might rest upon reputations at the Exchange: Mr Verbeeke and Mr Beverly, who in 1666 had been informed against 'by some Silke stockeinge weavers', were defended by the Lord Mayor of London who advised Secretary of State Williamson that 'upon the Exchange' they were 'esteemed verie honest p[er]sons, & affectionate to the English interest'.[75] Being well thought of on the Exchange, then, could open doors, and also keep some undesirable ones closed.

Reputations might also be damaged at the Exchange. In an attempt to clear his name in case it had been ruined at the Exchange Thomas Ludwell wrote to Secretary Williamson in November 1667 before departing for Virginia, concerned 'least my malitiously unjust enimies may have been as industrious to wound me by thire whippers upon the Exchange as I fear they have endeavored to doe at court'.[76] In their efforts to defend themselves, others too made a distinction between their reputation at the Exchange and elsewhere in London: Sir Thomas Lynch wrote from Jamaica, where he was lieutenant-governor, to Dr Benjamin Worsley in an attempt to save his reputation for he would have his 'Name Whyte at Villars Hous, how black soever Sr Bell's Partyzans have made itt on the Ex[change]'.[77]

Surviving depositions from a defamation case provide insight into how a reputation could be damaged, and what legal action could be undertaken in

---

72 N. Zahedieh, 'Credit, risk and reputation in late seventeenth-century colonial trade', *Research in Maritime History* xv (1998), 53–74.

73 *Pepys*, iii. 120.

74 Charles II to council of Barbados (draft), Jan. 1667, CO 1/21 fo. 3r. The petition is at 'The humble petition of the Planters and Merchants of Barbadoes', CO 1/20, part I, fo. 328r.

75 Tho[mas] Bludworth to Williamson, 4 Oct. 1666, SP 29/174, fo. 63r.

76 Thomas Ludwell to Secretary Williamson?, 9 Nov. 1676, CO 1/38, fo. 81r.

77 Sir Thomas Lynch to Dr Benjamin Worsley, CO 1/30, fo. 138v.

an attempt to recover it. On 8 October 1667 Mr Wych, part owner of a ship, met the master of the ship Mr Wyld, on the Exchange. In the case brought before the Consistory Court of London one deponent testified that Mr Wych said that he would do Mr Wyld, 'all the mischeife that hee could, and bid this dep[onen]t bid Mr Wyld to goe and looke after his whore, or whores, and Bastard or Bastards in Jamaica', and that the same words were repeated again at Change time. All three deponents defended Mr Wyld's reputation; the third ending his deposition by saying that Mr Wyld 'hath the reputation of a very honest man'.[78] Such an incident points to the importance for early modern traders of maintaining their sexual reputations in a commercial setting.

Could such episodes become physically violent within the Exchange? An incident in 1671 in which Alexander Frazer attacked James Shirley gives us some clues as to the limits of confrontational behaviour that were considered acceptable in the quadrangle. Examinations in the state papers record how Frazer, apparently carrying a 'great Cudgell', approached Shirley in the quadrangle and challenged him: 'You cowardly Rogue why did you not meet mee according to promise'. Frazer raised his cudgel at Shirley who 'stept back and laid his hand upon his sword, saying that, that was was not a place either for fighting or giveing any such base words'.[79] Shirley left the Exchange and when Frazer later followed him into the street they drew swords and 'severall passes were made by them at each other' before a soldier came between them.[80] Although the Exchange might be the venue for confrontation, then, there were limits as to what was considered acceptable behaviour in the Exchange quadrangle.

According to authors of merchant advice literature, reputations could be saved at the Exchange. John Vernon, in a manual for prospective apprentice merchants entitled *The compleat comptinghouse* (1678) observed that the reputation of a good substantial merchant could be ruined by failing to pay a bill of Exchange.[81] He gave instructions on the action to be taken when bills are not paid: 'you must go to the Exchange . . . and there you may enquire if any Person will pay such a Bill for the honour of the Drawer, or of any of the Endorsers: and there you will find some body undoubtedly that will, and he

---

[78] Consistory Court of London, deposition book, June 1679–June 1681, London, LMA, DL/C/239, fos 310r, 311v. My thanks to Jennifer Melville for telling me about this case and transcribing it for me.

[79] 'Examination of Capt. Roger Moore', 25 Mar. 1671, SP 63/330, fo. 176r.

[80] 'Ibid; 'Examination of Edward Bradston', 24 Mar. 1671; 'Examination of Roger Kelly', 24 Mar. 1671; 'Deposition by John Portlock', 24 Mar. 1671, SP 63/300, fos 176v–178r. James Shirley was tried for the rape of Mary Frazer, later Alexander's wife. He was found guilty but a retrial was ordered and later postponed: 'The king to the Lord lieutenant, and the king to Sir W. Domville', 27 Jan. 1671, TNA, SO 1/7, fo. 219r; 'Sir G. Rawdon to Viscount Conway', 13 July 1671, SP 63/330, part 2, fo. 97r; 'Order in council', 12 Jan. 1672, SP 63/331, fo. 5r; 'The king to the lord lieutenant', 16 Jan. 1672, SO 1/8, fo. 100r.

[81] John Vernon, *The compleat comptinghouse*, London 1678, 103.

must pay you the Principal and the Charges of the Protest, and Interest, if any due'.[82] The merchant on whose behalf the bill was paid had obligations and was 'bound by the Laws of Merchants' to pay the bill plus charges, and give 'thanks for stepping in, and so upholding his Credit'.[83] In an economy which comprised a fragile matrix of financial obligations it was in the interests of all that any individual did not renege on their agreements.

To lessen the chances of having unfulfilled obligations merchants were advised to visit the Exchange to determine the reputations of those with whom they were to do business. In a section on insuring ships, merchandise and housing, in the first edition of the pocket-sized commercial manual, *Comes commercii* (1699), Edward Hatton explained the place of the Exchange in the insuring procedure. After visiting the insurance office on the east side of the Royal Exchange, the 'next thing is to satisfy your self of the Solvency of those that are to insure, and in order to that you may desire the Office-keeper to give you the names of 6 or 8 of their best Men, which done, you may enquire after their Credit on the Exchange, or near the places of their abode'.[84] Indeed for some occupations official lists of approved or licensed individuals were displayed at the Exchange. In an attempt to regulate brokers in 1673 London's Common Council ordered that 'the Names and Surnames of all such Persons who are and shall be duly admitted and sworn Brokers as aforesaid, be speedily Printed or fairly Written in a Table, and published by being hung up at the Entrance of the Royal Exchange'.[85]

The themes explored in this section – the inseparability of the meanings of credit, as personal reputation and financial capacity, and the ways in which they were played out at the Exchange – are encapsulated in an anecdote in Roger North's biography of his brother Dudley, a merchant. Dudley North lost fifty pounds when the business of 'Lombard-street man', Benjamin Hinton, collapsed. His downfall 'made a great shake upon the Exchange', and was the end of a career which had begun when 'the banking goldsmiths came to him upon the Exchange, with low obeisances, "hoping for the honour" ' of keeping his cash.[86] Good credit was vital to success in business, and the Royal

---

82  Ibid. 104. Similarly, Edward Hatton in a section on bills of exchange in his *Merchant's magazine* described how, 'If the Bill is not yet paid, it is usual to go upon the Exchange to see if any Body will pay the said Bill, for the Honour of the Drawer': *The merchant's magazine*, London 1695, 176.

83  Vernon, *Compleat comptinghouse*, 105.

84  Edward Hatton, *Comes commercii*, London 1699, 291.

85  *Commune Concilium tentum . . .* [An act for the regulation of the brokers]. This regulation was enforced by a 1697 act of parliament, 8 and 9 William III, c. 32, which demanded that 'Brokers names and places of abode to be affixed on the Royal Exchange and in Guildhall'. This act was renewed in 1700 for seven years by 11 and 12 William, c. 13 and in 1707 the 1697 act was repealed and a new act was passed (6 Anne, c. 16) for regulating brokers. The 1707 act made no mention of the display of the names of brokers at the Exchange.

86  Roger North, *The life of the Honourable Dudley North*, in his *The lives of the Right Hon. Francis North, Baron Guilford; the Hon. Sir Dudley North; and the Hon. and Rev. Dr. John*

Exchange was the principal site in London where reputations of members of the business community were established, observed, determined, ruined and saved.

### 'the whole world's map': representing the Royal Exchange

As individuals sought to preserve their personal reputations at the Exchange, so efforts were made to maintain the Exchange's reputation by various parties that had vested interests in its trade – the Gresham Committee, the shop-keepers and the City authorities. For the Gresham Committee, part of maintaining the reputation of the Exchange was to ensure the smooth and orderly running of the Exchange. As has already been mentioned the Gresham Committee took measures to ease the congestion of foot traffic around the Exchange by trying to stop hawkers from selling printed materials and traders from dealing in Exchange Alley. The committee also attempted to prevent the crowding caused by the fruitsellers working at the north entrance to the Exchange for 'many Complaints are made of the Stoppages w[hi]ch are made by the Standing of their Baskets of fruite'.[87] Specific efforts were made to keep the surrounding alleys clear as well: Mr Sweeting, who let property in a passage at the east end of the Exchange, was asked to speak to his tenant 'the Vintner' who 'by Rolling his Casks of Wyne which breake the Stones, and Stop the passage Sometimes neare an whole day together'.[88] Similarly, the committee, along with other City authorities tried, apparently in vain, to stop hackney coaches waiting in front of the Exchange on Cornhill from obstructing access to the building.[89]

As well as taking steps to make approaching the Exchange easier the Gresham Committee and the city authorities tried to maintain proper order at the Exchange partly by attempting, as we have seen, to regulate the hours of trade, and to keep beggars and 'idle' people out of the building. The nature of the disorder such people could cause was made explicit in 1704 when the Common Council suggested that if the Exchange keepers were made constables they would be better able 'to keep the Royal Exchange cleare from all Beggars Vagrants & other loose and disorderly Persons who daily resort to that place & disturb the Merchants and others in negotiating their Affairs

North, ed. A. Jessopp, London 1890, ii. 175. On Hinton see F. G. H. Price, A handbook of London bankers: with some account of their predecessors, the early goldsmiths, London 1876, 77.
[87] Gresham repertory, 1669–76, p. 77. See also p. 203; Gresham repertory, 1678–1722, p. 507.
[88] Ibid. 1669–76, p. 150.
[89] Ibid. 1678–1722, p. 137; GL, MS 4069/2, Cornhill ward, 1652–1733, fos 300v, 311v, 315v–316r, 325v, 342r, 345r, 351r, 380v–381r, 383v, 389v, 393r, 396r, 400r, 411r, 417r, 420v, 424r, 427r, 430v, 435r, 443v, 456r, 460v, 464r, 467r, 470r, 474v, 477v, 481r, 484r, 487r; Pilkington Mayor [Order enforcing rules for hackney coaches] [London, 1691].

there'.[90] The city authorities also feared that the merchants were trading improperly, that they were transacting 'affaires, proper to the Exchange in tavernes Coffee-houses & places of Com[m]on Entertainment'. Not only was this seen to result in 'the disorder of trade & Familyes', but it also detracted from 'the reputation and fullnesse of that eminent concourse and meeting on the Exchange'.[91]

The Gresham Committee's very conscious conception of the existence and importance of the Exchange's reputation is particularly apparent in the discussion over how the Exchange was to be rebuilt after the Fire. Among the contentious issues was whether porticoes should be erected on the east and west sides of the Exchange, as well as on the north and south sides as they had been in the pre-Fire Exchange. At the end of March 1669, in the weighing up of the arguments, one of the arguments in favour of erecting all four porticoes, was 'what Fame hath Spake largely in the Eares of this City, the Kingdome & most forraigne Countreys of the Magnificence of this Structure'.[92] Part of the magnificence of the Exchange, from the committee's perspective, was its architecture. Before the Fire, the committee had responded to the complaints of two shopkeepers that customers avoided their shops because of a lack of light, that they could either enlarge an existing window, or construct a new one, 'provided they prejudice not the beauty of the Exchange, and by too much altering the uniformity'.[93]

Both the pre- and post-Fire Exchanges were appreciated for their architectural beauty and uniformity by writers of guide-books and histories of London, as well as by visitors. Thomas Delaune, in *The present state of London* (1681), described how the Exchange was rebuilt 'in a far more stately and Magnificent manner, of excellent Portland Stone, almost as durable as Marble, with such curious and admirable Architecture, especially for a Front, a Turret, and for Arch-work, that it far surpasseth all other Burses in Europe'.[94] Visitors to London sought out the Exchange to admire its architecture. According to the published Old Bailey proceedings, on a visit to London in February 1718 one Ambrose Walford (before having his purse stolen), 'willing to satisfy his Curiosity in viewing the Publick Buildings', visited the Royal Exchange where he 'gratified his Eye with that fine Structure'.[95] The Scotsman, John Macky, wrote in his *Journey through England* (1714), that of 'the Publick Buildings in London, the Exchange well deserves

90 CLRO, Rep. 108, 1703–4, p. 239. See also GL, MS 4069/2, Cornhill ward, 1652–1733, fo. 325v.

91 CLRO, Rep. 76, 1670–1, fo. 5v.

92 Gresham repertory, 1626–69, p. 368.

93 Ibid. p. 200. See also p. 197.

94 Tho[mas] Delaune, *The present state of London*, London 1681, 158–9. A very similar description of the Exchange appears in [Nathaniel Crouch] (pseudonym Richard Burton), *Historical remarques*, London 1681, 94–5.

95 *The proceedings on the king's commission of the peace, and oyer and terminer, and gaol-delivery of Newgate, held for the City of London, and county of Middlesex, at justice-hall in*

the first Place'.[96] Continental European visitors agreed. Henri Misson described it as 'un des plus beaux édifices de Londres', a visitor from Sweden as having a beautiful tower and an elegant clock, Samuel Sorbière as 'le mieux basti, & le plus regulier de Londres' and James Beeverell noted in some detail the fine architecture.[97] Controversy surrounds the authenticity of some of these accounts. John Macky, for example, in the dedication to his own book, criticises Beeverell who 'certainly had never been in England himself; for the Whole is only a wild Rhapsody collected from Cambden, and some other Authors, who have wrote the Natural History of distinct Counties'.[98] Whether or not writers described the Exchange in their own words from first-hand experience, an encomium to the Exchange was a standard feature of travel writing in this period, and the praise itself verged on the formulaic.

These testimonials to the Exchange's architecture were not only textual. Misson and Beeverell, for example, included detailed engravings of bird's-eye views of the Exchange in their books.[99] These were among many views of the Exchange engraved in this period, most of which were views of the exterior from such an angle that part of the interior courtyard could be seen.[100] Some representations were far more rudimentary, such as the print of the Exchange, part of a pair with Westminster Hall, bound into Delaune's *Present state of London*.[101] This print made the Exchange recognisable and distinguished it from other buildings but perhaps offered little more distinction.

One of the first to express reservations about the architectural magnificence of the Exchange in print was Colen Campbell in 1717 in his

the Old Bayly, on Wednesday, Thursday, Friday, and Saturday, being the 25th, 26th, 27th, and 28th of Feb., 1718, 5.

96 [John Macky], *A journey through England*, London 1714, 185.

97 [Henri Misson], *Memoires et observations faites par un voyageur en Angleterre*, The Hague 1698, 35 (published in English as *M. Misson's memoirs and observations in his travels over England with some account of Scotland and Ireland*, trans. [J.] Ozell, London 1719); Sven Bredberg, *Griefswald – Wittenberg – Leiden – London: Västgötamagistern Sven Bredbergs resadagbok 1708–1710 med inledning utgiven*, ed. H. Sandblad, Göteborg 1982, 112. My thanks to Daniel Grimley for translating this passage; [Samuel] Sorbière, *Relation d'un voyage en Angleterre*, Paris 1664, 35–6 (published in English as *A voyage to England*, London 1709); [James Beeverell], *Les Délices de la Grand' Bretagne et d'Irlande* [2nd edn], Leiden 1727, iv. 812.

98 [Macky], *Journey*, pp. ii–iii; D. Webb, 'Guide books to London before 1800: a survey', *London Topographical Record* xxvi (1990), 139. See also M. Blondel, 'French and English eighteenth-century guide-books to London: plagiarism and translations', *Notes and Queries* ccxxx (1985), 240–1; E. S. De Beer, 'The development of the guide-book until the early nineteenth century', *Journal of the British Archaeological Association* 3rd ser. xv (1952), 35.

99 [Misson], *Memoires*: 'Bourse De Londres', facing p. 34; [Beeverell], *Délices*, iv: 'La Bourse De Londres', facing p. 900.

100 See, for example, the particularly fine prints engraved by William Sherwin, 'The south-west prospect of the Royal Exchange of London'; 'Bursa Londini' (1668); 'The west prospect of the piazza of [th]e Royal Exchange, London', Department of Prints and Drawings, British Museum, London, Crace Collection, portfolio XXII, items 43–5.

101 Delaune, *Present state*, facing p. 161.

multi-volume work on British architecture, *Vitruvius Britannicus*, which was largely a survey of country house architecture lavishly illustrated with over two hundred folio engravings. In the text to accompany the plate of the Royal Exchange, it was noted that 'however inferior to those Pieces of Inigo Jones, yet [the Exchange] may very justly claim a Place in this Collection, being the most Considerable of this kind in Europe'.[102] For Campbell it was the building's status among bourses, rather than its place in the array of celebrated British buildings that merited its inclusion in this book. Like Campbell, others compared London's second exchange with those in continental Europe, and did not find it wanting: Zacharias Conrad Von Uffenbach, for example, in his visit to London in 1710 found it more elegant than the Amsterdam bourse.[103] Such comparisons were easy to make as the first Exchange building had been modelled on the continental bourses. After the end of the period there were further criticisms of the architecture. James Ralph, writing in 1734, found fault with the tower and the statues, and complained particularly that the building lacked a space in front of it from which to view.[104]

The reputation of the Exchange and indeed its 'magnificence' relied on more than its architectural qualities. It was known and celebrated perhaps more for being both the site of a great variety of luxury shops and a place where merchants gathered. The Gresham Committee took pains to ensure the smooth running of the shops and that the retailing did not interfere with the merchants' business nor bring the place into disrepute. They made efforts to limit 'annoyances', such as that experienced in 1677 by Mr Cooper and Mrs Baker, and the customers of their shops, from 'the Fumes from the Sifting of the pepper' at the bottom of the stairs leading to the cellars rented by the East India Company.[105] Restrictions were also placed on the sorts of businesses that could be run at the Exchange: in 1672, a tenant was prohibiting from subletting his shops 'to such p[er]sons as may therein Sell Wine, Ale, Coffee or other Liquors' for this would be 'to the annoyance of the M[er]chants, and disparragem[en]t of the Exchange'.[106] Indeed the honour and eminence that the shops were believed to bring the Exchange was a theme appealed to by all parties – tenants of the former shops, the pamphleteers who wrote on their behalf and the Gresham Committee – concerned about the reconstruction of the Exchange after the Fire whether

---

[102] Colen Campbell, *Vitruvius Britannicus*, London 1715–25, ii, sig. A1r.

[103] Zacharias Conrad Von Uffenbach, *London in 1710 from the travels of Zacharias Conrad Von Uffenbach*, ed. and trans. W. H. Quarrell and M. Mare, London n.d., 15.

[104] [James Ralph?], *A critical review of the publick buildings, statues and ornaments, in and about London and Westminster*, London 1734, 10–11. In 1768 it was contended that although the Exchange was 'a famous Building, it cannot stand the Test of a critical Enquiry' and that the 'Arcade or Walks with the Quadrangle hath something noble, but the upper Part is vile': *The London and Westminster guide*, London 1768, 29.

[105] Gresham repertory, 1669–76, p. 217.

[106] Ibid. p. 85.

they argued for or against having more shops in the building. Petitioners to the Gresham Committee claimed that the erection of a double pawn of shops would ruin the shopkeepers, and bring 'a Disreputation upon the place'.[107] Similarly, in a pamphlet supporting the construction of a double pawn, Henry Duke wrote that his interest lay in 'the benefit and advantage of the Royal Exchange', and his argument was imbued with the idea that the glory of the Royal Exchange rested on the great trade of the shops.[108] The Gresham Committee finally decided to build a double pawn of shops because 'itt will bee more Magnificent and pleaseing to his Ma[jes]ty and because itt will better answeare the charge of building'.[109] Perhaps, in the end, this had been a mistake as towards the end of the period the Gresham Committee was anxious about the number of shops left unleased. The request made to tenants in August 1716 was tellingly phrased: they were asked to propose remedies for this situation in order 'to Retreive the Credit of the Exchange'.[110]

Nevertheless, while the shops were thriving much was made of the immense variety and luxury of the commodities for sale. Contemporary writers went into lavish detail in their descriptions of the range and the qualities of the goods that were for sale. The author of *Great Britain's glory, or a brief description of the present state, splendor, and magnificence of the Royal Exchange* (1672) claimed that goods could be bought from the Exchange shops that were not available anywhere else in England, and went on to list gowns, caps, slippers, bonelace, gloves, garters, ribbons, cornelian rings and lockets among the goods that could be purchased.[111] The upper part of the Exchange, where the luxury shops were, was in Samuel Rolle's words 'the great Storehouse . . . where, might a man have seen the glory of the world in a moment'.[112] These writers captured the range of goods, many of which were imported, that were available for consumption in London in this period. The bringing together of a range of imported goods into a single image also appealed to other writers in this period. Joseph Addison in *The Spectator* employed the device of an imagined dress to explore the array of imperial goods sourced from different climates:

---

107 Ibid. 1626–69, pp. 329, 331; 1678–1722, p.1.
108 [Duke], *Londons-nonsuch*, sig. [B1v]. Henry Duke employed a similar line of argument in a later petition to the Gresham Committee on behalf of some of the tenants of the Exchange shops: DEHNKRVY [Henry Duke], *A brief memorial wherein the present case of the antient leasees . . . [is] truely, and impartially stated*, London 1674, 23. Henry Duke also presented these petitions to the Gresham Committee: Gresham repertory, 1669–76, p. 174.
109 Gresham repertory, 1626–69, p. 331.
110 Ibid. 1678–1722, p. 495.
111 Theophilus Philalethes, *Great Britain's glory*, London 1672, 17, 18–19.
112 Samuel Rolle, *[Shlohavot] or, the burning of London in the year 1666*, London 1667, pt III, 46.

The single Dress of a Woman of Quality is often the Product of an hundred Climates. The Muff and the Fan come together from the different Ends of the Earth. The Scarf is sent from the Torrid Zone, and the Tippet from beneath the Pole. The Brocade Petticoat rises out of the Mines of Peru, and the Diamond Necklace out of the Bowels of Indostan.[113]

Scholars have charted the capturing of various imperial goods in a single image, most notably in Dutch still-life paintings and Alexander Pope's description of Belinda's toilette in his poem, *The rape of the lock*.[114] As 'the empire of goods' might be captured in the image of a dress, or a still life, so too could it be contained in the image of the Exchange shops as 'the great store house' of imported luxury goods.[115]

Depictions of the Exchange as a microcosm of the trading world also drew on the powerful image of the quadrangle with the international assortment of merchants trading on the various walks, and in so doing drew attention slightly away from the consumption of goods to their exchange. The Exchange was described in a poem published in 1690 as a place 'Of Nations, and of Languages'.[116] Many others in this period remarked upon the gathering of merchants and traders of different nationalities there. In 1711 Addison described how he looked upon the Exchange as a 'great Council, in which all considerable Nations have their Representatives'. He referred to the merchants as 'Ministers of Commerce', and wrote that he had often 'been pleased to hear Disputes adjusted between an Inhabitant of Japan and an Alderman of London, or to see a Subject of the Great Mogul entering into a League with one of the Czar of Muscovy'.[117] For Voltaire, too, commerce could prevail over difference, and although he wrote after the end of the period his observations on the Exchange are worth quoting. It was 'a place more venerable than many courts of justice, where the representatives of all nations meet for the benefit of mankind'. As he wrote, 'There the Jew, the Mahometan, and the Christian transact together as tho' they all profess'd the same religion, and give the name of Infidel to none but bankrupts.'[118]

Earlier, Rolle had developed this theme of the gathering of nationals in a slightly different direction, to argue that the Exchange was a microcosm of

---

113 *The Spectator*, 19 May 1711, 213.

114 L. A. Landa, 'Pope's Belinda, the general emporie of the world, and the wondrous worm', *South Atlantic Quarterly* lxx (1971), 215–35; Nicholson, *Writing*, ch. i; S. Schama, 'Perishable commodities: Dutch still-life painting and the "empire of things" ', in Brewer and Porter, *Consumption and the world*, 478–88. See also K. Newman, 'City talk: women and commodification in Jonson's *Epicoene*', *English Literary History* lvi (1989), 503–18; Rabuzzi, 'Commercial mentalities', 180–2.

115 The phrase is Breen's: T. H. Breen, 'An empire of goods: the Anglicization of colonial America, 1690–1776', *JBS* xxv (1986), 467–99.

116 T[homas] D['Urfey], *Collin's walk through London and Westminster*, London 1690, 63.

117 *The Spectator*, 19 May 1711.

118 De Voltaire, *Letters concerning the English nation*, London 1733, 44.

the trading world. Rolle reflected on the first Exchange after its destruction in 1666:

> Was not that the Center in which these lines met, that were drawn from all parts of Europe? rich Merchants, I mean, and other eminent Trades-men and great Dealers, not onely English, but Spanish, French, Dutch, Portugueze, Danes, Swedes. Was not the place a little Epitomie, or rather Representative of all Europe (if not the greatest part of the trading World) renewed every day at such a time, and for so many hours?[119]

As Addison captured the empire in his image of a dress, Rolle saw it recreated each day at this hub of the commercial world for a few hours. Authors saw parallels between the Exchange and maps of the world. The anonymous author of a poem published in 1674 to celebrate the rebuilding of London, described the Exchange, 'the eighth great wonder of the world', thus:

> This is the Centre of Commerce for here
> Nations from the circumference appear;
> Here we see, point and meet the worlds extream's,
> Just like the lines we see in printed schemes.[120]

The author of *Hickelty pickelty*, a one penny 'medly of characters', published in 1708, took the parallel further. The Exchange might be a microcosm of Great Britain, or even the world: it 'Is the Land's Epitome, or you might call it the little Isle of Great-Britain, did the Waters encompass it. It is more, 'tis the whole World's Map, which you may here discern in its perfectest Motion, justling and turning.'[121] Tellingly this 'character' of the Exchange was lifted directly from John Earle's *Micro-cosmographie*, first published in 1628, and repeatedly republished until the early twentieth century.[122] For Earle, however, this was a character of St Paul's Walk; as the Exchange had in some ways, as noted above, usurped the role of St Paul's Walk, it had, in at least one author's opinion, also taken on its 'character'.

Visitors to the capital were encouraged to visit the Exchange where the jostling merchants could be viewed from above. Not all experienced the Exchange in person but were taken by authors, like the writer of an encomium to the Exchange who led readers by the hand: 'Come Reader then, let us joyn hand in hand, / And take a view of this rich Piece of Land.'[123] Those visitors to London who read François Colsoni's *Le Guide de Londres pour les*

119  Rolle, *Burning of London*, pt III, 45.
120  *Troia rediviva*, London 1674, 31.
121  *Hickelty pickelty*, 10.
122  John Earle, *Micro-cosmographie*, 9th edn, London 1669, 218–21. The author of *Hickelty pickelty* does omit some parts of Earle's account of Paul's Walk. On the various editions of *Micro-cosmographie* see G. Murphy, *A bibliography of English character-books, 1608–1700*, Cambridge 1925, 35–44.
123  Philalethes, *Glory*, 5.

*estrangers* (1693) were instructed in French that the first thing to see was the Royal Exchange.[124] Among its attractions were the merchants, and he informed his readers of when they gathered at the Exchange. So keen was Colsoni on the Exchange that in the grammar (with eight pages of 'dialogue familier') bound to some of the 1710 editions of his guide were such useful phrases as 'I must go to the Royal Exchange' and how to ask directions to the Exchange, and the times of the afternoon exchange.[125] Colsoni recommended that his readers went to the upper part of the Exchange and stood on one of the balconies from where 'l'on peut voir le monde qui est à la Bourse d'en bas, qui sy' promene ou passe à travers'.[126] These balconies had been constructed partly to 'add much to . . . the pleasure of the Customers', and indeed visitors did enjoy the display of merchants as a spectacle.[127] Béat Louis de Muralt, from Switzerland, viewing the Exchange quadrangle from one of the balconies, saw below him 'the World in Epitome', and how the merchants 'stir about like a Swarm of Ants', and hum 'like a Swarm of Bees'.[128] Of course, the association between bees and commerce had been well rehearsed by the time Muralt visited the Exchange, most notably by Bernard Mandeville.[129] Similarly for the author of *Hickelty pickelty*, 'The Noise in it [the Exchange quadrangle], is like that of Bees; a strange Humming or Buzzing, or walking Tongues and Feet; it is a kind of a still Roaring, or loud Whisper.'[130] Ned Ward's London Spy also commented on the noise at the Exchange: 'an Incessant Buz, like the Murmurs of the distant Ocean, stood as a Diapason, to our Talk, like a Drone to a Bagpipe'.[131] For Steele, in *The Spectator*, listening to the merchants in the Exchange quadrangle below 'all the several Voices lost their Distinction, and rose up in a confused Humming'.[132]

Such images of busy merchants buzzing around a world in miniature were also employed in the description of at least one provincial place of trade. Admirers of regional market places in the period usually limited their praise to the simple descriptors of 'commodious' or 'convenient'. However, the Tolzey at Bristol where merchants conducted trade was described in 1712 in the following glowing terms:

> I humble Subjects leave, by higher led
> To view the City's Trade at Fountain Head,

124 F[rançois] Colsoni, *Le Guide de Londres pour les estrangers*, London 1693, 1–2.
125 'Dialogue familier', 7, 8, 16, ibid. 3rd edn, London 1710.
126 Colsoni, *Guide* (1693), 1–2.
127 Gresham repertory, 1626–69, p. 360.
128 [Béat Louis de] Muralt, *Letters describing the character and customs of the French and English nations*, 2nd edn, London 1726, 80 (published in French as *Lettres sur les anglois et les françois*, Cologne 1725).
129 Bernard Mandeville, *The fable of the bees*, London 1714.
130 *Hickelty pickelty*, 10.
131 [Edward Ward], *The London Spy*, Jan. 1699, pt III, London 1699, 13.
132 *The Spectator*, 11 Aug. 1712.

Where working Brains from diverse Quarters meet,
And wealthy Commerce drive in eager Heat:
As burning Glasses scatter'd Rays unite
In central Point, then raise a kindling Light.
Tho' distant Worlds in largest Compass run
From Pole to Pole from East to Western Sun;
The whole Extent, where trading Actions reigns,
This busy Spot, as in a Map, contains.[133]

Like the authors of *Hickelty pickelty* and *Troia rediviva*, William Goldwin uses the device of a map to describe the concentration of the trading world in a single arena. For Goldwin a powerful image is needed to describe the 'jostling and turning' at the Tolzey and from natural philosophy he borrows the device of the concentration of light using a lens to start a fire to describe the intensity of the 'wealthy Commerce' driven 'in eager Heat' by the 'working Brains from diverse Quarters'.

Such a world was not only to be celebrated by writers, or enjoyed by spectators, it also offered a classroom for the sorts of educational programmes proposed by political arithmeticians, among others, with their keen interest in knowledge about trade. Among William Petty's manuscript papers is a proposal, 'How by the present greatnes & state of London, to make it supply the use of forain Travell to the Youth of England.' He recognised the Exchange as a microcosm of the trading world, and suggested that experiencing it would be a substitute for the foreign travel which was a fundamental element of a gentleman's education in this period. 'The Exchange of London will furnish men every day who have fresh concerne & correspondance with all parts of the knowne world & with all the Commodityes growing or made within the same.' According to Petty, in the areas around the Court, the Exchange and the Inns of Court were people 'as different as in 8 severall Cittyes or nations'.[134]

Not only were such conceptions of the Exchange pursued with unrelenting regularity by writers, they were also captured visually in a number of engravings of the interior courtyard of the Exchange, in the form of either a view or a plan, on which were indicated the names of the different walks where the merchants met.[135] Even in prints unpopulated by merchants the

---

133 William Goldwin, *A poetical description of Bristol*, London 1712. Interestingly, in the 1712 edition the footnote to this section refers to the Tolzey. By the time of the 1751 edition (revised by I. Smart) the Exchange in Bristol had been built and the footnote refers to this instead.

134 William Petty, 'The uses of London', in *The Petty papers*, ed. the marquis of Landsdowne, London 1927, i. 40–1, 42.

135 'A view of the inside of the Royal-Exchange in Cornhill London as it now is 1712 describeing the walks used by the merchants of divers nations, and representing the statues of all the kings and queens', in Joseph Smith, *Nouveau Theatre de la Grande Bretagne*, London 1724, iv, plate 24. Another version of this engraving, attributed to Sutton Nicholls, with two additional inset pictures of the Exchange ('A view of the interior of the

floor plan of the Exchange quadrangle could stand in for the trading world as a whole. Here one plan, from Pepys's collection, is the focus of this discussion (*see* Figure 1).[136] It was produced by Wapping-based John Seller, in Coolie Verner's estimation 'an entrepreneur with lofty ambitions', who made instruments as well as producing nautical maps.[137] He had a shop on the west side of the Exchange from 1682 to 1686, and this print probably dates from no earlier than 1684 when the statue of Charles II was placed in the middle of the quadrangle.[138] The caption states that it could be bought from Seller's shop at the Exchange and indeed the shop's location is marked on the left-hand side of the print at the east entrance to the Exchange.

The print was more than a simple advertisement for his shop. As a guide for those visiting the Exchange, the accuracy and elaborateness of the plan were more than sufficient. As some visitors to the Exchange paced out the dimensions of the quadrangle so this 'ichnographical draught or ground plat' was drawn to scale, and more than likely accurately represented the patterns of the cobbles in the open part of the quadrangle and the marble floor tiles in the covered walks.[139] Such precision and detail advertised the quality of Seller's goods. Pepys, a regular at the Exchange, and acquaintance of Seller, certainly thought it was worthwhile putting in his collection of prints alongside six other prints of the interior and exterior of the Exchange, and a print of the statue of Charles II.[140]

Exchange at Cornhill') can be found in the Crace Collection, portfolio XXII, item 48, and in the London Guildhall Library Print Room, La.Pr.512/ROY(2)int. It is reproduced in Saunders, *Royal Exchange*, fig. 36 at p. 141. See also 'Interior view of the Royal Exchange, 1720', drawn by D. Chodowiecki and engraved by Schleuen, Crace Collection, portfolio XXII, item 54. Other prints with labelled walks date from after 1720.

136 John Seller, 'An ichnographical draught or ground plat of the Royall Exchange in London', Pepys Library, Magdalene College, Cambridge, 2972/68, 69. No other copy of this print has been traced. Richard Gough noted it in his survey of prints of the Exchange: *British topography*, London 1780, i. 710.

137 C. Verner, 'Engraved title plates for the folio atlases of John Seller', in H. Wallis and S. Tyacke (eds), *My head is a map: essays and memoirs in honour of R. V. Tooley*, London 1973, 23.

138 Idem, 'John Seller and the chart trade in seventeenth-century England', in N. J. W. Thrower (ed.), *The compleat plattmaker: essays on chart, map, and globe making in England in the seventeenth and eighteenth centuries*, Berkeley 1978, 138; K. Gibson, ' "The kingdom's marble chronicle": the embellishment of the first and second buildings, 1600–1690', in Saunders, *Royal Exchange*, 155. On John Seller see also R. A. Skelton, *County atlases of the British Isles, 1579–1850: a bibliography*, London 1964–70, v. 246; S. Tyacke, *London map-sellers, 1660–1720*, Tring 1978, 139–40.

139 Admittedly Sutton Nicholls may have had this print in front of him when he engraved his view of the Exchange in 1712 but it is worth noting that the patterns of the floor tiles and cobbles are the same: 'A view of the interior of the Exchange at Cornhill', 1712. On the laying of the tiles see Gresham repertory, 1626–69, p. 375.

140 Various connections between Pepys and Seller can be established: Pepys possessed a number of maps and charts published by Sellers, and references to the mapmaker in Pepys's papers suggest that they were acquainted: *Samuel Pepys's naval minutes*, ed. J. R. Tanner, London 1926, 370; A. W. Aspinall, *Catalogue of the Pepys Library at Magdalene College*

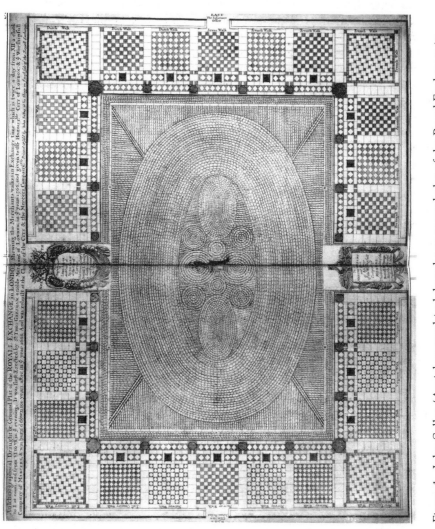

Figure 1. John Seller, 'An ichnographical draught or ground plat of the Royal Exchange in London' (1669). Pepys Library, Magdalene College, Cambridge, 2972/68 & 69. Reproduced by permission of the Pepys Library.

The print was 'humbly dedicated and Presented' to the bodies in charge of the Exchange – the Mercers' Company and the Lord Mayor and Court of Aldermen – their arms were carefully engraved above the elaborate cartouches containing the dedications which were placed on the plan at the north and south entrances to the Exchange.[141] Such dedications and gifts would probably have oiled the wheels of patronage for Seller and not only because he was a tenant at the Exchange. For one whose livelihood depended on selling instruments and nautical maps an opportunity not only to bring his name in front of influential City traders but also to be seen to be doing so might have brought Seller more business. Perhaps such a print could not have been produced without their endorsement: certainly straight after the rebuilding of the Exchange the Gresham Committee took pains to control who published prints of prospects of the structure.[142]

Seller's print honoured the Mercers and the City for paying for the rebuilding of the Exchange, as well as celebrating the building's long history and its founder, Thomas Gresham, as detailed in the caption. Seller also provided information about the meeting of the merchants at the Exchange: he gave the Change times in the caption, and the location of the walks on the plan. As writers struggled to capture the concentration of international merchants at the Exchange in words, Seller's print simply *is* a map of the trading world at the Exchange. By locating the walks of the colonial traders, the Baltic traders, the Scandinavian trade, the Scots, the Irish, the continental European traders, as well as the Jewish traders in the Exchange quadrangle he had created 'the whole World's map' on a single sheet of paper.

The only other plan that can be dated to this period is one that Edward Hatton included in his two-volume *A new view of London* published in 1708. Hatton was also the author of *Comes commercii* and some other commercial manuals which will be discussed in chapter 3. Certainly he was well acquainted with the operation of trade in London. Hatton's account of the Exchange in his description of London had something in it for each of the groups he claimed would benefit from his book: 'useful not only for Strangers,

---

*Cambridge*, III: *Prints and drawings* I: *General*, ed. R. Latham, Woodbridge 1980, 15; R. Latham (ed.), *Catalogue of the Pepys Library at Magdalene College Cambridge*, IV: *Music maps and calligraphy*, Woodbridge 1989, 8–11, 15–17, 33–4, 37, 41, 48–50. On Pepys's collection of Exchange-related prints see Aspinall, *Catalogue of the Pepys Library*, iii/I, 4.

141 Two plans of the Exchange quadrangle survive from later in the eighteenth century which were also designed to be presented to the authorities in charge of the Exchange: 'A Plan of the Royal Exchange . . . Humbly Dedicated to the Right Hon[our]ble the Lord Mayor & the Worshipful the Grand Committee . . . . By . . . . Sam[ue]l Walter & Joseph Threlkeld. Exchange Keepers', and 'The Elevation, Plan, and History, of the Royal Exchange of London . . . To the R[igh]t Hon[oura]ble S[i]r Crisp Gascoyne . . . and to the Worshipful Company of Mercers . . . by . . . R. Forrest' (1752–3?), London Royal Exchange Assurance PLC.

142 Gresham repertory, 1669–76, p. 77. See also the tantalising entry on p. 3 where unfortunately the page has been trimmed.

but the Inhabitants [of London], and for all Lovers of Antiquity, History, Poesie, Statuary, Painting, Sculpture, Mathematicks, Architecture and Heraldry'.[143] He ends his account of the inside of the Exchange noting that 'for the more facile expediting the Affair of Negoce, Merchants dealing in the same Commodities have by custom fixed on these different parts of the Exchange to meet one another, called their Walk. I cannot otherways make it so briefly intelligible as by this short Sketch of the Plan of this Royal Burse'.[144] This engraving was less ornate than Seller's, more clearly labelled and although it could be argued it might have been more effective as a guide to the location of walks it was no less effective as an image that captured this international world.

These are the only two plans of the Exchange quadrangle on which the walks were labelled that can be dated to this period. Later in the eighteenth century guide-books and histories of London often included engraved plans of the Exchange quadrangle indicating the location of the walks.[145] In his *History of London* (1739), Maitland, for example, having described how the 'the Area of the Royal Exchange is canton'd out into a great Number of Parts or Places, call'd Walks', justified his inclusion of a plan: 'But as a Represent-ation therefore to the Eye, as well as to the Mind, is necessary, I have thought fit to subjoin a Plan thereof, for the better Information of the Reader.'[146]

These conceptions collapsed the trading world into a single image. Whether it was a plan of the Exchange quadrangle, a description in verse of the merchants of different nationalities gathered there, or an imagined dress, the extensive, exotic and complicated trading world was captured, defined and understood, and to some extent made imaginable through these images.

### 'a gaming table': speculation and scandal at the Royal Exchange

In the images discussed so far, commerce at the Exchange was characterised as involving international merchants trading in tangible, and mostly luxury, goods.[147] Admittedly, the Exchange was sometimes associated with the less tangible areas of insurance and bills of exchange but the 'elusive' trade in stocks was usually located by writers in Exchange Alley (even if it was being undertaken in the Exchange quadrangle), and, particularly in 1720 when the South Sea Bubble burst, satirists made much of the speculation frenzy there.[148] But occasionally the Exchange itself was also associated with the

---

143 Edward Hatton, *A new view of London*, London 1708, i, title page.
144 Ibid. ii. 617.
145 Harris, 'Exchanging information', 192.
146 Maitland, *History of London*, 467.
147 Pocock, *Machiavellian moment*, 456.
148 [Daniel Defoe], *The anatomy of Exchange-Alley*, London 1719; M. Hallett, *The spectacle of difference: graphic satire in the age of Hogarth*, New Haven 1999, 57–61.

trade in stocks, even after the brokers had supposedly left the quadrangle. Defoe invoked the common rebuke of stocks as lacking foundation in his attack on 'the Interests of Elections Jobb'd up on Exchange for Mony' during the turn-of-the-century general election in which the conflict between the Old and New East India Company became embroiled.[149] Defoe's free-holder argued that 'all Men whose Eyes are to be open'd with Reason and Argument' should find the growth of the 'Scandalous Mechanick Upstart Mistery of Job-brokeing' and their growth in England abhorrent. The perpetrators 'can turn all Trade into a Lottery, and make the Exchange a Gaming Table: A thing, which like the Imaginary Coins of Foreign Nations, have no reality in themselves; but are plac'd as things which stand to be Calculated, and Reduc'd into Value, a Trade made up of Sharp and Trick, and manag'd with Impudence and Banter'.[150] Like the many other attacks on the stock market, and credit in general, in this period the trade in 'imaginary' goods was feared and condemned.[151] The dishonest ways of stockjobbers on the Exchange were pursued by other writers. Brown poked fun at the stockjobbers in the quadrangle and joked that they sold 'Upright Honesty or Down-right Dealing' as 'they are dead Commodities'.[152] Indeed some narratives turned on the idea that stockjobbers in the Exchange could only be trusted to be untrustworthy. In an inversion of the established country person outwitted by city folk trope, the eponymous heroine of the ballad *The country girl's policy* arrives from Herefordshire at the Royal Exchange with her illegitimate baby hidden in a basket under the necks of two geese. Handing the basket to some stockjobbers to look after while she goes up the stairs apparently to admire the pictures displayed above, the jobbers run off with the basket believing they have duped the girl out of her geese. Of course, the last laugh is on the jobbers when they, in front of their wives, discover the baby and it is only with feigned anger that the girl declares: 'I'll never come to the Royal Exchange, any more to sell my Ware: / For by a couple of cheating Knaves, alas I am undone.'[153] For, of course, that the knaves were 'cheating' had allowed her to regain her honour.

---

[149] P. Gauci, *The politics of trade: the overseas merchant in state and society, 1660–1720*, Oxford 2001, 195; R. Walcott, 'The East India interest in the general election of 1700–1701', *EHR* lxxi (1956), 223–39.

[150] Daniel Defoe, *The free-holders plea against stock-jobbing elections of parliament men*, 2nd edn, London 1701, 10, 21. With less emphasis on the illusory stock market and more on the dangers of credit transactions, the 'Country Spy' critically described the Exchange after the end of this period: 'Here bargains are made without Money, and Debts contracted that will never be paid: One Tradesman takes Goods from another upon Credit for six Months, and becomes a Bankrupt before five of them are expired': *The country spy or a ramble thro' London*, London 1730?, 31.

[151] John Pocock's discussion of this subject remains the most influential; *Machiavellian moment*, ch. viii.

[152] Brown, *Amusements*, 31.

[153] *The country girl's policy*, [London 1701?].

For detractors of trade at the Exchange, cheating, unlike the irredeemable stockjobbing, left open the possibility of future reform. Rolle, from whose book quotations on the glory of the Royal Exchange have been taken in this chapter, couched his criticisms of the *way* trade was carried out at the Exchange with such reform in mind. He argued that the 'craft and covetousnesse' of the merchants in the courtyard, and the 'pride and prodigality' of those shopping above, were the sins that providentially led to the destruction of the Exchange in the Fire.[154] This view was not inconsistent with his encomium of the Royal Exchange however, for he concluded with the hope that another Exchange would be used only for 'honest Merchandise', and that men and women who shop there would use it to put 'them and theirs, into a decent equipage, befitting their respective qualities'.[155]

Such tensions between the Exchange as a palace of wonder, excitement and glorious commerce and as a site for frauds, cheats and misdeals fit into a long tradition of London being figured as a place of both 'vanities' and 'vices'.[156] In much writing in this period the two were inextricably linked and this association is apparent in the writing about the Royal Exchange. For Tom Brown, the Exchange was at the same time 'a Magnificent building' and a place where political trouble might be stirred up, stockjobbers could be relied on to be cheats and all sorts of other amusing mischief could be observed. Brown and his companion witnessed the striking of fraudulent insurance deals, a broker teasingly approached about the sale of 'Spiders Brains, Philosophers Guts . . . [and] Hens Teeth', 'a Publick Notary tied to an Inkhorn' and a 'Hunger-starv'd Usurer in quest of a Crasie Citizen for Use and Continuance-Money'.[157] Brown celebrated 'all this Hodge-Podge [as] a Pleasant Confusion, and a Perfect Amusement'.[158] Besides the amusement to be got from observing the errant commercial dealing Brown also pokes fun at other scandalous behaviour playing on the well-worn themes of the dangers of gaming and the upstart merchant's rapacity for gentry status:

See, there's a Beau that has Play'd away his Estate at a Chocolate-House, going to Sell himself to Barbadoes, to keep himself out of Newgate, and from Scandalizing his Relations at Tyburn. . . .

Behind that Pillar is a Welch Herald deriving a Merchant's Pedigree from Adam's Great-Grandfather, to entitle him to a Coat of Arms, when he comes to be an Alderman.

154 Rolle, *Burning of London*, pt III, 48.
155 Ibid. 49.
156 The expression is Ned Ward's and is cited by P. Slack in his 'Perceptions of the metropolis in seventeenth-century England', in P. Burke, B. Harrison and P. Slack (eds), *Civil histories: essays presented to Sir Keith Thomas*, Oxford 2000, 179. See also P. Lake, 'From Troynouvant to Heliogabulus's Rome and back: "order" and its others in the London of John Stow', in J. F. Merritt (ed.), *Imagining early modern London: perceptions and portrayals of the city from Stow to Strype, 1598–1720*, Cambridge 2001, 217–49.
157 Brown, *Amusements*, 26–9.
158 Ibid. 29.

Brown also highlights another popular theme, the sexual exploits negotiated at the Exchange: 'Look! Yonder's a Jew treading upon an Italian's foot, to carry on a Sodomitical Intrigue, and Bartering their Souls here, for Fire and Brimstone in another World.'[159] As Brown could describe such goings on as taking place in a 'Magnificent building' so too could the author of *Hickelty pickelty*, for whom the Exchange was celebrated as 'the whole World's Map' moving in its 'perfectest Motion', locate it as a site of debauchery. 'Is a Man a Whore-master, he may here be furnish'd with dry and wet Nurses for his Bastard; and even amongst this Crowd of Reformers, there are Bills stuck up here and there, to encourage Debauchery.'[160] The upper floor of the Exchange, where the luxury shops were located, many of which were run by women, was most closely associated with 'debauchery'. As the narrator's companion in Ned Ward's serialised exploration of London, *The London Spy*, noted, having climbed the stairs to the upper pawn: 'This Place is a Nursery for Wives, the Merchant's Seraglio.'[161]

The difficulties writers had in distinguishing such shopkeepers selling wares from purveyors of consolation, have been usefully explored by James Grantham Turner in an account of the exchange women at the New Exchange, the Strand's two-storied luxury shopping centre and one of the Exchange's competitors.[162] For some writers the two roles were so entangled that they entertained the idea that 'illicit sexuality drives the entire machine of polite society, fashionable assembly, luxury consumption, and cultural-discursive display'.[163] That illicit sexuality and thriving commerce could be connected might go some way towards helping us to understand how writers could at the same time entertain such apparently conflicting views of the Royal Exchange. As Peter Lake suggests, we should also be wary that such ideas are in conflict: 'as many a godly preacher complained, the profane and ungodly were only too adept at repackaging drunkeness and gluttony as good fellowship or hospitality, at relaunching greed as prudence and proud and wasteful conspicuous consumption as the fitting display of status and wealth'.[164] Indeed, in an issue of the organ of politeness, *The Spectator*, attributed to Steele's editorship, in a ramble around London to 'tire my Imagination' the writer indulges himself with a visit to the upper floor at the Exchange where the pleasure he takes in the women there leaves perhaps

159  Ibid. 31–2.
160  *Hickelty pickelty*, 10.
161  [Ward], *London Spy*, Jan. 1699, pt III, 14.
162  J. G. Turner, ' "News from the New Exchange": commodity, erotic fantasy, and the female entrepreneur', in Bermingham and Brewer, *Consumption of culture*, 419–39. The New Exchange, built in 1608–9, had been opened by James I as Britain's Burse and its popularity, especially in the late seventeenth century, may have contributed to the declining trade of the shops in the upper pawn of the Royal Exchange.
163  Ibid. 426; Slack, 'Perceptions', 179.
164  Lake, 'Troynouvant', 219.

only just enough room for readers to pretend they are unaware of his inclinations:

> it was not the least of the Satisfactions in my Survey, to go up Stairs, and pass the Shops of agreeable Females; to observe so many pretty Hands busie in the Folding of Ribbands, and the utmost Eagerness of agreeable Faces in the Sale of Patches, Pins, and Wires, on each Side the Counters, was an Amusement, in which I should longer have indulged my self, had not the dear Creatures called to me to ask what I wanted, when I could not answer, only To look at you.[165]

If his actions were restricted to only looking (indeed he claimed that 'the greatest Pleasure I receive at my Eyes') then the ambiguity of the reference to the sale of patches suggests the gaze was not innocent. Patches were used to disguise the marks left by venereal disease and by listing them amongst the goods sold he alluded to prostitution.

Even if we might still be attached to the attempt to separate vices and vanities, or to put it another way, to establish that there is some sort of significant gap between *The Spectator* and, say, Ward's *London Spy*, then we still need to attend to the enormous amount of ground they have in common. For the burlesque writer Ward, as for the polite Addison, the Exchange was an international gathering; Addison applauded the 'Ministers of Commerce' and Ward described the home to 'sundry Nations': 'Bumfirking-Italians', Spaniards who were recognised by their smell 'for they Stink as strong of Garlick as a Polonian Sausage', and Jews who were 'so accurs'd for their Infidelity, that they are generally the Richest People in all Nations where they dwell'.[166]

For the Gresham Committee, always intent on preserving the magnificence of the Exchange and protecting its reputation, it remained a struggle to keep the vices and vanities separated. Not only did they try to prevent the disorder caused by the congestion around the Exchange but they also made efforts to deal with 'nastinesse' and 'scandalous papers'. The committee was called upon to deal with the 'great annoyances' and 'the noysome smell' caused by people urinating: 'the little Vacuity or Nooke at the foot of the Eastermost of the Fower Great Collumns on the South side of the Exchange is made a comon pissing place in the day time & every morning . . . it is like a Comon Jakes filled with nastinesse'.[167] Part of the Exchange stood in Cornhill Ward and the ward authorities were also involved in trying to keep order around the Exchange. The ward's raker, Robert Alsop, was presented at the wardmote in 1662 for having neglected his duties, one consequence of

---

[165] *The Spectator*, 11 Aug. 1712.

[166] [Ward], *London Spy*, Jan. 1699, pt III, 14.

[167] Gresham repertory, 1678–1722, pp. 80, 498–9, 310.

which was 'a dunghill before the Exchange to the great offence of the Inhabitants and of Merchants and other passengers'.[168]

The Gresham Committee, London's Common Council and the Cornhill wardmote all made attempts to keep people they considered undesirable out of the Exchange. These included beggars, vagrants and 'loose' people. The Society for the Reformation of Manners was particularly concerned about the sort of 'Sodomitical Intrigue', the 'Swarthy Buggerantoes' and 'Preternatural Fornicators' later satirised by Brown and Ward, that they believed was undertaken at the Exchange.[169] In their campaign against moral vice, members of the Society entrapped suspects at the Exchange who were later brought to trial. As Rictor Norton has argued, the Exchange was one of London's principal gay cruising grounds.[170]

The advertisements for 'a dry Rogue', 'Wet and Dry Nurses' and the 'Bills stuck up here and there, to encourage Debauchery' that so amused Ward, Brown and the author of Hickelty pickelty also concerned the Exchange authorities.[171] The Exchange keepers were reminded in 1717 of their particular duty to 'prevent Scandalous papers being Pasted upon the Pillars of the Exchange' and ordered to 'suffer no Advertisements to be Fixed upon the Pillars of the Excha[nge] except such as are usefull to Merchants that resort thereto'.[172]

Despite the repeated efforts to remind the Exchange keepers of all their duties in these matters throughout the period, and that their failure would be 'on forfeiture of their places', there was still blunt and public criticism of the 'Neglect' of the Exchange by Steele in The Spectator.[173] 'Instead of the Assembly of honourable Merchants, substantial Tradesmen, and knowing Masters of Ships, the Mumpers, the Halt, the Blind, and the Lame, your Venders of Trash, Apples, Plumbs, your Raggamuffins, Rakeshames, and Wenches, have justled the greater Number out of the former Place.'[174] The 'Royal Exchange is a Fabrick that well deserves to be so called, as well to express that our Monarch's highest Glory and Advantage consists in being the Patron of Trade, as that it is commodious for Business, and an Instance of the Grandeur both of Prince and People' and its decline signalled that the City itself was in decline. Steele associated the Exchange with the monarch, the City and the 'People' even if in this case it did not bring glory to these.

---

168 GL, MS 4069/2, Cornhill ward, 1652–1733, fo. 287v.

169 Brown, Amusements, 31; [Ward], London Spy, Jan. 1699, pt III, 13.

170 The tryal and conviction of several reputed sodomites, London 1707. See also John Dunton, The he-strumpets, 4th edn, in his Athenianism, London 1710, ii. 95, and R. Norton, Mother Clap's molly house: the gay subculture in England, 1700–1830, London 1992, 50. I am grateful to Faramerz Dabhoiwala for the reference to Norton's book.

171 [Ward], London Spy, Jan. 1699, pt III, 14; Brown, Amusements, 33, Hickelty pickelty, 10.

172 Gresham repertory, 1678–1722, pp. 498–9.

173 Ibid. p. 294.

174 The Spectator, 14 Oct. 1712.

What Steele is pointing towards here is the wider resonance of the Exchange. What is the significance of the Exchange more generally? How does it fit into images of the city, the nation and the monarch?

## 'Englands king, the city, and the nation': the Exchange's glory in wider context

The Exchange's trading reputation reverberated in the city's reputation, and the success of the city's trade was couched in terms of its partial dependence, as it was for individual merchants, on the preservation of a good reputation. As discussed above, the practice of merchants trading outside the Exchange was considered by the City authorities to damage the Exchange's reputation. This was seen to be 'to the scandall of this citty', and in 1668, it concurred 'with those great Distresses and Difficulties which the Divine Justice hath inflicted, and our own Folly and Iniquities have drawn upon us, to abate and diminish the ancient Splendour, Esteem and Honour of the City'.[175] The importance of the smooth running of trade in the city, and an untarnished trading reputation, was a general concern of the City authorities, and not just in relation to the Royal Exchange. In 1674, for example, the Lord Mayor attempted to curb the behaviour of 'divers rude and disordered Young-men, Apprentices and others' who by their actions were driving out of the city 'all Persons of Quality (upon whom the Trade of this City does very much depend)'. The City's failure to prevent such practices was to 'the great Dishonour of the Magistracy of this City, the great Prejudice and Hindrance of the Trade thereof, and the Scandal of this once renowned City in all civilized parts of the World'.[176]

The Exchange, both through its architecture and its trade, made a positive contribution to London's reputation; in 1667 during discussion about rebuilding the Exchange the surveyor-general Sir John Denham relayed to the Gresham Committee Charles II's opinion that the Exchange was 'soe publiq[ue] and Eminent a Concerne for the Honour of the City'.[177] The date and context of Charles's comment are significant as the rebuilding of the Exchange was later to signal London's recovery after the Fire. The frontispiece to the first five editions of Nathaniel Crouch's survey and history of London, *Historical remarques*, first published in 1681, depicted London both during and after the Fire and makes this point very effectively (*see*

175 CLRO, Rep. 76, 1670, fo. 4v; Turner, *Martis vicesimo sexto die Januarii, 1668*. [Order respecting the hours of meeting].
176 By the Maior, *Whereas divers rude and disordered young-men, apprentices and others . . .* [An order prohibiting the throwing about of squibs and fireworks in the streets and public passages], London 1674.
177 Gresham repertory, 1626–69, p. 303.

Figure 2. [Nathaniel Crouch] (pseudonym Richard Burton),
*Historical remarques, and observations of the ancient and present
state of London and Westminster*, London 1681, frontispiece.
British Library, shelfmark G. 13203. Reproduced by permission
of the British Library.

Figure 2).[178] In the upper scene, entitled 'London, in Flames', a woman sits amongst rubble in the foreground with her simple unadorned dress falling off one shoulder, exposing her breast. Buildings are on fire in the background. The lower scene, titled 'London, in Glory' includes the same figure. However, here she sits with composure in an ornate dress on the right of the image gesturing towards the Royal Exchange behind. With the dragon and arms of London at her feet in both scenes there can be no doubt that the figure represents London.[179] In fact, the figure in the upper scene very closely resembles a figure that appeared in Gabriel Caius Cibber's sculptural relief on the base of the Monument erected to commemorate the Fire. The similarities between the posture and dress of the two figures, and the positioning of the same symbolic objects (sword, dragon and shield), suggest that the Crouch frontispiece is making a direct reference to the figure in Cibber's relief. In the caption to an engraving of the relief made by Nicholas Goodnight the figure of the woman is identified: 'the first female figure represents the City of London, sitting in ruins, in a languishing posture, with her head dejected, hair dishevelled, and her hand carelessly lying on her sword'.[180]

Like the relief, Crouch's frontispiece is concerned with both the destruction of London and its post-Fire recovery. In the case of the frontispiece the recovery is articulated with particular reference to the Exchange. Although the Monument also appears in the background, the focus is on the larger and

---

[178] Crouch wrote this book under the pseudonym Richard Burton. Two editions were published in 1681 and three more in 1684, 1691 and 1703: B. Adams, *London illustrated, 1604–1851: a survey and index of topographical books and their plates*, London 1983, 21–2. On Nathaniel Crouch see R. Mayer, 'Nathaniel Crouch, bookseller and historian: popular historiography and cultural power in late seventeenth-century England', *ECS* xxvii (1994), 391–419.

[179] L. Manley, *Literature and culture in early modern London*, Cambridge 1995, 133–4, 253–4, 287; J. Dallas, 'The City of London and its dragons', *Journal of the British Archaeological Association* xix (1913), 97, 101; A. C. Fox-Davies, 'Domine dirige nos', *The Genealogical Magazine* ii (1898–9), 249. For the arms of London see also [Crouch], *Historical remarques*, 80. It is possible that the figure in the lower frame, at least, is wearing a fur cap, which, like the dragon, often accompanied the arms of London: Fox-Davies, 'Domine dirige nos', 255; Richard Wallis, *London's armory accuratly delineated*, London 1677. The most likely alternative is that she is the Mercers' Company virgin who was depicted on their buildings (including the Exchange), their seal and their arms. However, textual descriptions and visual depictions all mention a jewelled crown and an abundance of straight (flaxen) hair which do not appear here. For textual descriptions see M. Taubman, *London's yearly jubilee*, London 1686, 9–10; Elkanah Settle, *The triumphs of London, for the inauguration of the right honourable Sir William Gore*, London 1701, 3. For a visual depiction see [Crouch], *Historical remarques*, 81. See also Gibson, ' "The kingdom's marble chronicle" ', 167; W. Herbert, *The history of the twelve great livery companies of London*, London 1836–7, i. 254–59; and A. F. Sutton, *I sing of a maiden: the story of the maiden of the Mercers' Company*, London 1998.

[180] Nicholas Goodnight, 'Allegory of the Great Fire of London', London 1700; Hallett, *Spectacle of difference*, 210–11. I am grateful to Mark Hallett for directing me to the monument.

more detailed image of the Exchange, and it is to this that the figure directs our attention.

There were fears that if the City was not rebuilt quickly then trade would suffer. The Derbyshire MP John Milward, for example, wrote in his diary that the general opinion of the Commons was:

> that if some speedy way of rebuilding the City was not agreed upon that the City would be in danger never to be built, for if the citizens found a difficulty in it, and that things were not speedily provided for, the merchants and wealthiest of the citizens would alter their course of their life and trade and remove themselves and estates into other countries so the City would remain miserable for ever.[181]

The committee in charge of the Exchange was very eager to complete the rebuilding of the Exchange 'for the Tradesmen and Merchants and incourageing of the City in Gen[er]all'.[182] In the context of these anxieties then, the rebuilding of the Exchange and the fact that it was one of the first prominent buildings to be completed signalled the success of the recovery of London's trade and served to symbolise London's return to glory.[183] The emphasis in Crouch's book on London's trade, both in the text, and in the accompanying woodcuts of 'the Arms of the Sixty Six Companies of London, and the time of their Incorporating', reinforces the importance of the associations introduced in the frontispiece between trade and the glory of London.

The use of a visual image of the Exchange as a symbol for London can also be seen in an early eighteenth-century almanac produced as a single sheet. Entitled *London almanack for the year of our Lord 1706* it included a list of recent Lord Mayors, as well as a calendar for the year. At the top of the single sheet below the motto 'Our Loyalty is the High-Road. To a full Trade, at home & abroad', is a small engraving of the Royal Exchange.[184]

Of course, the Exchange was not the only symbol of London; it rivalled the Tower, and from its completion in 1710, St Paul's Cathedral in the attention it received from travel writers and authors of descriptions of London and its history. For Herman Moll, in his *A system of geography* (1701), it was ranked third in a list of eight notable London buildings after the Tower and

181 John Milward, *The diary of John Milward Esq*, ed. C. Robbins, Cambridge 1938, 9.

182 Gresham repertory, 1626–69, p. 383.

183 T. F. Reddaway, *The rebuilding of London after the Great Fire*, London 1951, 122.

184 *London almanack for the year of our Lord 1706*, London 1706. Images of the Royal Exchange also featured on trade cards, tokens, and later on the fire marks of the Royal Exchange Assurance Company. See, for example, the trade card advertising the discharge of bills of exchange, in Peter Murray Hill Ltd, *Catalogue* lxxxii (1962), 57, and plate v (a copy of the relevant pages is held at MCA, Misc. MS 14.10); R. H. Thompson, 'Tokens of the Royal Exchange', in Saunders, *Royal Exchange*, 239–49; Supple, *Royal Exchange Assurance*, fig. 3, after p. 90.

Gresham College, 'a most noble Ornament to the City, as well as a singular convenience to Merchants'.[185]

The significance of the Exchange in conceptions of London some years earlier can be gauged by considering the proposals for rebuilding the city after the Fire.[186] In his plan Christopher Wren, for example, located the Royal Exchange in its pre-Fire position and placed it prominently on the right-hand vertex of the main z-shaped street structure. It was to form the hub of the eastern part of the city with ten streets radiating out from the area around it towards the river, St Paul's, the Custom House, and other parts of the city.[187] Similarly, on a plan attributed to Robert Hooke, the Exchange, as the counterpart to the Guildhall, was to dominate the eastern part of the city. The proposed Exchange was to have a large forecourt and a long vista down to the fish market by the Thames.[188] In Richard Newcourt's plans the Royal Exchange was one of the few buildings that he intended to be built in the central square of his proposed London, which was to be the site of 'the most noble & most Magnificent Structures of all'.[189]

John Evelyn, who had been an admirer of the pre-Fire Exchange (he described it as he clambered over the 'mountains of yet smoking rubbish' on 7 September 1666 as 'the Sumptous Exchange') drew up at least three different plans for London, on two of which he marked the buildings.[190] On the earlier of these he placed the Royal Exchange at the end of one of the principal north–south roads by the river: 'I should think the Royal Exchange might front the quay betwixt Queenhithe and the Bridge, about the Steel-yard I conceive were a proper place, respecting the goodliest river in the world, where the traffic, and business is most vigorous (but for this I submit to better judgements).'[191] On the later plan he intended the Exchange

[185] Herman Moll, A system of geography, London 1701, 22.

[186] Valentine Knight's proposal is not discussed here as he did not consider the location of the Royal Exchange, or many other buildings: Proposals for a new modell for re-building the City of London, London 1666.

[187] Christopher Wren's drawing of his final plan in 1666 is reproduced in S. Perks, 'London town-planning schemes in 1666', Journal of the Royal Institute of British Architects xxvii (1919), 72, and in T. F. Reddaway, 'The rebuilding of London after the Fire', part I, Town Planning Review xvii (1937), 205–11, plate 38. Labelled engravings of the plan were made later and are reproduced in both these articles and in A. Saunders, 'The second Exchange', in her Royal Exchange, 123.

[188] 'Model, wie die Abbgebrante Statt London widrüm Büttgebaüwet werden solle', St Paul's collection, 4/18. This print is also reproduced in Perks, 'London town-planning', 76.

[189] Ric[hard] Newcourt, 'An explanation of the mapps', GL, Manuscripts, MS 3441, p. 3. Richard Newcourt's plan, and that of Valentine Knight, are reproduced in J. Hanson, 'Order and structure in urban design: the plans for the rebuilding of London after the Great Fire of 1666', Ekistics lvi (1989), 25.

[190] Evelyn, Diary, iii. 457, 460; John Evelyn, London revived: consideration for its rebuilding in 1666, ed. E. S. De Beer, Oxford 1938, plates following pp. 28, 56; the earlier plan is also reproduced in Saunders, 'Second Exchange', 122.

[191] Evelyn, London revived, 42.

to be built in almost the same place it had been before the Fire and at the junction of roads that were to lead to the bridge, the Guildhall and out of the city to the north. All these planners in different ways gave the Exchange a more prominent role in the city's structure than it had had before the Fire, confirming what historical geographers, like Emrys Jones, have said about the Exchange being one of the centres of London.[192]

Like the River Thames, celebrated for its extensive shipping, the Exchange was central to the larger discourse that identified London with its trading activities.[193] When Joseph Addison, in *The Spectator*, described London as 'a kind of Emporium for the whole Earth' he was drawing on a very well established discourse that celebrated London's commerce.[194] John Ogilby and William Morgan had described London in 1677 in the index to their map of London as a 'Celebrated Emporium, which for Situation, Extent, Government, Magnificence, Plenty, Riches and Strength, may Challenge any European City whatsoever'.[195] Travellers like Misson agreed: 'Personne n'ignore, je pense, que Londres ne soit une des Villes du Monde du plus riche & du plus vaste Négoce'.[196] Although there were concerns about the favourability of England's balance of trade with its continental neighbours and about the superiority of Dutch commercial institutions and trading methods, the rhetoric of London's pre-eminence in world trade, with the Exchange as a central component, was articulated throughout this period.

The Exchange symbolised and brought glory not only to London but also to England. Rolle, writing of the first Exchange, made links between the building, the metropolis and the nation: 'As London was the glory of England, so was that Royal Exchange one of the greatest Glories and Ornaments of London.'[197] Links between the Exchange and the nation were also established through the imitation of the building's architecture in the design of civic buildings in provincial cities. Although Peter Borsay has cautioned against adopting a 'dominance model of cultural change' to describe the relationship between London and provincial towns, and instead proposes a pluralist one, he does demonstrate that 'the capital's example exerted a powerful influence'.[198] The Exchanges in Bristol and Liverpool were built, to some extent at least, in imitation of London's Royal Exchange, and reinforced the image of the Exchange as a glorious national icon.[199] In a

---

192  E. Jones, 'London in the early seventeenth century: an ecological approach', *LJ* vi (1980), 129.
193  Manley, *Literature*.
194  *The Spectator*, 19 May 1711.
195  John Ogilby and William Morgan, *London survey'd*, London 1677, sigs a1r–a3r.
196  [Misson], *Mémoires*, 306.
197  Rolle, *Burning of London*, pt III, 45.
198  P. Borsay, 'The London connection: cultural diffusion and the eighteenth-century provincial town', *LJ* xix (1994), 31.
199  Idem, *Urban renaissance*, 287, 109; Wood, *Description*, 37–8.

speech at the opening ceremony of the Bristol Exchange in 1741, for example, specific reference was made to the Royal Exchange:

> As our Metropolis with great Reason, justly boasts that the Exchange there, was first built in the glorious Reign of Queen Elizabeth, who honoured it with her Presence, and dignified it with the Title of the Royal Exchange: So may this Second City of England, with no less Reason Glory in her Happiness, that this Exchange is here built, and open'd, under the auspicious Reign of his Present Majesty.[200]

Such an account of the opening of the Exchange by Elizabeth I and her bestowal of the name the Royal Exchange featured in many accounts of the Exchange in histories, guides and travel writing in the late seventeenth and early eighteenth centuries.[201] As the monarch lent glory to the Exchange so the Exchange glorified the monarch. George Elliott's verse in 1671 on the reaction of foreigners to the Exchange suggested associations between the Exchange, London, the nation and the monarch:

> French, Spanish, Dutch, the Noble Tuscanite,
> The Portugall, the Mighty Muscovite,
> The Swede, the Dane, and from all Christendome
> Which from beyond the Sea to our City came,
> Stands gazing on it with delighted Eyes,
> Sayes, 'Tis the stateliest Structure under Skies;
> Takes Pen in hand, writes in the Commendation
> Of Englands King, the City, and the Nation.[202]

Other royal connections were also emphasised, such as Charles II's influence in the design of the second Exchange, and the laying of foundation stones by him, the Duke of York and Prince Rupert.[203] The most visible connection, however, between the monarchy and the Exchange was in the statues of former and current monarchs that were placed in niches on the upper level in the interior of the Exchange in the first and second buildings.[204] As Rolle writes of the statues in the first Exchange, they were set up 'in the most conspicuous and honourable place (as well as receiving lustre from the place

---

[200] Wood, *Description*, 34. See also the comparison (p. 12) made with the Royal Exchange in the description of the laying of the foundation stone of the Exchange.
[201] Most accounts follow John Stow, *Survay of London*, London 1598. On the most important reworking of Stow, John Strype's 1720 edition, see J. J. Morrison, 'Strype's Stow: the 1720 edition of A *survey of London*', *LJ* iii (1977), 40–54.
[202] George Elliott, *Great Brittain's beauty*, London 1671.
[203] Gresham repertory, 1626–69, pp. 302, 303, 305, 331, 333, 381; John Stow, *A survey of the cities of London and Westminster*, rev. John Strype, London 1720, i. 137; [Simon Ford], *London's resurrection*, London 1669, 6–7.
[204] Gibson, ' "Marble chronicle" '; I. Roscoe, ' "The statues of the sovereigns of England": sculpture for the second building, 1695–1831', in Saunders, *Royal Exchange*, 174–87.

where they stood, as giving lustre to it)'.[205] Indeed part of the attraction of the Exchange was the statues, and guide-book writers as well as visitors, went to the trouble of compiling lists of these statues.[206]

It was the statue of Charles II by Grinling Gibbons erected in the centre of the Exchange in 1684, however, that received the most attention from engravers, guide-book writers and poets in the late seventeenth century.[207] The statue made classical allusions by portraying Charles II in Cæsar's image wearing classical robes, and also national ones by being placed on a pedestal decorated with images of the three kingdoms.[208] Engravings of the statue appeared in published travel accounts and descriptions of England, like the volumes written by Misson and Beeverell.[209] The significance of the location of the statue was highlighted in one anonymous poem:

> . . . the Figure with the Place agrees,
> Where else should stand the Monarch of the Seas?
> Then let the World's united Treasure meet
> T'enrich Their Bank, with each returning Fleet,
> Who lay their Hearts and Wealth at Cæsar's Feet.[210]

The image of Charles as Neptune and master of the seas had featured in his coronation procession through the City, where the links with trade had been made more prominently. As he processed, Charles passed by a number of arches, the second of which, positioned adjacent to the Exchange, had a naval theme. On it there was an image of the Exchange, and on the upper storey were 'eight living Figures, representing Europe, Asia, Africk, and America, with Escutcheons, and Pendents, bearing the Arms of the Companies trading into those parts', and in four niches stood 'living figures . . . representing Arithmetick, Geometry, Astronomy, and Navigation'.[211] As Charles stood by this arch, a figure representing Thames addressed the king:

> Hail, Mighty Monarch! whose Imperial Hand
> Quiets the Ocean, and secures the Land;
> This City, whom I sever with Neighb'ring Floods,
> Exporting Yours, importing Foreign Goods,

---

205 Rolle, *Burning of London*, pt III, 47.

206 William Schellinks, *The journal of William Schellinks' travels in England, 1661–1663*, ed. M. Exwood and H. L. Lehmann, London 1993, 52; Hatton, *New view*, 615–16.

207 Gibson, ' "Marble chronicle" ', 151–7.

208 *A poem upon the new marble statue of his present majesty*, London 1684, 1.

209 [Misson], *Memoires*, 'Charles II au milieu de la Bourse', facing p. 388; [Beeverell], *Délices*, IV, 'Charles II dans le milieu de la Bourse', illustration for 837, 812, 814.

210 *Poem upon the new marble statue*, 4.

211 John Ogilby, *The entertainment of His Most Excellent Majestie Charles II*, London 1662, 67, 96, and the engraving of the arch facing p. 43; S. J. G. Reedy, 'Mystical politics: the imagery of Charles II's coronation', in P. J. Korshin (ed.), *Studies in change and revolution: aspects of English intellectual history, 1640–1800*, Menston 1972, 26–8.

With anxious Grief did long Your Absence mourn;
Now with full Joy she welcomes Your Return
. . .
You are our Neptune, every Port, and Bay
Your Chambers: the whole Sea is Your High-way.[212]

This was followed by three seamen singing a shanty which called on Charles, as Neptune, to rig the navy. Successful trade depended on control of the seas, and this shanty, as Gerald Reedy argues, was an attempt to obtain a more fulsome backing from Charles.[213] Such associations between the monarch and trade, as we have already seen in Steele's lament in the *The Spectator* of the Exchange's decline, continued into Anne's reign.

The Royal Exchange, a trade and information entrepôt, was one of the most important sites where the dynamics of reputation were played out amongst those in London's trading circles. Although it is unconventional to explore ideas about trade by focusing on a single building, and its associated discourses, this approach has served also to illuminate the resonances that the Exchange had in images of London, and indeed, to some extent, in imaginings of the nation. The Exchange was important in its own right, not only for its role in trade but also because its image was constructed, both in words and pictures, to represent the whole of the trading world in miniature. Such images provided a way of imagining the extensive and complicated trading world as contained and to some extent ordered.

This idea of places of international trade as microcosms of the trading world where merchants of different nationalities came together to 'traffick', and where goods from all over the world could be bought from the shops, accorded with a commonly held conception of trade in this period. Its essence was that trade merely redistributed the products of some countries to others where they were not available. Interpretations emphasised the 'mutual intercourse' that resulted. Addison, in expounding a version of this model in his account of the Exchange in *The Spectator*, developed it to argue that such mutual intercourse led to 'the Natives of the several Parts of the Globe' being dependent upon one another and becoming 'united together by their common Interest'.[214] Preachers also explored this model of the trading world: such redistribution made 'the Blessings of our bountiful Creator as diffusive, as he intended them'.[215]

[212] Ogilby, *Entertainment*, 104.
[213] Reedy, 'Mystical politics', 28.
[214] *The Spectator*, 19 May 1711; John Hughes, *A sermon preach'd before the right honourable George earl of Berkley, governour, and the company of merchants of England trading in the Levant Seas*, London 1683, 11. Interestingly, both Addison and Hughes use the term 'mutual intercourse'.
[215] Hughes, *Sermon*, 10.

# 2

# 'The Surest and Straitest Way to Wealth': Preaching Before the Levant Company

Lori Anne Ferrell and Peter McCullough argue that early modern '[s]ermons were not simply words on a page, but instruments of policy, documents of religious change, and expressions of public life'. They stimulated action. The sermons preached to promote the Virginia Company's enterprise in the early seventeenth century, for example, were believed to be 'themselves acts in the foundation of the new commonwealth' because, in John Donne's formulation of the classical principle, 'every man, that Prints, Adventures'.[1] The vibrancy of sermons in political culture, Tony Claydon argues, was sustained into the late seventeenth and early eighteenth century. He contests the model of a secularised public sphere and suggests that in the late seventeenth century it was 'still dominated by actively preaching clerics'.[2]

This chapter explores the sermons preached before the Levant Company in the period 1660–1720. Preachers competed for the position of chaplain at one of its three factories in Turkey, and part of the competition involved the preaching of a trial sermon before the company. The company ordered many of the sermons preached by the successful candidates to be printed. Other trading companies, like the East India Company and the Russia Company, also appointed chaplains to serve their merchants, and officials, overseas but none held preaching competitions in this period.[3]

The printing of these sermons coincides with the period 1660–1720; only one sermon was printed outside this period, in 1724, after which, although the Levant Company's fortunes declined, it continued to appoint chaplains.[4] Indeed, these sermons were a high profile part of the Levant Company's presence in late seventeenth- and early eighteenth-century print culture and carried the company's endorsement. What did preachers say at the sermons that they hoped would secure them a prestigious and profitable job? What

[1]   L. A. Ferrell and P. McCullough, 'Revising the study of the English sermon', in idem. (eds) *English sermon revised: religion, literature and history, 1600–1750*, Manchester 2000, 11 and A. Fitzmaurice, ' "Every man, that prints, adventures": the rhetoric of the Virginia Company sermons', ibid. 37.
[2]   T. Claydon, 'The sermon, the "public sphere" and the political culture of late seventeenth-century England', in Ferrell and McCullough, *English sermon revised*, 225.
[3]   G. Yeo, 'A case without parallel: the bishop of London and the Anglican Church overseas, 1660–1748', *Journal of Ecclesiastical History* xliv (1993), 468.
[4]   Charles Burdett, *A sermon preach'd before the right worshipful the deputy-governour and the company of merchants trading to the Levant Seas*, London 1724.

messages were in the sermons that the company was keen to be seen both listening to and endorsing? Many of the preachers gave sermons that touched on themes that had particular resonances with a mercantile audience: charity, conduct in trade, and how wealth and piety could be reconciled. At times, and especially in the dedications to the sermons, issues of the moment were raised and the company's position defended.

This chapter is in four sections. In the first two, the procedure of appointing Levant Company chaplains is examined followed by an analysis of the opportunities the position opened up and the careers of successful candidates. The third section looks at the relationship between the printed sermon and the preached sermon. The content of the sermons, both the main text and the dedication, is discussed in the final section. For many of these preachers, wealth and piety were compatible, and merchants, partly because of their wealth, had special duties and responsibilities as God's stewards on earth.

## Preaching before the Levant Company: making appointments

The Levant Company was a regulated trading company which held a monopoly of trade with Turkey.[5] Its general courts were held in London and it had factories in Turkey at Aleppo, Constantinople and Smyrna where merchants and employees of the company were based. The company appointed a chaplain for each of the factories to serve both the factory and the crown's representative: the ambassador at Constantinople and the consuls at Aleppo and Smyrna.[6]

Henry Maundrell (1665–1701), chaplain to the company at Aleppo at the end of the seventeenth century, gives an idea of the congregation at the factory there:

> Pious, Sober, Benevolent, devout in the Offices of Religion . . . exhibiting in all their Actions those best and truest signs of a Christian Spirit, a sincere and cheerful friendship among themselves, a generous Charity towards others, and a profound reverence for the Liturgy, and Constitution of the Church of England. It is our first Employment every morning to solemnize the dayly Service of the Church, at which I am sure to have always a devout, a regular, and full Congregation.[7]

---

5  For general histories of the company see A. C. Wood, *A history of the Levant Company*, Oxford 1935, and R. Walsh, *An account of the Levant Company; with some notices of the benefits conferred upon society by its officers, in promoting the cause of humanity, literature, and the fine arts*, London 1825.

6  Company to Mr Hughes, 30 Oct. 1684, SP 105/114, p. 321.

7  Hen[ry] Maundrell, *A journey from Aleppo to Jerusalem at Easter, A D. 1697*, 2nd edn, Oxford 1727, dedication.

The congregation might also include not just English merchants: Robert Frampton (1622–1708) preached to German Lutheran merchants at Aleppo in the early years of this period.[8]

Chaplains had been appointed by the Levant Company to positions in Turkey from at least as early as 1599, and in the six decades following the Restoration thirty-two different ministers were appointed to these posts.[9] Most vacancies arose when an incumbent requested to return home, often because of illness, and occasionally because of death, or, in the case of Constantinople, the chaplain often left with the ambassador. On only one occasion in this period, which will be discussed below, was the minister sent back to England. Usually, vacancies were announced at meetings of the general court of the company, and a date was set for the next meeting where candidates for the post could present themselves.

For most appointments candidates were asked to preach a sermon before the company; the earliest such preaching is recorded as having taken place in 1615.[10] As Frampton recorded many years after he preached his trial sermon, it was 'a specimen of his ability to instruct young men of which the factory generally consists', at a time and place, and quite often on a text specified by the company.[11] The Levant Company was not the only trading company to ask its prospective chaplains to preach, as in the early seventeenth century trial sermons were also preached before the East India Company and the Virginia Company.[12] By the late seventeenth century, however, the East India Company had abandoned this practice and relied instead on obtaining 'the best information they can' of candidates' 'Ministerial Abilities & good Conversation'.[13]

Tony Claydon argues that in the early eighteenth century 'attendance at sermons was still a key part of the social round'.[14] The Levant Company trial sermons were apparently well attended and congregations included those who were not members of the company, as Samuel Pepys witnessed in 1662:

---

8  Robert Frampton, *The life of Robert Frampton bishop of Gloucester deprived as a non-juror 1689*, ed. T. S. Evans, London 1876, 40.

9  Alfred Wood notes that the chaplain in Aleppo in 1599 had a predecessor: *History*, 22.

10  J. B. Pearson, *A biographical sketch of the chaplains to the Levant Company, maintained at Constantinople, Aleppo and Smyrna, 1611–1706*, Cambridge 1883, 46.

11  Frampton, *Life*, 23. Supposedly Frampton listed a number of texts that he considered 'hard to be understood' in the preface to his trial sermon and that these texts were given to subsequent candidates 'till that stock of texts were spent'. I have not been able to trace this sermon but the texts apparently listed in the preface – 1 Cor. xv. 29 and 1 Peter iii.19 – were preached upon by the successful candidates, John Luke and Thomas Smith, at two subsequent appointments. In the case of John Covel (who was appointed before he preached) it was left up to him to choose his 'owne text': Eliab Harvey to John Covel, 17 Mar. 1669, BL, MS Add. 22910 fo. 29.

12  L. B. Wright, *Religion and empire: the alliance between piety and commerce in English expansion, 1558–1625*, New York 1965, 65; Yeo, 'Case without parallel', 452.

13  India Office Records, B/31, p. 36.

14  Claydon, 'Sermon', 213

'seeing many strangers and coaches coming to our church and finding that it was a sermon to be preached by a probacioner for the Turky Company, to be sent to Smyrna, I returned thither. And several Turky Merchants filled all the best pews (and some in ours) in the church.'[15] Frampton described how in 1655 he preached 'to the full satisfaction of the company as well as other their friends then present'.[16] At the meeting of the general court following the sermon, candidates submitted their testimonials and heard sections of them read aloud to the court. After candidates had withdrawn, they were 'put in nomination' – an election by a show of hands – but when the votes for candidates seemed close, a ballot box was used and the candidate for whom the highest number of balls were cast was appointed. The results of such ballots, recorded in the court's minutes, suggest that nearly a hundred people might cast a vote.[17]

Appointments to the position of chaplain at Constantinople were not always made in this way as the minister appointed was also the ambassador's private chaplain. The ambassador's chosen candidate was generally rubber stamped by the general court.[18] Out of the twelve chaplains appointed to positions at Constantinople in the period 1660–1720, four were recommended by the ambassador, one of whom did not want to go, and the company supported the other three recommendations. Four were chosen by the conventional procedure, and for the remaining four details about the circumstances of their appointment either have not survived, or were not recorded in the company's minutes.

Out of the thirty-two appointments made in the period 1660–1720 candidates for at least twenty-five of them preached sermons before the Levant Company.[19] For the period up to 1706, for which the minutes of the company's general court survive, quite a full picture of the appointment procedure can be constructed. For thirteen of these appointments there were at least two candidates. Most candidates were required to preach before the company, even on the occasions when there was only one candidate.[20]

15 *Pepys*, iii. 259–60.
16 Frampton, *Life*, 24.
17 At the election of John Luke in 1664, 59 balls were cast in his favour and 45 for his contender. At the election of Mr Guyse in 1681, 49 balls were case in his favour and 45 for his contender: SP 105/152, p. 241; SP 105/154, p. 270.
18 Wood, *History*, 223;
19 Of the seven appointments made in the period 1706–20 (for which the minute books of the general court do not survive) three of the candidates published their sermons (William Crosse, Laurence Hacket and Bernard Mould). Whether the other four candidates preached is not known. There were three reappointments in this period: Thomas Andrews having served at Constantinople, 1717–19, then had a brief interlude in Aleppo before returning to Constantinople; Samuel Lisle served in Smyrna, 1710–16, and then Aleppo 1716–18; and John Luke served in Smyrna twice, in 1664–9 and 1674–83.
20 For two of the uncontested positions special circumstances account for why they did not preach: Thomas Rawlins, who was appointed to the position in Smyrna in 1692, had preached in 1689 when Edward Smith had been appointed. When Smith resigned

Preaching a sermon was recognised as an important part of becoming a chaplain for the Levant Company, even if it was not always given as part of the selection process; in three cases chaplains appointed to Constantinople offered to preach after their appointment.[21]

Frequently the company requested the successful candidate to have his sermon printed, usually ordering him £5 to cover the costs, and in the period 1660–1720, fifteen sermons were printed. On one occasion, in 1665, when the preacher unusually delivered a manuscript to the general court and they arranged for its printing, it was recorded that the governor 'requested that 500 of them might be left with him to be distributed unto the Members of the Company'.[22] Whether the sermons were always distributed amongst the members of the company, of which in 1676 there were almost 350, is hard to say. Were they read by non-company members? John Hughes (b. 1651?), in the dedication of his sermon to the governor and the 'Company of Turkie Merchants', did think that there might be others 'who may possibly throw away so much time as to read this Discourse'.[23] Certainly, a couple of sermons found their way into White Kennett's library.[24]

It is not easy to generalise about the sort of preachers appointed by the company. When the general court did say what sort of appointment it wished to make, as it did in 1701, it rehearsed platitudes: 'it was recommended to ye Court to make Choice of Such a One as is of known Ability, Orthodox in Religion, and well affected to the present Governm[en]t'.[25] Appointments

Rawlins's candidacy was uncontested. In 1683 the position of chaplain at Smryna was filled by Thomas Smith, who was already resident in the Levant. His appointment was confirmed in 1684 when the general court received a reference from John Luke, the previous incumbent.

[21] Henry Denton offered to preach after he had been appointed in 1664, as did John Covel in 1670. William Hayley was appointed on 11 Nov. 1686 to go to Constantinople and although he promised to give a sermon on his return he preached on 30 Jan. 1687: SP 105/152, p. 241; SP 105/153, p. 40; SP 105/155, p. 26.

[22] SP 105/152, p. 254. This was the standard size for an early modern print run.

[23] Hughes, *Sermon*, dedication. That Thomas Hearne read Edmund Chishull's sermon ('there is little Judgm[en]t in w[ha]t he says, as appears from w[ha]t he has publish'd of [tha]t nature in a certain Sermon preach'd when he went Chaplain to [th]e Factory') indicates that these sermons in their published form reached an audience beyond that composed of members of the Levant Company: *Remarks and collections of Thomas Hearne*, ed. C. E. Doble, Oxford 1885–1921, i. 290.

[24] Edm[und] Chishull, *A sermon preach'd before the honourable company of merchants trading to the Levant-seas*, London 1698 (Huntington Library, Los Angeles, shelfmark 209509). John Luke, *A sermon preached before the right worshipful company of the Levant merchants at St. Olav's Hart-street London*, London 1664 (Huntington Library shelfmark 209510). Amongst Kennett's projects was a history of Christianity in the American colonies and it was perhaps in this connection that he was interested in these sermons.

[25] SP 105/156, p. 90. Before the Restoration, the historian, James Anderson, claims that the company 'had been careful to send out, as their Chaplains, some of our ablest and most devoted Clergy': *The history of the Church of England in the colonies and foreign dependencies of the British empire*, 2nd edn, London 1856, ii. 117.

were made independently of any ecclesiastical authority, unlike those made by the East India Company.[26] In the late 1670s the East India Company had come under pressure from the bishop of London to license chaplains and although some chaplains had begun to seek licences from the bishop, until new charters in 1698 and 1702 made them mandatory, the company maintained their right to appoint chaplains who were not licensed.[27] In a rather different religious and political environment two decades earlier, the Levant Company was quite resistant to having their chaplains licensed. At Frampton's appointment in 1655 the suggestion that he should be sent to the 'Tryers', was objected to as the company 'had never been obliged to submit their chaplains to the examination, approbation or licence of a Bishop, much less were they to ensnare themselves under a new found authority, but thought it much better to depend upon Mr Frampton's episcopal ordination and excellent character'.[28] In the early eighteenth century such resistance to the influence of the bishop of London can perhaps still be detected: of the three candidates recommended by him only one was appointed.[29]

Identifying the religious affinities of all these chaplains is not straightforward. Although, according to Gary De Krey, there was 'a significant dissenting presence in the Levant trade' it appears that there was at times little sympathy for nonconformity amongst the chaplains.[30] One, Charles Hickman, attacked dissent in the sermon he preached before the company in 1681. He begged the 'favour and patience' of his audience for being led 'by the method of my Text; to touch upon some of those sores which so unhappily afflict us' and he hoped that 'none will be offended at this uncharitable design, especially in defence of that Church whereof we all here profess our selves to be Members'.[31] He admonished 'our Dissenting Brethren . . . who by a new and strange Interpretation have forced this expression of Worshipping in the Spirit to signifie only Extempore Prayer'.[32] Their 'Assemblies', he suggested, were animated not by 'the Spirit of Prayer, but the Spirit of Ostentation'.[33]

Not all the chaplains appointed launched such attacks, and indeed the picture is made more complicated by the Broadgate incident.[34] John

26 Pearson, *Biographical sketch*, 10.
27 Yeo, 'Case without parallel', 460, 468.
28 Frampton, *Life*, 23.
29 SP 105/156, pp. 92, 131, 245.
30 He estimates that almost 30% of Levant traders were dissenters: G. S. de Krey, *A fractured society: the politics of London in the first age of party, 1688–1715*, Oxford 1985, 102, 104.
31 Charles Hickman, *A sermon preached before the right honourable George earl of Berkeley, governour, and the company of merchants of England trading into the Levant Seas*, London 1681, 17–18.
32 Ibid. 31.
33 Ibid. 35.
34 Earlier in the seventeenth century there had been problems with some chaplains, partly on religious grounds but also on others: Pearson, *Biographical sketch*, 14, 29–30.

Broadgate (b. 1628) was appointed by the company on 4 December 1662 to the position of chaplain to the factory at Smyrna.[35] It was probably Broadgate's sermon that Pepys heard and dismissed as 'most pitiful'.[36] He was supposedly 'palmed . . . upon the Turkey Company' by a gentleman who had been offended by Broadgate's 'unfitness and ill carriage'; two years after his arrival in Turkey he was sent home.[37] In the biography of Dudley North, who was at this time a Levant merchant, Broadgate was described as 'a fanatic and a whimsical pedant; and accounted to himself . . . that he ought to erect a discipline and make a Presbyterian reform amongst them; in order to which he had framed a Catechism and had it printed'.[38] Although there were other causes of friction that centred on Broadgate at Smyrna, his religious beliefs and practices were in conflict with those of the consul and the senior officials at the factory, as well as Heneage Finch, earl of Winchelsea, who at this time was the ambassador at Constantinople.[39] In Steven Pincus's words, Winchelsea led an 'Anglican crusade' against Broadgate as a 'first step' in an ultimately unsuccessful campaign 'toward easing the Presbyterians out of positions of influence within the Levant Company'.[40] The general court in London were certainly frustrated by what had happened in Smyrna and chastised the officials there for overstepping the bounds of their authority in sending Broadgate home. Certainly this incident highlights religious differences and tensions within the company but did it lead the general court to appoint more orthodox chaplains to prevent discord at the factories? By 1681, as we have seen, a preacher was appointed who explicitly attacked dissent in his sermon, but by then the general religious-political atmosphere had changed making it far more difficult to appoint someone unorthodox, than it had been two decades earlier.

In the letters to consuls and ambassadors introducing their new chaplains, the admirable qualities of the successful candidates were outlined, with emphasis placed on their general worth, learning, sobriety, orthodoxy and piety.[41] Occasionally practical considerations also played a part in making

[35] Broadgate presented testimonials from St John's College, Cambridge. An untraceable Mr Harison also preached before the company for this position and a Mr Coxe was asked to preach but presumably because no further mention of him is made in the minutes he did not: SP 105/152, pp. 72, 79, 88, 92, 96.

[36] *Pepys*, iii. 260.

[37] Roger North, *The life of the right hon. Francis North, Lord Guilford*, in his *Lives*, i. 43.

[38] Idem, *Dudley North*, ii. 41; Grassby, *English gentleman*, 203–4. Some records suggest that Broadgate had probably been ejected at the Restoration; if indeed he had, did the company know this in 1662?: A. G. Matthews, *Calamy revised: being a revision of Edmund Calamy's account of the ministers and others ejected and silenced, 1660–2*, Oxford 1934, repr. 1988, 77.

[39] S. P. Anderson, *An English consul in Turkey: Paul Rycaut at Smyrna, 1667–1678*, Oxford 1989, 102.

[40] S. C. A. Pincus, *Protestantism and patriotism: ideologies and the making of English foreign policy, 1650–1668*, Cambridge 1996, 328.

[41] For example, Company to Consul Rycaut, 1 Sept. 1670, SP 105/113, fo. 119r; W[illia]m Hussey and others to Consul Metcalf, June 1688, SP 105/114, p. 432.

appointment decisions, as candidates were sometimes asked when they could be ready to leave, as a ship was about to depart for Turkey.[42] Realising the company's eagerness to retain chaplains in post, one candidate, Thomas Rawlins, who had been defeated for the position at Smyrna in 1689, presented himself in August 1692, and 'proffered his Service to the Court promising if hee should bee chosen to remain there [Smyrna] 5 years, if required'.[43] Not surprisingly given the Broadgate incident, the general court was also concerned how prospective chaplains related to other people; in letters to officials in the Levant the court repeatedly expressed a desire for harmonious relations between the officials, the factors and the minister.[44]

Patronage may have been a deciding factor in many appointment decisions. Many candidates were introduced and recommended to the general court by members of the company. Such patronage was in fact encouraged, as in August 1683 when the position of chaplain at Constantinople became vacant; the minutes of the general court record that the members of the company were 'desired to inform themselves of some fitting persons to recommend'.[45] A number of the preachers had influential connections: Henry Brydges (1676?–1728), who was chaplain at Aleppo in the early eighteenth century was the second son of James Brydges, the eighth Lord Chandos, who had been ambassador at Constantinople in the 1680s. Brydges's predecessor at Aleppo, Henry Maundrell, was related to both Sir Charles Hedges, judge of the Admiralty Court, and Sir William Hedges, who had been treasurer of the factory in Constantinople in the 1660s. There is evidence that Charles Hedges, at least, attempted to exert his influence for his nephew's advantage by asking the then governor of the company, William Trumbull, not to support other contenders.[46]

### 'he cannot but live well, and grow rich': the careers of the Levant chaplains

From the candidates' perspective, a Levant chaplaincy was an attractive position to hold. Ministers were provided with food and lodging for themselves, and a servant, at the consul or ambassador's house. They were paid four hundred Lyon dollars, half of which was considered to be a salary and the other half a gratuity.[47] This totalled approximately ninety pounds, and

---

42 SP 105/156, p. 67.
43 SP 105/155, pp. 94, 219.
44 SP 105/113, p. 96.
45 SP 105/154, p. 369.
46 D. Howell, 'Introduction', to Henry Maundrell, A journey from Aleppo to Jerusalem in 1697, Beirut 1963, p. xxiii n. 1. Howell also suggests (pp. xxix–xxxi) that Maundrell's family may have been keen to see him obtain an appointment outside England because of an apparently unsuitable involvement with a woman.
47 SP 105/152, pp. 96, 241.

compared favourably with the estimate, by the governors of Queen Anne's Bounty, that in 1708 half of the incumbents of parish livings in England and Wales received at least eighty pounds.[48] The chaplain also received twenty pounds 'towards the furnishing himself for the voyage', and extra sums in the form of gifts and bequests from the factors.[49] When in the Levant chaplains might be very well respected; as Roger North wrote in the biography of his merchant brother: 'if their chaplain be a venerable and prudent good man, [the factories] revere him entirely, and calling him Pappas, which is the term in the Levant, given to their priests, not only observe and honour but present him very considerably, so as he cannot but live well, and grow rich'.[50]

Financially, a Levant chaplain was certainly comfortable, but it was perhaps more the commercial, intellectual and career opportunities offered by the post that attracted candidates to present themselves for consideration by the company. The chaplains were permitted to trade and a number of transactions are recorded in the company minutes. John Tisser (b. 1665/6), the chaplain at Smyrna in the early eighteenth century, arranged for £200 from his fellowship at Oxford to be invested in cloth and sent to him at Smyrna. More significant, however, was the company's decision to allow him to pay duties at the lower rate paid by company members.[51] Edward Smyth, according to his eighteenth-century biographer, noted that the years he spent as chaplain at Smyrna (1689–92) were 'to the great Advancement of his Private Fortune'.[52]

Perhaps most important for many chaplains, an interval in the Levant also offered the possibility to pursue scholarly interests.[53] Edward Browne, who was chaplain at Constantinople in the late 1670s, was in awe of the opportunities for scholarship he had there. He wrote to John Strype in 1676, 'I am confident that there are not such advantages for study to any other Englishman abroad in all the world, as I have here'; he particularly valued the conversations he had with a couple of 'learned Gentlemen', as well as the key to their library.[54] Such scholarship often built on existing language skills and

---

[48] Richard Grassby suggests a conversion rate of 4s. to 1 Lyon dollar. However, conversion rates of 4s. 6d., and 5s., to 1 Lyon dollar are mentioned in the minutes from this period: *English gentleman*, appendix, 342; SP 105/152, p. 316; SP 105/153, p. 254. Eighty pounds was regarded 'as an income just large enough to enable a gentleman with manageable obligations to maintain the bare subsistence and the minimal trappings of gentle status': G. Holmes, *Augustan England: professions, state and society, 1680–1730*, London 1982, 95.

[49] SP 105/154, p. 226; Anderson, *English consul*, 102.

[50] North, *Dudley North*, ii. 41.

[51] SP 105/156, p. 175. Sonia Anderson notes that the chaplain at Smyrna could use a warehouse if he wanted to trade: *English consul*, 102.

[52] James Ware, *The works of Sir James Ware concerning Ireland revised and improved*, I: *The history of the bishops of that kingdom*, Dublin 1739, 215.

[53] A. Hamilton, 'The English interest in the Arabic-speaking Christians', in G. A. Russell (ed.), *The 'Arabick' interest of the natural philosophers in seventeenth-century England*, Leiden 1994, 41–3.

[54] Edward Browne to John Strype, 17 Mar. 1676, CUL, Add 1, fo. 135r.

interest in oriental studies. Laud had been well aware of the potential value of the Levant Company for furthering such studies and had proposed a scheme in the mid-1630s, although ultimately unsuccessful, that each ship should return with a manuscript from the Levant. More successful, however, was his establishment of a Chair of Arabic at Oxford, the first holder of which was the former Levant Company chaplain at Aleppo, Edward Pococke (1604–91).[55] Aleppo was the safest place for Europeans at this time and the most conducive to scholarship; indeed most of the chaplains the company appointed to positions there during this period had graduated from Oxford, and a number were students of Pococke.[56] Among them was Robert Huntington (1636–1701), who was urged to apply for the position of chaplain by Pococke. Huntington, according to Thomas Smith (1638–1710), was 'always possessed by a searching indefatigable curiosity of seeing rarities' and travelled extensively, visiting Syria, Palestine, Egypt and Persia in his eleven years as chaplain to the company at Aleppo.[57] Despite the disappointment at finding so few books on foreign travel in the library at Aleppo, Huntington made the most of the scholarly opportunities.[58] He gathered manuscripts for himself, and others including Narcissus Marsh, John Fell, Thomas Marshall, Edward Barnard, Thomas Hyde, William Guise and Pococke, and in the early 1690s the Bodleian paid more than £1,100 for around 600 of Huntington's manuscripts: a massive addition to the collection.[59]

Huntington's 'lifelong friend', Thomas Smith, was also an Oxford graduate and a precocious scholar of oriental studies publishing, only two years after attaining his BA, a study of Aramaic translations of parts of the Old Testament.[60] The trial sermon he preached before the Levant Company in 1668 for a position at Constantinople demonstrated his abilities in both Hebrew

[55] G. J. Toomer, *Eastern wisedom and learning: the study of Arabic in seventeenth-century England*, Oxford 1996, 108–9, 111–12.

[56] Hamilton, 'English interest', 41–2.

[57] Thomas Smith, 'The life and travels of the right rev. and learned Dr Robert Huntington', *Gentleman's Magazine* xcv (1825), 11–12. This is a translation of Thomas Smith, *Admodum reverendi & doctissimi viri, D. Roberti Huntingtoni, S. theologiæ doctoris, et episcopi rapotensis, epistolæ*, London 1704. On Huntington see Toomer, *Eastern wisedom*, 281–6, and M. Feingold, 'Oriental studies', in N. Tyacke (ed.), *The history of the University of Oxford*, IV: *Seventeenth-century Oxford*, Oxford 1997, 491–2.

[58] '[T]he report of a great Library here, kept me from bringing any along w[i]th me . . . but they are all Books of another nature; & what little hopes I have to be furnished from England y[o]u will conjecture, when I can't get so much of a Letter hence': R[obert] Huntington to John Covel, 25 Jan. 1671?, BL, MS Add. 22910, fo. 79r.

[59] Smith, 'Robert Huntington', 13; Dr Twells, *The lives of Dr Edward Pocock*, London 1816, 289–9, 292–6, 298–302, 318; I. G. Philip, *The Bodleian Library in the seventeenth and eighteenth centuries*, Oxford 1983, 60–1, 125 n. 52.

[60] Thomas Smith, *Diatriba de chaldaicis paraphrastis, eorúmque versionibus, ex utroque Talmude, ac scriptis rabbinorum concinnata*, Oxford 1662; Feingold, 'Oriental studies', 470–5, 492, quotation at p. 492.

and Aramaic.[61] Following in Pococke's footsteps, Smith presumably wanted the position so that he could further his language skills.[62] While he was in Constantinople, however, G. J. Toomer suggests, Smith gave up his Arabic and Hebrew studies but maintained his interest in the Greek Orthodox Church.[63] He published his impressions of the Turks on his return to England, first in Latin and then in English: to him '[t]he Turks are justly branded with the character of a Barbarous Nation'.[64] Likewise other chaplains were interested in the eastern Churches and John Covel (1638–1722) published a book on the Greek Church in 1722 which was 'the Product of my Studies, during my Residence at Constantinople' in the 1670s.[65] Robert Frampton, Huntington's predecessor at Aleppo, became proficient in Arabic while in the Levant. He collected manuscripts and made a 'laborious collection of the Arabick proverbs with an account of their original and present use and application, with a parallel of the European in various languages'.[66]

John Luke (1635?–1702) was chaplain at Smyrna from 1664 until 1669, and for a further seven years from 1674. During his time in the Levant he asked the company to pay a quarter of his salary in England 'to be disposed of in Bookes to be sent to him'.[67] Despite such interests and that on his return to England in 1683 he was elected Fellow of Christ's College, Cambridge, and two years later became professor of Arabic, his career in oriental studies was undistinguished.[68]

Some of the chaplains' interests might better be described as natural philosophical. Huntington gathered 'the apples of cedars, the nuts of the Egyptian cypress and sycamores, and the berries of Assyrian shrubs for the use of those of his friends who took a delight in the study of gardens'. Among the recipients of such specimens was Jacob Bobart, the *horti praefectus* of the Botanic Garden at Oxford.[69] The chaplain at Smyrna between 1689 and 1692 was Edward Smyth (1665–1720), a graduate of Trinity College, Dublin. He was elected to the Royal Society in November 1695 and was admitted in April 1696 when he presented 'a parcel of Earth' originating from a place near

---

61 Tho[mas] Smith, *A sermon preached before the right worshipful company of merchants trading into the Levant*, London 1668.

62 Toomer, *Eastern wisedome*, 243.

63 Ibid. 245–6.

64 Tho[mas] Smith, *Remarks upon the manners, religion and government of the Turks*, London 1678, 1.

65 John Covel, *Some account of the present Greek Church*, London 1722, dedication.

66 Frampton, *Life*, 38–9, quotation at p. 39.

67 SP 105/152, p. 316.

68 Toomer, *Eastern wisedome*, 270; P. M. Holt, 'Background to Arabic studies in seventeenth-century England', in Russell, *'Arabick' interest*, 24, and 'The study of Arabic historians in seventeenth-century England: the background and the work of Edward Pococke', *Bulletin of the School of Oriental and African Studies* xix (1957), 444.

69 Smith, 'Robert Huntington', 118; R. Desmond (ed.), *Dictionary of British and Irish botanists and horticulturists: including plant collectors, flower painters and garden designers*, London 1994, 367.

Smyrna where it was used to make soap.[70] He was a 'fairly active' member of the Society and in addition to the account of this 'strange kind of earth' he also wrote an account of his experiments with 'the most famous Opium Eater' near Smyrna; both were published in the *Philosophical Transactions*.[71] Although a less active member of the Royal Society, the oriental scholar Thomas Smith also had some studies published in the *Transactions*, including a description of his journey to Constantinople in 1668 and historical observations of Constantinople (where he had been chaplain).[72] Smith was also involved in the publication of William Halifax's (1655?–1722) account of his voyage from Aleppo (where he was chaplain) to Palmyra in the *Philosophical Transactions*.[73]

Perhaps more widely read was Henry Maundrell's narrative of his journey from Aleppo to Jerusalem, written partly at the insistence of his uncle who hoped its distribution amongst prominent clerics would improve Maundrell's prospects on his return to England.[74] The travels were first published in Oxford in 1703, two years after Maundrell's early death in Aleppo, and although dismissed by the divine and antiquary William Nicolson as having 'nothing in 'em extraordinary, but many borrowed Accounts which are false', the book reached a seventh edition by the end of the eighteenth century.[75] Maundrell's book was advertised on the reverse of the title page of the sermon Laurence Hacket preached before the company in 1707, suggesting an overlapping audience (at least in the printer's eyes) for the sermons and the travel writings of company chaplains.[76]

70 Royal Society, Journal books of scientific meetings, vol. 8, p. 348; R. P. Stearns 'Fellows of the Royal Society in North Africa and the Levant', *NRRS* xi (1954), 77.

71 M. Hunter, *The Royal Society and its Fellows, 1660–1720: the morphology of an early scientific institution*, 2nd edn, Oxford 1994, 223; Edward Smith, 'An account of a strange kind of earth, taken up near Smyrna, of which is made soap, together with the way of making it', *PT* xix (1695–7), 228–30, and 'Of the use of opium among the Turks', *PT* xix (1695–7), 288. From Smyrna, Smith also sent Robert Plot two substances and an account of their uses (hair removal and colouring nails) which Plot presented in Oxford and reported in the *Transactions*: 'Extract from the minutes of Philosophical Society at Oxford , Feb. 8. 1684 concerning Rusma and Alcanna', *PT* xx (1698), 295.

72 Tho[mas] Smith, 'Historical observations relating to Constantinople', *PT* xiii (1683), 335–46; 'An account of the city of Prusa in Bithynia, and a continuation of the historical observations relating to Constantinople', *PT* xiv (1684), 432–54; and 'Journal of a voyage from England to Constantinople, made in the year 1668', *PT* xix (1695–7), 597–619.

73 William Halifax, 'A relation of a voyage from Aleppo to Palmyra in Syria; sent by the Reverend Mr. William Halifax to Dr. Edw. Bernard (late) Savilian Professor of Astronomy in Oxford, and by him communicated to Dr. Thomas Smith. Reg. Soc. C.', *PT* xix (1695–7), 83–110.

74 Howell, 'Introduction', pp. xxv–xxvi. One of the two letters of dedication is addressed to Maundrell's uncle, Sir Charles Hedges.

75 William Nicolson, *The London diaries of William Nicolson bishop of Carlisle, 1702–1718*, ed. C. Jones and G. Holmes, Oxford 1985, 319. See also Edmund Chishull, *Travels in Turkey and back to England*, London 1747.

76 Laurence Hacket, *A sermon preach'd at St. Bennet-Finct Church*, London 1707, facing title page.

Becoming a chaplain to the Levant Company not only offered commercial opportunities, and the chance to pursue scholarly interests, but it was also one of the first rungs on a ladder to a successful clerical career. Most chaplains were at the beginning of their careers; on average they were just over thirty-one years old when they first went out to the Levant.[77] All but one of the chaplains had a degree, and they went out to the Levant within, on average, seven years of graduating.[78] The strength of oriental studies at Oxford is perhaps reflected in the preponderance of Oxford graduates amongst the chaplains: over two thirds of the chaplains were Oxford alumni, one from Trinity College Dublin, and the remainder from Cambridge.

Compared to the Leicestershire parish incumbents in this period, studied by John Pruett, the Levant Company chaplains were very well qualified. Pruett found that in 1670 and 1714, 5 and 3 per cent respectively, of the parish incumbents held the BD, and possibly also the DD degree.[79] At their appointment 14 per cent of the Levant chaplains held the BD degree. A substantial proportion of the thirty-two chaplains appointed in this period became doctors of divinity and five went on to hold bishoprics: Charles Hickman (1648–1713), chaplain at Constantinople in the early 1680s, became bishop of Derry; Samuel Lisle (1683–1749), who was chaplain at both Smyrna and Aleppo in the early eighteenth century, became bishop of St Asaph, and then in the last years of his life bishop of Norwich; Edward Smyth became bishop of Down and Connor only six years after his return from the Levant; Robert Huntington, who had served at Aleppo for eleven years, became Provost of Trinity College, Dublin, and then in 1701, just before his death, bishop of Raphoe; and Robert Frampton, Huntington's immediate predecessor, became bishop of Gloucester in 1680.[80] Three former Levant chaplains became chaplains to the monarch, one of the 'most

77 All but three were between twenty-seven and thirty-four years old.

78 Joseph Foster, *Alumni oxonienses: the members of the University of Oxford, 1500–1714: their parentage, birthplace, and year of birth, with a record of their degrees*, Oxford 1891–2; Pearson, *Biographical sketch*; J. Venn and J. A. Venn, *Alumni cantabrigienses: a biographical list of all known students, graduates and holders of office at the University of Cambridge, from the earliest times to 1900*, Cambridge 1922–7. It should not be assumed, however, that the four who remain obscure lacked a formal education, for their common names have made them hard to identify. Moreover, by the late seventeenth century very few ordained Anglican clergy were not university graduates.

79 J. H. Pruett, *The parish clergy under the later Stuarts: the Leicestershire experience*, Urbana 1978, table 'Leicestershire degree-holders', at p. 43.

80 Although Frampton was deprived of the see in 1691 as a non-juror, the newly instituted clergy of the diocese continued to seek his ratification of their appointments: ODNB. Gordon Rupp notes that Frampton 'seems to have been the only bishop seriously to consider easing the situation by resignation, and in the last years of his life ceased correspondence which would involve him in controversy with the more extreme Non-Jurors': *Religion in England, 1688–1791*, Oxford 1986, 14.

distinguished' preaching positions in London, and a number of chaplains advanced to the position of dean.[81]

As holding the post of Levant chaplain could lead to a successful clerical career, so a disgraceful departure from the company's service could potentially signal its ruin. After being sent back to England from Smyrna in 1664, Broadgate 'lived very poorly upon his trade, that is conventicling' and repeatedly petitioned the company for financial support.[82] Others went to some lengths to protect themselves from the damage that being thought to have been dismissed from the company's service might have. William Halifax had been chaplain at Aleppo for seven years beginning in 1688. In 1702 he was accused of improperly influencing elections to the Lower House of the 1701 Convocation and his detractors described him as having been dismissed by the Levant Company as a result of misbehaviour. When this came to the attention of the general court it quickly moved to prepare a certificate for him to use to clear his name attesting that he had left of his own accord.[83]

That holding the post of chaplain to the Levant Company was a first stage in a career leading to positions amongst the upper clergy is indisputable. Maybe it was a case of well-qualified candidates fulfilling their potential or maybe it was that the prestige of the position with the company, and the patronage network chaplains became involved in, opened doors. For Samuel Lisle at least, there is evidence that his Levant Company connections furnished opportunities for preferment, as following his time as chaplain at Smyrna and then Aleppo, he became chaplain to the son of a former governor of the Levant Company.[84]

The position did not lead to good fortune for all. Almost one in eight died while they were in Turkey and many chaplains claimed deterioration in their health as their reason for desiring to return home. Others were acutely aware of the dangers of the Levant. John Covel, who did make it back to England, wrote from Constantinople to his father about the threat of plague: 'it is certaine they t[ha]t drank hardest escaped best. I was not at all afraid yet I have been in danger a 1000 times, sometimes very desperately'.[85]

[81] Ibid. 41. In 1711, a decade after he left Smyrna, Edmund Chishull became chaplain to Queen Anne. Charles Hickman, who had been chaplain at Constantinople, became chaplain to William and Mary as did Edward Smyth on his return from the Levant. Henry Brydges became chaplain to Queen Anne.

[82] North, Dudley North, ii. 42; SP, 105/152 fos 116r, 117r, 188r–v, 120v, 123v, 123r, 134v, 173r, 173r; SP 105/156, pp. 18, 92, 103.

[83] SP 105/156, p. 98; William Halifax, A sermon preach'd at Old Swinford in Worcester-shire, London 1702, and A letter to a clergyman in the City concerning the instructions lately given to the proctors, London 1702.

[84] ODNB.

[85] John Covel to his father, 4 Apr. 1674, BL, MS Add. 22910, fo. 129r.

## From pulpit to print

Before moving on to consider the sermons themselves I want to discuss the difficulties of the relationship between the preached sermon and the printed sermon. If the appointment of a preacher was partly determined by his trial sermon then it was not just what he said that mattered. Delivery was crucial, as manual writers, in the 1670s alone, reminded their readers: '[t]he Voice should be lively and earnest; but without any affected tone. . . . You should avoid a droning dulness of speech on the one hand, . . . and a boisterous noise on the other.'[86] Joseph Glanvill also instructed readers that gesture mattered too: 'it hath a considerable share in the influence on the hearers, who are moved by the Eye as well as by the Ear'. Glanvill's recommendation of 'a sutable and moderate motion . . . such as is free and natural' was not unlike James Arderne's prescription: 'let it comply with the things and sentences delivered, let it be grave, and decorous, free from apish postures and distorted looks'.[87]

Some of the successful candidates were noted for their oratorical skills. Frampton was described by John Evelyn as 'excellent in the Pulpet; for the moving affections' and was considered to be among the best preachers of the period.[88] Pepys, who had been unable to stay to hear Frampton preach on the fast day for the Fire in October 1666 because 'the crowd so great', heard him preach in 1667 when the chaplain was in London. He found

> the church crammed by twice as many people as used to be; and to my great joy find Mr. Frampton in the pulpit. So to my great joy I hear him preach, and I think the best sermon, for goodness – oratory – without affectation or study – that ever I heard in my life. The truth is, he preaches the most like an Apostle that ever I heard man. And was much the best time that ever I spent in my life at Church.[89]

Frampton's trial sermon of 1655 does not survive; even if did it could not fully convey the style of delivery which so captivated Pepys.

How did what was said relate to what was printed? Scholars used to think that the convention in the Restoration period was to preach from memorised notes and outlines; and in the eighteenth century to read the full sermon.[90] This is, of course, an unlikely disjuncture and even if this chronology could be sustained, individual practice probably varied quite substantially and

---

86 [Joseph Glanvill], *An essay concerning preaching*, London 1678, 78.

87 Ibid. 80; [James Arderne], *Directions concerning the matter and stile of sermons*, London 1671, 95–6.

88 Evelyn, *Diary*, iii. 629.

89 *Pepys*, vii. 316; viii. 21.

90 W. F. Mitchell, *English pulpit oratory from Andrewes to Tillotson: a study of its literary aspects*, London 1932, 26; Rolf P. Lessenich, *Elements of pulpit oratory in eighteenth-century England (1660–1800)*, Cologne 1972, 135.

possibly even across one career. Indeed manuals recommended particular practices for less experienced preachers: they should keep 'close to [their] written notes, without taking the liberty to speak . . . sudden and undigested thoughts: 'tis true, you may after long exercise in preaching, adventure upon *extempore* enlargements'.[91] There are a few clues as to the variety of preaching practices of the Levant Company chaplains across the period. A number of years after his return from being chaplain at Smyrna, and eight years after he preached his trial sermon, Edmund Chishull (1671–1733) was observed to preach from memory: his 'way of Preaching is by heart'.[92] Perhaps John Luke's reluctance to have his sermon printed, and his delay in delivering a copy of it to the company, can partly be explained by his having preached it not from a written copy but from a memorised outline.[93] Other preachers were in the habit of writing out their sermons in full. Two surviving manuscript volumes of the sermons of the Smyrna chaplain Bernard Mould (b. 1683), including the dates when, and places where, they were preached, suggest that at some stage, at least, he wrote his sermons in full, but not necessarily that he read from a manuscript in the pulpit.[94] Even if preachers gave their sermons from a complete copy, it may have been an amended version that was handed to the printer; some of the sermons preached before the House of Commons in the eighteenth century, as James Caudle has argued, were substantially revised before publication.[95]

The sermons as preached by the successful candidates represented something that the general court of the Levant Company approved of and thought was appropriate for their factors overseas to hear. The preachers got the job partly because of the merits of their sermons. Even if we cannot know the nature of the gaps between the preached and the printed sermons, or even how much weight the company placed in their appointment decisions on what was said, rather than the way it was said, the printed sermons can be read on their own terms. The company was keen to be seen to be endorsing

---

91 [Arderne], *Directions*, 94. Similarly, Glanvill recommended that a young divine should make himself the 'perfect Master of your Sermons, get them fully into your memory, and indeavour to keep them there: This is indeed painful, but 'tis a labour that I reckon necessary in the beginning, and such as will beget facility and ease, in the future course of your Ministry': *Essay concerning preaching*, 85.
92 Hearne, *Remarks and collections*, i. 290.
93 SP 105/152, pp. 241, 248.
94 Unfortunately, this volume does not contain a manuscript version of the sermon preached before the Levant Company. Although the author of these sermons has not previously been identified, the places and dates prefacing the sermons correspond to the various positions that Mould held on his return from Smyrna, and so it is with confidence that they can be attributed to him: [Bernard Mould], 'Texts of sermons preached at St. Alban Wood Street; St. Bartholomew by the Exchange; Newport, Essex; Quendon, Essex; Widdington; Holwell, Beds and Smyrna, Turkey', GL, Manuscripts, MS 330; Foster, *Alumni oxonienses*, iii. 1042.
95 J. Caudle, 'Preaching in parliament: patronage, publicity and politics in Britain, 1701–1760', in Ferrell and McCullough, *English sermon revised*, 235–63, at p. 253.

the sermons. As we know from Pepys's diary entry these were occasions on which Turkey merchants invited their friends; and others might also be present, like Pepys. These wealthy and important merchants were seen to be listening to such sermons and ordering their publication took this one step further. Readers of the sermons were left in no doubt that the company had witnessed the sermon being preached, that it had been printed at the company's command and that it was dedicated to them. As Mould wrote in the dedication in his sermon to the company: 'It was preach'd by your Appointment, it was heard with your Approbation, and is now published by Your Direction.'[96] Whether or not there is anything to be read into the fact that of the, at least, twenty-five appointments for which sermons were preached, only fifteen sermons were printed, that the sermons were endorsed by the company must have mattered to readers. No evidence has been found of debate by the courts of the Levant Company over whether to print a sermon, unlike in the House of Commons where whether to give thanks for a sermon preached before it and order it to be printed, was at times disputed.[97]

Charles Hickman, for one, articulated his concern that his sermon might affect the company's reputation. His denunciation of dissent, and the controversies it had apparently provoked, affected the company. Since the 'censures must in some manner reflect upon you also, who have been pleased to afford me a more favourable Character; I find myself bound in honour, as well as in gratitude and obedience, to vindicate both you, and my self, by this Publication'. Rather than addressing the objections to his sermon specifically Hickman argued that the defence was in the printed sermon: he stated that 'every rational man will be satisfied by reading the sermon'.[98] For Hickman, then, the printed sermon was a chance to defend both himself and the company.

### 'the surest and straitest way to wealth'

For at least two-thirds of the appointments to Levant chaplaincies candidates preached before the company, and fifteen of the sermons by the successful candidates were printed. These fifteen sermons, and another sermon by William Hayley (1658–1715) which was preached very soon after his appointment to the post of chaplain to the ambassador and factory at Constantinople at the end of 1686, are considered in what follows.[99]

---

[96] Bernard Mould, A sermon preach'd before the right worshipful the deputy governor and the company of merchants trading to the Levant-seas, London 1717, dedication.

[97] Caudle, 'Preaching', 245–50.

[98] Hickman, Sermon, dedication. Similarly, Hughes expressed his concern that the faults of his sermon would reflect upon the company: Hughes, Sermon, dedication.

[99] In the minutes it is recorded that William Hayley was appointed at the same meeting as the vacancy was announced. There is no mention of his preaching before the company

Although they were published throughout the period, the sermons better represent the later period as half were published in the first forty years after the Restoration and the other half in the first two decades of the eighteenth century.

What then were the messages that the company was so keen to be seen to be endorsing in print? The sermons focused on here are those concerned with wealth and the compatibility of commerce and Christianity, and those that contained portrayals of merchants. However, sermons were also preached on other topics. Thomas Owen (b. 1678/9) was asked to preach on Psalm cxix.59: 'I thought on my Ways; and turned my Feet unto thy Testimonies'. From the text he propounded that thinking was the way to combat the flesh, the devil and the world, which were the three 'great enemies'.[100] Some preachers in their sermons were concerned with issues of particular contemporary relevance. In his sermon in 1718, Thomas Payne (1688/9–1759), appointed chaplain to the factory at Constantinople, preached on the text 'I counsel thee to keep the King's Commandment, and that in regard of the Oath of God'.[101] He called on his audience to be loyal to George I as they were bound to be by 'Duty and Conscience', and not to be 'guilty of so base a Prevarication as directly or indirectly to espouse the cause of an abjur'd Pretender'.[102] Not all preachers took advantage of such opportunities for political reflection. William Hayley, who delivered a sermon on 30 January 1687, the anniversary of the death of Charles I, however chose not to mention it.[103]

The sermons preached before the Levant Company in this period on the subject of wealth, its acquisition and enjoyment, encompassed quite a range of positions, and cannot be treated as a unified and harmonious discourse. John Tisser, for example, preached before the company in 1701 on a text from Matthew, chosen by the company, which begins 'What is a Man profited, if he shall gain the whole world, and lose his own Soul.'[104] This was a much preached upon text in this period: when Tisser preached in 1701 at least five sermons had been published on this text, and by 1720 at least another nine

although he did offer to preach on his return. However, the sermon published in 1687 was supposedly preached before the company at the end of Jan. 1687 and in the Epistle Dedicatory Hayley remarked that the publication was commanded by the company. No mention is made of his sermon in the company minutes: William Hayley, A sermon preached before the right honourable George Berkeley governour, and the company of merchants of England trading into the Levant seas, London 1687, ep. ded.; SP 105/155, p. 26.

[100] Thomas Owen, A sermon preach'd before the honourable company of merchants trading to the Levant-seas, London 1706, 12. Thomas Smith also preached a sermon largely unrelated to mercantile themes: Sermon.

[101] Ecclesiastes viii.2.

[102] Thomas Payne, A sermon preach'd before the right worshipful the deputy governour and the company of merchants trading to the Levant seas, London 1718, 23.

[103] Hayley, Sermon.

[104] Matthew xvi.26.

had been printed.[105] Tisser argued that it would be imprudent to part with one's soul, and the eternal happiness of heaven, in exchange for worldly pleasures, including riches: 'let us not foolishly chuse Darkness before light, Hell before Heaven, eternal Woe before eternal Happiness, nor the transitory Things of this World before the never-fading ones of the next'.[106] According to Tisser there was nothing in the world that was 'truly valuable, nothing worth laying out ourselves upon'.[107] At their deaths the wealthy 'must change their gorgeous Robes for the filthy garments of Corruption . . . and then, they who now cringe to them, may trample on their Graves'.[108] The rich man may appear happy in this world but he hides his torment:

> the mighty Man, rais'd to boundless Possessions, by Cheating, Bribery, or Oppression . . . may, notwithstanding all his ill-gotten Wealth and specious Prosperity, be overwhelm'd with pining Melancholy and heart-rending Despair: And tho' the deluded World, gazing on the richness of his Attire and the splendour of his Equipage . . . may imagine him most transcendently Happy, yet he may know, and secretly feel himself to be most desperately wretched . . . He may be harrass'd with such tormenting Cares and grievous Reflexions, so justly terrifying, as may pall all his Pleasures, make his Honours cumberson, and his Riches a burthen to him.[109]

According to Tisser, the 'mouldering Treasures of this World therefore . . . should be beneath our care'.[110] Considering the possibility of throwing away one's soul or 'forfeit[ing] our Interest in God, and our Inheritance in Heaven', should 'deter us from all unjust and unlawful Dealings, from heaping up Riches by Fraud and Oppression, which we know not who shall gather, from gratifying our Desires by wicked Means, and from building upon other Mens Graves, raising our selves by the ruine of others'.[111] Even for those who obtained their riches with 'great Care, and kept [them] with greater Fear', the riches 'either make Wings to themselves, and fly away, or else, if kept are not enjoy'd'.[112] For Tisser then, riches were associated with corruption and led neither to earthly happiness nor heavenly riches. How much was Tisser going out of his way to shape his sermon for his audience? Certainly other sermons published on this text in this period did not devote quite the same amount of

---

[105] Sampson Letsome, *The preacher's assistant*, London [1753], 122–3. Letsome's listing of sermons published since 1660 is a reliable, but not comprehensive, guide: N. E. Key, 'The political culture and political rhetoric of county feasts and feast sermons, 1654–1714', *JBS* xxxiii (1994), 226.

[106] John Tisser, *A sermon preached . . . before the honourable company of merchants trading into the Levant-seas*, London 1702, 17.

[107] Ibid.

[108] Ibid. 19.

[109] Ibid. 11.

[110] Ibid. 20–1.

[111] Ibid. 24–5.

[112] Ibid. 20.

attention to wealth in their discussions of what fools might consider exchanging their souls for.

Tisser's views were out on a limb when compared to those of the other Levant preachers, but perhaps we should not be so surprised that he should address wealthy merchants in this way. Sermons were often controversial, even those that were critical of those who endorsed them. As Claydon has argued, 'Even clerics of the state Church – and even as they performed on state-sponsored events – were willing to use the pulpit to criticise the regime.'[113] Tisser was not the only candidate for the position in Smyrna (a Mr Woodford also preached), and even if he had been the only appointable candidate, the company did not have to order the printing of his sermon.[114] Perhaps it was in the interests of the Levant Company to be seen to be listening to, and endorsing, a message such as Tisser's?

Edward Smyth, who had preached in 1689 on the text of Isaiah xxvi.10 'For when thy Judgments are in the Earth, the Inhabitants of the World will learn Righteousness', just over a decade before Tisser preached his sermon, also denounced worldly pleasures. He suggested that one of the ends of divine judgements was to:

> beget in us a thorough Contempt of the World, and its fatal Dalliances: to enforce the Divine Precepts of setting Our Hearts on things above. For do not the Divine Judgments teach us; either how fugitive and uncertain, or how unsatisfying and empty all sublunary Beings are.[115]

He appealed to 'Common Prudence' and noted that daily 'the great emptiness and uncertainty of all worldly enjoyments' can be observed.[116] Later in the sermon he encouraged his audience to consider the 'necessary and natural consequents' of 'Luxury and Intemperances'. These sins 'sow the Seeds of all Distempers', and lead to 'decay of Estate, [and] a Crassed Body'. These consequences alone 'would be Amulet against them to a considering Man', but divine judgements like a plague or famine should shock all into repentance.[117]

Such interventions, according to Smyth, were sent from Heaven 'to frighten us from the gilded Poyson, and wean us by frequent disappointments from any fondness we may have for earthly things'.[118] Like Tisser, Smyth invited his audience to consider the rich person tormented by his sins, who when faced with judgement complained 'Had I laid up my Treasure in Heaven, it would not have been in the power of any outward accident now to

---

113 Claydon, 'Sermon', 220.
114 SP 105/156, fos 90r, 92r.
115 Edward Smyth, *A sermon preached before the right worshipful the deputy-governour, and the company of merchants trading to the Levant-Seas*, London 1689, 19.
116 Ibid.
117 Ibid. 28.
118 Ibid. 21.

deprive me of him' and repented 'Farewel then all ye deceitful Vanities; tho' I plac'd my Riches next my Heart. . . . Tho I preserved my Beauty with all Extravagance of Art; I must lose it this instant.'[119] He invited his audience to embrace the resolutions of the rich person who faced judgement and promised to 'lay up my Treasure in Heaven . . . be no longer cheated with imaginary good, but . . . make provision for the true and everlasting happiness' for then the Soul will be 'possessed of the only valuable Riches of Grace and Vertue'.[120]

Unlike Tisser, who denounced riches almost outright, Smyth's condemnation was largely limited to luxury and intemperance. Using an analysis familiar to his listeners, he interpreted the earthquake and subsequent fires that had recently occurred at Smyrna as a providential punishment.[121] He acknowledged the role of their sins in provoking such a divine judgement:

> let us not flatter our selves, or run into that dangerous mistake; that the Infidelity of the Jew and Mahometan, that the Idolatry and Superstition of Popery are the only provocations which brought down this heavy Judgment. Our sins, alas, are but too much the ingredients, and its wounds and scars yet bleeding afresh, are but too strong an intimation that we are still in our sins.[122]

However, Smyth did not pursue the complete condemnation of wealth.

Laying up treasures in Heaven rather than concentrating on acquiring riches in this world was a precept frequently employed in these sermons. Laurence Hacket, like other preachers, described the emptiness of riches: 'tho' Riches and Honour, and the Affluence of these World's Goods may dazle the eyes of unthinking mortals, yet have they no Essential Happiness in themselves'. Likewise he presented the conventional portrait of a rich man in distress: 'Let but the greatest favourite of fortune have his mind fill'd with the Apprehensions of Death and Future Torments, and he will think Job upon the dunghill the more happy Man.' Yet, unlike Tisser and Smyth, Hacket pursued the notion of happiness in this world from the starting point that 'since all our happiness flows from God, he can only be happy with whom God is well-pleased'. As 'the happiness of mankind, even in this Life, consists in the peace and tranquility of his mind', he allowed the possibility, more explicitly than Tisser or Smyth, that the rich could be happy on earth.

> The Happy Man . . . is only he whose conscience is at peace, whose mind is sedate and quiet, who is not afraid to look into the past actions of his Life . . . his Worship and Adoration of God having been constant and regular, and what proceeded from due and right Conceptions of the Deity, must needs be the genuine effect of Love and Duty, and not of the Place and Custom; for the

---

119 Ibid. 24.
120 Ibid. 25.
121 Claydon, 'Sermon', 219.
122 Smyth, *Sermon*, 35.

mind being rightly instructed, the heart and affections will yearn and tend towards the Chiefest Good.[123]

He ended his sermon, however, by cautioning his audience about the 'false notion of the present good that makes us so fond of the varieties and follies of this World'. For Hacket, like others, 'Profit and Pleasure' were 'mistaken' notions that 'makes Men act so desultorily and inconstant in Religion and Vertue; and the too great value and estimation they have of the things of this Life, which makes them so little regard a future happiness, and so very negligent of laying up Treasures in Heaven'.[124] Similarly, Joseph Soley (1690–1737), addressing the Levant Company at St Peter's Poor in Broad Street in 1719, preached a sermon on the acceptable performance of public worship using the text of Ecclesiastes v.1.[125] He exhorted the congregation not to put 'improper Petitions' to God: 'Which our Duty forbids us to ask, and the Honour of God to grant. As when we beg to be gratify'd in our Sensual Appetites and Passion; in our Covetousness, our Pride, Revenge, &c. Or when we pray for temporal Prosperity, without submitting it to the Wisdom of God, if he sees it best for us.'[126] Also especially relevant to his mercantile audience was his instruction to 'Let neither Sloth, nor Pleasure, nor unnecessary ill-tim'd Business, or any such unwarrantable Causes, ever keep us from God's House.'[127]

William Hayley, in his sermon preached before the company in 1687, undertook the most thorough consideration of the subject of the acquisition of wealth and how it could be reconciled with piety. Hayley stressed the importance of piety, and proposed, using the text from Proverbs 'Riches and Honor are with me, yea durable Riches and Righteousness', that wealth and piety could be pursued in harmony, and were indeed mutually reinforcing:[128]

> How troublesome, how unsatisfactory, yea and how pernicious too all our worldly goods are, is too too evident, when they are not directed by prudence, enjoyed with sobriety, and managed according to the dictates of Justice and Charity; and particularly Wealth and Riches, which are so eagerly prosecuted by mankind, as the instrument of all our necessaries and conveniences, are indeed but heavy incumbrances and unprofitable lumber, if they are not made use of to reward the good, to excite the diligent, and to relieve the oppressed.[129]

---

123 Hacket, *Sermon*, 13–14.
124 Ibid. 26.
125 'Keep thy Foot when thou goest into the House of God, and be more ready to hear, than to offer the Sacrifice of Fools; for they consider not that they do Evil': Ecclesiastes v. 1.
126 Joseph Soley, *A sermon preach'd before the right worshipful the deputy governour and the company of merchants trading to the Levant-seas*, London 1719, 18.
127 Ibid. 20.
128 Proverbs viii.18.
129 Hayley, *Sermon*, 2.

Although he admitted that there may be exceptions and God may let the sinful be rich and deprive the godly, in general 'Piety is the most effectual means . . . To gain riches certainly'.[130] This position was supported with four arguments. First, riches were the gift of God and so 'those that serve him religiously, and endeavour to please him' could 'reasonably hope' to receive God's gifts.[131] The notion that fortune was a gift, or a blessing, directly from God was stated in a number of these sermons.[132] Secondly, he argued that piety, because it is no more than 'the habitual practice of Moral and Divine Vertues', is 'naturally productive of Riches and Plenty'.[133] He listed these various virtues and showed how each could enrich those who practised them. As wealth could not flourish in wartime, 'Peace, concord and Brotherly love', for example, promoted prosperity on a large scale. On a smaller scale, mutual help 'makes every person of a double strength, and interchangeable kind offices and good turns help to exalt all together without the downfall of any'.[134]

Hayley's third argument concerned credit and reputation and appealed to contemporary understandings. All people involved in commerce, he preached, 'make it their business to conserve a good name and a fair reputation', as any whose name has been wronged is deprived of wealth. The only solid foundation for this necessary good name is sincere piety and virtue.[135] This was a point that Hacket had also explored. He noted that men avoided dealing with those who 'have little or no fidelity and honesty', and one that was identified as such 'generally becomes the scorn and contempt of the World' and received no pity, offended man and God. For Hacket:

> Doing Justly not only establishes Men's Characters in the World, makes Men Love and esteem them, but is the most effectual way to encrease their Wealth and Riches, one would think there needed no exhortation to the practice of it, since Honour and Riches are so much the darling objects of Mens desires; but yet we find Men must be courted to their own happiness, woo'd and entreated to do themselves good.[136]

Lastly, Hayley claimed, in a vein similar to that of this passage from Hacket, that piety and virtue lead to wealth as 'they direct to the use of those methods which are honest and lawful, and abominate all such as are false and unjust'.[137] Hayley appealed to his audience's knowledge of God's nature, and human experience, to confirm that honest means are the most productive of

---

130 Ibid. 6.
131 Ibid. 11.
132 Chishull, *Sermon*, 25; Hughes, *Sermon*, 26.
133 Hayley, *Sermon*, 11–12.
134 Ibid. 13.
135 Ibid. 15.
136 Hacket, *Sermon*, 27–8.
137 Hayley, *Sermon*, 18.

riches.[138] Other preachers acknowledged that there were ways of acquiring wealth that were consistent with Christian practices. Among the questions that Edmund Chishull, for example, proposed that individuals should ask themselves as part of a self-examination was 'Have they been fair and just in all their Dealings?'[139]

Congregations were accustomed to the high esteem in which a fair-dealing merchant was held. Sermons preached at the funerals of merchants, including those who were members of the Levant Company, praised the same virtues espoused in the printed sermons by the Levant Company chaplains. The published sermon given by John Scott in 1688 at the funeral of the one-time deputy governor of the company – Sir John Buckworth – paid tribute to his commercial conduct: 'I believe that all that knew him, will allow him this Character, That he was a Gentleman of great Integrity and Fidelity to his Trust; of exact Justice and Righteousness in his Commerce and Dealings'.[140] Other merchants were commended for having been 'skilful, diligent, and just and faithful' in their business.[141] Funerary monuments cele- brated the same virtues. In St Stephens, Coleman Street, on a monument erected for Henry Vernon, who died in Aleppo in 1694, he was praised for being 'a Person of strict Virtue and exemplary Piety, just in his Dealings, dutiful to his Parents, and kind to his Relations'. His father, who erected the monument, recommended his son's life 'as a Pattern worthy the Imitation of our young Merchants' at home and abroad.[142] Maintaining the chains of credit that linked early modern individuals was singled out in such orations. Not only was the merchant, Lucas Lucie, 'a Punctual and Just man' but 'he did not break Artificially to cheat his Creditors, and fill his own purse; But he studied to thrive by ingenuous and honest Arts'.[143]

Although maintaining credit was vital to success for all traders, Hayley's (and others') emphasis on honesty may have struck a particular chord with the Levant merchants in his audience. At the beginning of the period the company's profits were much reduced by the factors' strategies to divert money from the company coffers into their own pockets.[144] The problem of the factors' abuses in Turkey was addressed from a number of angles. Under the new charter in 1661, the consuls and ambassador 'were authorized to

[138] The 'Anglican instructed business men to serve themselves by being godly . . . sound economic practice was elevated from the realm of common sense to the heights of heavenly duty': R. B. Schlatter, *The social ideas of religious leaders, 1660–1688*, London 1940, 203.

[139] Chishull, *Sermon*, 25.

[140] John Scott, *A sermon preach'd at the funeral of Sir John Buckworth*, London 1688, 27.

[141] Edward Lawrence, *Two funeral sermons of the use and happiness of humane bodies*, London 1690, 74.

[142] Hatton, *New view*, i. 553.

[143] Nathanael Waker, *A sermon preached at the funeral of Mr. Lucas Lucie*, London 1664, 37.

[144] Wood, *History*, 58; Grassby, *English gentleman*, 55–6. Such problems were common in other companies: A. M. Carlos and S. Nicholas, 'Agency problems in early chartered companies: the case of the Hudson's Bay Company', *JEcH* i (1990), 853–75.

administer to all factors, ships' captains, and pursers an oath to make true entries of all goods consigned to or by them or carried by them'.[145] Factors who refused to take the oath were not employed and the transactions of those that did could, to some extent, be checked by the officer employed in the custom house in London.[146] The measures were successful and the company's fortunes recovered.[147]

The difficulties of regulating the factors' behaviour were compounded in the 1670s by problems with the repayment of debts. In the early 1670s a particular problem emerged with the credit that the factors in Turkey had extended to merchants when they bought cloth: large debts had been contracted and they were proving difficult for the factors to collect. The company's response was the controversial measure of forbidding credit sales in the factories with the factors pressurised to take an 'oath against trusting'.[148] There were ways to evade the measure and the company was well aware that the factors took mortgages and pawns as security instead. In 1701 another oath which took account of such practices was introduced which, almost until the end of this period, was resisted but eventually took effect.[149] It was therefore crucial throughout the period for the company to endorse the messages that debts were not to be undertaken lightly and that business should be transacted honestly.

Some of the Levant preachers also addressed how wealth that had been acquired honourably should be used. As Hayley put it 'Wealth and Riches . . . are indeed but heavy incumbrances and unprofitable lumber, if they are not made use of to reward the good, to excite the diligent, and to relieve the oppressed'.[150] Again Hayley emphasised piety, and associated it here with using riches honourably. Honour cannot arise properly from anything that is not directed by piety, proposed Hayley, and so riches can only be used honourably under the guidance of piety.[151] Of the virtues that naturally promoted prosperity he listed charity. In using money in this way, a person gained supporters which led to greater prosperity.[152] Chishull too exhorted his audience to question 'Have they been Charitable to the Distressed according to their Ability?'[153] It was also argued that charity was a means of glorifying God and, using a variation on the analogy from an often cited verse from Matthew, to obtain 'one Pearl of great Price', eternal salvation.[154] The

145  Wood, History, 94; Anderson, English consul, 120.
146  Anderson, English consul, 120.
147  Wood, History, 97.
148  Anderson, English consul, 205; G. Ambrose, 'English traders at Aleppo (1658–1756)', EHR 1st ser. iii (1931), 254–6.
149  Ambrose, 'English traders', 255–6.
150  Hayley, Sermon, 2.
151  Ibid. 6.
152  Ibid. 14.
153  Chishull, Sermon, 25.
154  Matthew xiii.45, 46.

chaplain at Aleppo at the beginning of the eighteenth century, Henry Brydges, preached in his sermon on this text before the Levant Company:

> To be rich to the World in this use of our Worldly prosperity, is the best and wisest method of being rich towards God. . . . If they who are rich in this World . . . do good, if they be rich in good Works, ready to distribute, willing to communicate; according to the decision of the Great Apostle, they are laying up in store for themselves a good foundation against the time to come, that they may lay hold on Eternal Life.[155]

Merchants were indeed praised in funeral sermons for having been charitable. The Levant merchant James Houblon was lauded for his 'universal Charity for all good and worthy Men' and the preacher at the funeral of the merchant Thomas Bowyer listed the charitable instructions in his will.[156] In the dedication prefacing Hayley's sermon he paid tribute to the Levant Company: it had demonstrated to him 'exemplary Vertue, so frequent Charities, so constant and regular a Devotion, and so profound a respect for all things that are Sacred'.[157] The company had realised the ideals Hayley went on to expound in the sermon. Other virtues of the company were praised and held up as exemplary in the dedications prefacing other published trial sermons. Two years later Edward Smyth echoed Hayley's sentiments, observing that it was to the company's 'Industry and Ingenuity, [that] the English Nation in a great measure owes those extraordinary Advancements of Wealth and Reputation abroad, this last Century has made. Whose most eminent Vertues, exemplary Charity, and signal Services to your Country, have rais'd you up to be the Ornament of your own, as the Envy of all neighbouring Nations.'[158] Hayley and Smyth preached these sermons in the early 1680s when the Levant Company had been suffering declining fortunes for some years for which they blamed the East India Company's encroachment of the Levant trade.[159] Hughes, in his dedication to the Levant Company in

---

[155] Henry Brydges, A sermon preached at St. Mary Aldermanbury, London 1701, [21–2]. These themes were pursued in other sermons preached before merchants in this period. See, for example, Charles Brent's sermon preached before the 'society of merchants' in Bristol: Honour thy Lord with they substance, London 1708.

[156] Gilbert Burnet, A sermon preached at the funeral of Mr. James Houblon, London 1682, 31; Nath[aniel] Hardy, Carduus Benedictus, the advantage of affliction, or the reward of patience: unfolded in a sermon preached at the funeralls of Mr Thomas Bowyer Merchant, London 1659, 33.

[157] Hayley, Sermon, dedication.

[158] Smyth, Sermon, dedication.

[159] Competition from the East India Company was seen as the major reason for the decline in the Levant Company's trade since the late 1670s but there were others connected to French and Dutch competition and later conditions in Turkey and war with France: Wood, History, 102–12. See, for example, The allegations of the Turky Company and others against the East-India-Company, [London 1681].

1683, spoke to the context most directly in alluding to the absence of crown backing for the Levant Company:

> So that, not to speak of the Benefits we at present enjoy from the Levant trade, the merits of its past services have been so incomparably great to the whole Nation, that I doubt not, but they'll be an argument to Authority to continue the protection, and encouragement of it; as they ought to be, to all English men to wish, and pray for its prosperity.[160]

In the early eighteenth century too, preachers were keen to defend and promote the company's reputation. In their dedications to the company prefacing their published sermons both William Crosse (b. 1683/4) and Bernard Mould drew on Isaiah xxiii.18 to applaud the merchants as princes. William Crosse, in the dedication to the 'Governour and Company', which preceeded his sermon on angels wrote: 'I shall not cease to Offer up my Hearty Wishes, and Fervent Prayers, for the Wealth and Prosperity of Your Illustrious Body; That Your Merchants may be in this Crowning City, as those in Tyre of Old, like Princes, and Your Traffickers the Honourable of the Earth.'[161] Mould drew upon the same verse from Isaiah to frame his tribute to the company in terms of the honour of trade: 'May the Almighty take Your Honourable Company under his Protection, preserve and prosper You, the Credit and Glory of this Trading Nation, the Ornament of this . . . Crowning City! May Your Merchants still rival Princes in every Thing that is truly great, and may Your Traffickers still continue the Honourable of the Earth and Seas.'[162] As the Royal Exchange was seen to bring glory to London, so too did the Levant Company merchants.

In these sermons many of the preachers adopted a language of commercial terms and trading analogies. John Hughes gave a sermon before the company on the text 'They that go down to the Sea in Ships, that do business in great waters: These see the Works of the Lord, and his Wonders in the Deep.'[163] This may appear an obvious choice for the company to direct a candidate to preach on but as Chishull (who was also asked to preach on this text) notes it was an 'occasional and peculiar subject' and these two sermons were the only ones published on this text in the period.[164] In his introduction Hughes announced that he would not give a discourse on sailing or merchandise as this would be a very 'undecent undertaking, with respect to the Audience'. He hoped that ''twill not be esteemed a Fault' that he chose not to use the terms of these subjects. He regarded doing so as ostentatious since 'It being a very easie thing for any one to pick up some Phrases of a Science, and Strut

---

160 Hughes, *Sermon*, dedication.
161 William Crosse, *The nature and office of good angels, set forth in a sermon, preach'd before the honourable company of merchants trading to the Levant-seas*, London 1713, dedication.
162 Mould, *Sermon*, dedication.
163 Psalm cvii. 23, 24.
164 Chishull, *Sermon*, dedication; Letsome, *Preacher's assistant*, 52.

with a few terms of an Art, that he has no competent knowledge of.'[165] That Hughes was so conscious that the 'arts' of sailing and merchandise had their own terminology indicates an awareness that different groups of people adopted different vocabularies, a topic pursued in more detail in chapter 3.

Other preachers used trading terms with less restraint. Tisser, in his discussion of losing one's soul and gaining the world, used commercial terms like exchange, barter and consign.[166] Other preachers intricately wove together the themes of commerce and piety using trading analogies. Henry Maundrell, in his sermon in 1695, considered the River Thames as the basis for commerce and a model for piety:

> A Christian Zeal must imitate that friendly and propitious River upon which this City stands, and to which you are so much indebted for your Traffick and Grandeur: It must proceed in a still and gentle Course . . . be pleased to learn the due Moderation of your Piety: And derive this double Advantage from its Waters, to make it the Pattern of your Zeal, as it is the great Fountain of your Riches. 'Tis such a Calm, and Even, and Deep Current of Religion, which alone can quench the burning Discords that are between us; and Import as great an Increase of true Piety amongst us, as that other does of Wealth and Splendor.[167]

So, for some of the Levant chaplains, piety and wealth were completely compatible, and were in fact mutually reinforcing. In his study of best-selling religious literature of the late seventeenth century John Sommerville has considered the applicability of the Weber thesis. He found that it was amongst Anglican writers, rather than dissenters, that the notion of diligence in one's calling was most prevalent.[168] What was being preached before the Levant Company, however, was that piety led to salvation, and fortune was the outcome of pious behaviour. Working, but not necessarily diligently, in one's calling, although this notion was not emphasised, could lead to salvation. However, and this is where these preachers differ most from the writers Sommerville considered, it was not the work itself that would lead to salvation but that rational individuals worked for their own happiness which brought glory to God and their own salvation. Edmund Chishull argued a well developed version of this position. He demonstrated that the 'Glory of God is no other that our own Happiness', and therefore as individuals 'we need not then be directed to aim at the Glory of God in all our Undertakings: for as we are Men, and Masters of right Reason, we shall be sure so to do'.[169]

In the text of the sermons, some preachers explored the position and

---

[165] Hughes, *Sermon*, 4–5.
[166] Tisser, *Sermon*, 16.
[167] Henry Maundrell, *A sermon preach'd before the honourable company of merchants trading to the Levant-seas*, London 1696, 23–4.
[168] C. J. Sommerville, 'The anti-Puritan work ethic', *JBS* xx (1981), 78.
[169] Chishull, *Sermon*, 9.

responsibilities of merchants. The amount of wealth individuals owned was decided by God, according to Hacket, and 'whatever may be the reasons' why upon some were bestowed 'the affluence and plenty of these worlds goods' and others 'fall into want and penury, trouble and affliction . . . we are not to enquire'. Rather this was 'an opportunity for us, to shew forth our Thankfulness to God, for the Blessings he has bestowed upon us, and the Plenty he has endow'd us withal'.[170] Although Hacket did not develop the notion of the calling as fully as other preachers in this century he did appeal to its central tenet in bidding: 'Let us every one in the station God has plac'd us in, fully resolve to obtain his own good and happiness, and heartily set about it, since God hath shewed us what this Good is, and the conditions requir'd are so very easy and agreeable to our Natures.'[171] In his sermon Hacket described how those who were rich, and by implication merchants, had special responsibilities:

> Riches, and Honour, and Power are given unto Mankind, for no other end, but to Do Good, and Shew Mercy; and he who frees the Poor and Oppressed out of the hand of the Oppressor and Extortioner, acts God-like in his Station, and imitates that Supreme Being who has delegated that Power to him to use to his Glory and Praise, which is no otherwise perform'd but by such actions.[172]

Doing good and loving one another, Hacket writes, 'is the Essential and Distinguishing Character of Christians, and every Man has it more or less in his Power; but those who have the frequentest Opportunities, and the largest Means, have an inestimable Blessing bestow'd upon them, if they will but make the right use of it'.[173] Quoting from Luke vi.36, Hacket went on to exhort his audience to imitate God in showing mercy.[174] In describing how God's power was delegated to the rich and that in their actions they should imitate him, Hacket was appealing to the notion of stewardship which other Levant preachers pursued. For example, one of the questions Chishull suggested that the members of his congregation consider was 'Have they approv'd themselves as wise and faithful Stewards to their great Master, and manag'd the good Things of this Life to the Glory of him who lent them?'[175]

Not only were merchants seen as God's stewards because of their wealth, but also because they were traders involved in commerce abroad. John Hughes in 1683 preached to the Levant Company on the value of

---

170 Hacket, *Sermon*, 16.
171 Ibid. 27.
172 Ibid. 16–17.
173 Ibid. 17.
174 Ibid.
175 Chishull, *Sermon*, 26. Compare with John Locke on stewardship: 'God requires him [Man] to afford to the wants of his Brother': *Two treatises of government*, ed. P. Laslett, 2nd edn, Cambridge 1967, 188.

navigation. Navigation, and by implication merchants, made it easier to supply 'the wants of every Country, out of the abundance of others . . . And thereby making the Blessings of our bountiful Creator as diffusive, as he intended them'.[176] This was a providential arrangement: 'in the great Oeconomy of the World, by the Wisdom of Providence, to encourage Industry, and promote a mutual Intercourse, and good Correspondence amongst Mankind, those parts that abound most, and with the noblest Productions, do yet as much want some of the Commodities of the less fruitful Countries'.[177] Hughes's depiction of commerce as a world of exchange and redistribution is perfectly in line with much that was written about commerce across the period in all genres. Take Joseph Addison writing in his periodical *The Spectator* in 1711, for example, echoing Hughes in his use of the phrase 'mutual intercourse': 'Nature seems to have taken a particular Care to disseminate her Blessings among the different Regions of the World, with an Eye to this mutual Intercourse and Traffick among Mankind, that the Natives of several Parts of the Globe might have a kind of Dependance upon one another, and be united together by their common Interest.'[178]

Merchants, because they were involved in 'traffick', were seen to have a special duty to promote Christianity in the countries to which they travelled. Hughes implored God to influence all those that went abroad 'that by their just and honest dealings, their innocent and holy Lives, they may adorn the Profession of the Gospel, and win over strangers to the Love of it; or at least make them asham'd to blaspheme it'.[179] Chishull, preaching on the same text from the Psalms as Hughes, portrayed merchants as having a greater responsibility; for if those travelling after the merchants did not find the Christian faith revered as a 'Holy, Sincere, and Heavenly Profession' it would be the merchants who were at fault.[180]

He also argued that as merchants were employed as traffickers and travellers they had peculiar opportunities 'of being serviceable to the Glory of God'. Not only because they were God's stewards but also because their travelling acquaints the inhabitants of England with the 'Works of Creation', and the 'Dispensations of Providence'.[181] These opportunities were accompanied by a duty to set an example to the English on their return from their travels. 'Otherwise', argues Chishull, 'there never will be wanting such weak and unwary Persons, who being less acquainted with the Dispensations of Providence, will be led by these great Authorities into the like remisness of Obedience.'[182]

---

176 Hughes, *Sermon*, 10.
177 Ibid. 12.
178 *The Spectator*, 19 May 1711.
179 Hughes, *Sermon*, 26.
180 Chishull, *Sermon*, 23.
181 Ibid. 12, 13, 15–17. Compare with Hughes, *Sermon*, 16.
182 Chishull, *Sermon*, 23–4.

Here then merchants were being judged on the basis of their trading activities. Their interaction with countries abroad gave them opportunities to promote God's glory, and entailed a duty to redistribute God's provisions, and to set an example, both at home and abroad, to promote the Christian religion. Merchants were being judged against a religious ideal, and not a business ideal, but equally they were able to measure up to this ideal partly because of their trading activities.

In those sermons preached before the Levant Company in this period, with only a few exceptions, wealth and merchants were portrayed in a positive light. For those hoping to get a position preaching to a mercantile community, this comes as no surprise. What is more intriguing is how preachers set out to portray merchants in a positive light to impress their audience. Merchants were depicted as wealthy in a context where wealth was largely sanctioned, and was in some preachers' eyes compatible with piety. Moreover, trading and owning wealth were accompanied by the special responsibilities of being God's stewards and presented opportunities to bring glory to God. In appointing the preachers of these sermons, and ordering the printing of these sermons, the general court of the Levant Company, to some extent, endorsed these messages.

# 3

# 'The Compleat Comptinghouse':
# Manuals for Merchants

In 1684 Richard Steele, in his book *The trades-man's calling*, instructed readers to study the Bible and to 'Read also such other good Books, whereof there is store, to make you wise. But add withal serious consideration of men and things, whereby you will vastly improve in godly Wisdom; for every thriving and decaying Tradesman will be a Book, to teach you something.'[1] This chapter is about the largely technical and secular manuals written to instruct and inform readers about commerce, which were perhaps in Steele's category of 'other good Books', rather than the education gained from 'serious consideration of men and things'. However, although most authors of manuals did not hesitate to make grand claims about the scope of their books and the benefits of studying them, some did acknowledge that traders might instruct, not least in their choice of book titles: *The exact dealer, The compleat tradesman, The gentleman accomptant, The accurate-accomptant*.

Texts advising merchants were part of a large body of publications which were concerned to advise, inform and instruct readers in the early modern period on almost every area of conduct and knowledge from gardening to writing poetry, from music to cosmetics.[2] If images of the Royal Exchange somehow offered the promise of capturing and containing the trading world and making it seem understandable, then, so too might merchant manuals, with their claims to being comprehensive and accessible guides to the world of trade. Bookkeeping instruction, with which many manuals were concerned, in particular, is one way in which these texts offered some command over commerce. Building on studies of prescribed accounting techniques, scholars have debated the role of double-entry bookkeeping in the 'rise of capitalism'.[3] Methods of double-entry bookkeeping, it has been argued, were promoted to make records 'orderly and complete'; they

---

[1] Richard Steele, *The trades-man's calling*, London 1684, 76.
[2] N. Glaisyer and S. Pennell (eds), *Didactic literature in England, 1500–1800: expertise constructed*, Aldershot 2003.
[3] B. S. Yamey, H. C. Edey and H. W. Thomson, *Accounting in England and Scotland: 1543–1800: double entry in exposition and practice*, London 1963, 155–79; J. R. Edwards, *A history of financial accounting*, London 1989, 59–63. For a contribution which considers arithmetics, rather than accounting texts see N. Z. Davis, 'Sixteenth-century French arithmetics of the business life', *Journal of the History of Ideas* xxi (1960), 18–48.

'promised . . . initiates an unprecedented sense of control over the intimi-
dating universe of credit, debt, and cash-flows'.[4]

As well as offering techniques like bookkeeping, that made commerce
comprehensible, containable and profitable, manual writers also offered their
readers exhaustive knowledge. Writers compiled lists of commodities, coins,
goods, fairs, coaches and numerous pre-calculated prices and interest
payments. A few authors also provided their readers with dictionaries of
commercial terms, and it is these which will be examined in some detail in
this chapter.

Contemporary commentators, like Daniel Defoe, remarked on the
specialist terminologies amongst mechanics and handicrafts traders: 'every
trade has its nostrums, and its little made words, which they often pride
themselves in, and which yet are useful to them on some occasion or other'.[5]
The 'compleat English tradesman' should know all these different languages
'as the beggars and strollers know the gypsy cant, which none can speak but
themselves'.[6] Defoe also noted that stockjobbers had their own specialist
language: stockjobbers 'can ruin men silently, undermine and impoverish by
a sort of impenetrable Artifice, like Poison that works at a distance, can
wheedle Men to ruin themselves, and Fiddle them out of their Money, by the
strange and unheard of Engines of Interests, Discounts, Transfers, Tallies,
Debentures, Shares, Projects, and the Devil and all of Figures and hard
Names'.[7] Authors attempted to arm their readers with knowledge about all
areas of commerce, not least specialist terminology, to defend themselves
against being cheated.

There were a number of ways in which a vocabulary of trading terms might
be seen in the late seventeenth and early eighteenth centuries to promise an
entry into the world of commerce and perhaps even an expertise in trade.
Glossaries and dictionaries were common in other didactic texts and
compiling vocabularies was an important part of the Royal Society's
programmes to write the history of trades. In the context of the challenges
posed by the emerging financial world of the 1690s to the status and capacity
of language, the definition of commercial terms has particular significance
and can be interpreted as part of attempts to legitimate the new financial and
commercial realms with their new forms of credit. Moreover, the construction of a commercial language (for authors also prescribed writings and
conversation styles, as well as providing vocabularies) in these texts helped to
demarcate commerce as an area of knowledge which was worthy of study by
various groups, including gentlemen.

The vocabularies, like the manuals as a whole, may have allowed readers

---

4  M. Chatfield, A history of accounting thought, Hinsdale, Il. 1974, 57–61; Hunt, Middling
sort, 58.
5  [Defoe], Complete English tradesman, 38.
6  Ibid. 34.
7  [Idem], The villainy of stock-jobbers detected, London 1701, 22.

to take imaginary journeys into the world of commerce, just as the Royal Exchange offered the chance to those on the balconies to be spectators of commerce. The evidence for such reading practices is slight but many of the didactic strategies employed by the authors of merchant manuals opened up opportunities for such spectating. Other evidence of owning and reading these texts survives and is also examined below.

The connections with the first chapter are also more prosaic. As we have seen some manuals provided guidance on negotiating credit at the Exchange, and as we will see below, one of the bookshops that specialised in this genre was located at the Exchange. Indeed the chapter begins by placing these manuals in the context of the contemporary print culture of the period to examine their publication and marketing, before moving on to consider in the second and third sections the contexts in which they were read, their authors and the claims made about readership. The fourth section deals with the identity of the merchant constructed within these texts, focusing principally upon the construction of his commercial language, through glossaries and stylistic precepts, and its significance. The ways in which these texts offered a vicarious experience of commerce and evidence of reading and owning them are explored in the final two sections.

## Publishing and marketing merchant manuals

With the European-wide expansion of print culture in the early modern period there was an increase in the publication of materials concerned directly with trade and commerce.[8] Printed material in the form of stationery, newspapers, books, pamphlets and broadsides was available to inform, instruct and aid those with an interest in trade.

Advertisements provide some indication of the range of the often ephemeral printed commercial stationery available in late seventeenth- and early eighteenth-century England.[9] The bookseller Nathaniel Brooke advertised on the final page of Thomas Browne's *The accurate-accomptant* (1670) the

---

[8]  D. Grote, J. Hoock and W. Starke, 'Handbücher und Traktate für den Gebrauch des Kaufmanns, 1470–1820: Bibliographie und Analyse des Wandels einer literarischen Gattung', *Tijdschrift voor Geschiedenis* ciii (1990), 279–93. My thanks to Alex Baer for translating this article. For general surveys of a variety of contemporary printed literature concerned with trade and commerce see A. H. Cole, 'Conspectus for a history of economic and business literature', *JEcH* xvii (1957), 333–88, and J. Raven, 'Imprimés et transactions économiques: réprésentation et interaction en Angleterre aux XVIIe et XVIIIe siècles', *RHMC* xliii (1996), 234–65. I am grateful to David Jones for assistance with translating this article.

[9]  J. Lewis, *Printed ephemera: the changing uses of type and letterforms in English and American printing*, Woodbridge 1962, repr. 1990, 41, 85, 172–3, 195, 198. On commercial ephemera in the eighteenth century see A. Heal, *London tradesmen's cards of the xviii century: an account of their origin and use*, London 1925; Hunt, *Middling sort*, 182–8.

sale of 'all Sorts of Bonds single or double, Releases, Indentures for Leases, or for Apprentices, Policies of Insurance, Bills of Lading of all sorts' at his shop at 'the Angel' in Cornhill.[10] Many of the booksellers who published and sold mercantile manuals also stocked commercial stationery, including a wide range of pre-printed forms. The stationer Christopher Coningsby, for example, advertised that he sold at his shop at the 'Ink-Bottle' in Flower de Luce Court, Fleet Street, 'All sorts of Blank Bonds, Writts, Warrants, Licences, and other usefull Blanks'.[11]

Serial publications, as will be shown in the next chapter, provided readers with diverse financial and commercial information. Although, for pragmatic reasons, the discussion of merchant manuals is separated from the discussion of newspapers in this book, it must be remembered that the distinction should not be too strictly drawn. As will be seen in the next chapter some newspapers had explicitly didactic elements. Likewise, commercial manuals provided much 'current' information with details of coaches and fairs, and almanacs, in particular, offered many details specific to a particular year. Some wrote for both types of publication. The brokers John Castaing, Jr and Sr, like Alexander Justice, introduced in the next chapter, were involved in producing both commercial newspapers and manuals. Moreover, mercantile manuals were also advertised in specialist commercial newspapers and some manuals included sections devoted to explanations of the content of specialist commercial newspapers.

Printed stationery and serial print were only two segments of this substantial market. Books, pamphlets and broadsides were published on a wide variety of topics related to the exercise of trade in England, and it is upon these that this chapter concentrates. As a genre it included commercial arithmetics, multi-lingual dictionaries for foreign traders, letter-writing guides, commercial law manuals, commercial almanacs, navigation texts and guides to merchants' accounts, bills of exchange and general business affairs, such as the procedures at the custom house.[12]

---

10 Thomas Browne, *The accurate-accomptant*, London 1670, final page. On Brooke see Plomer, *Dictionary, 1641 to 1667*, 34. On Thomas Jenner, who carried a similar stock at his Exchange printshop, see Worms, 'Book trade', 215 n. 33.

11 'Chr[istopher] Coningsby, trade card', Bodleian Library, Oxford, John Johnson collection, booktrade trade cards 4. Christopher Coningsby traded from 1687 to 1720 in various London locations. According to imprints, he traded from this address from at least as early as 1700 and as late as 1707. The same advertisement appeared facing the title page of William Edler, *The modish pen-man*, London 1691 (which was sold by Coningsby). However, here he advertised as trading from the Golden Turks Head against St Dunstan's Church in Fleet Street where he was based, according to imprints, from 1691 to 1710. See also A. Heal, '17th-century booksellers' & stationers' trade-cards', *Alphabet and Image* viii (1948), 51–62.

12 As well as J. Hoock and P. Jeannin, *Ars mercatoria: eine analytische Bibliographie*, II: *1600–1700*, Paderborn 1993, other specialist bibliographies can be used to identify this literature: J. Robertson, *The art of letter writing: an essay on the handbooks published in England during the sixteenth and seventeenth centuries*, London 1942.

Some of these commercial publications can be classified as instruction and advice manuals, like John Vernon's *The compleat comptinghouse* (1678). Its subtitle advertised its scope: *The young lad taken from the writing school, and fully instructed . . . in all the mysteries of a merchant, from his first understanding of plain arithmetick, to the highest pitch of trade*.[13] Others, like *England's golden treasury* (1691), largely provided information relating to trade. In this particular pocket-sized book readers could consult tables 'of Accompt, Trade, Merchandize, Merchants Goods, Weights and Measures of all kinds. . . . An Exact Table of the Moveable Terms and Feasts for Twelve Years to come. Tables of Interest, Annuity, Wages and Expences: Reducing Pounds into Pence, Shillings, Farthings. . . . An exact Catalogue of the Fairs of England and Wales . . . Prizes of Post Letters and Post-Days'.[14] Most works, however, cannot be so easily categorised as they offered their readers both instruction and information.

Jochen Hoock and Pierre Jeannin have shown in their bibliography of European *ars mercatoria* that there was a steady increase in the number of commercial titles that were published and republished in London during the seventeenth century, from ten texts in the first decade of the century to seventy-two in the last, with the period after the Restoration witnessing the establishment of this type of publication as an important genre.[15] The interpretation of these figures must inevitably be limited and cautious, however, since a full sense of the popularity of such books can only be achieved by probing the difficult issues of republication, print run sizes and readership practices.

If the numbers of editions works went through can give some sense of the popularity of a particular text then some, like *The merchants map of commerce* by Lewes Roberts, a survey of trading conditions across the world, which was first published in 1638 and had reached a fourth edition by 1700, remained popular for decades.[16] *Lex mercatoria*, a treatise on commercial legal practice by the Antwerp-born merchant Gerard Malynes, was published five times between 1622 and 1686.[17] Similarly, William Webster's *Essay on book-keeping* went through over fifteen editions between 1719 and the end of the eighteenth century. Other works were republished far more quickly: *The accurate-accomptant* by Thomas Browne was issued six times in the single

---

[13] Vernon, *Compleat comptinghouse*.

[14] *Englands golden treasury*, London 1691, title page.

[15] Hoock and Jeannin, *Ars mercatoria*, ii, table 2 at p. 649. Hoock and Jeannin have also compiled tables for the numbers of publications in English which are similar to those compiled for the numbers of publications in London: table 6 at p. 655. They exclude periodical publications and almanacs from the bibliography but they employ a broad definition of commercial literature including, for example, a large number of commercial arithmetics (pp. xxx–xxxi).

[16] C. J. Sommerville makes a case for republication as an indicator of popularity in his study of religion: *Popular religion in Restoration England*, Gainesville, Fl. 1977, 9–15.

[17] Gerard Malynes, *Consuetudo, vel lex mercatoria*, London 1622.

decade following 1668. Edward Hatton's books, *The merchant's magazine* and *Comes commercii*, both went through comparatively rapid and regular republications, the latter reaching a twelfth edition in 1766. Republication, however, may not always indicate the popularity of a book, as stationers sometimes repackaged unsold copies of old editions as if they were new editions.[18]

The reliability of the number of editions a work went through as an indicator of its popularity can be improved if the sizes of print runs are also known. Although the size of most print runs in the early modern period can only be guessed at, figures are available for two of Edward Hatton's publications.[19] The booksellers of *Comes commercii* did claim that the second edition (1706) had a print run of 2,000 and the third edition (1715) 3,000.[20] Assuming a conservative estimate of 1,000 copies for the first edition (1699), and that the figures the booksellers provided can be trusted, and were not merely a puff for promotional purposes, then between 1699 and 1722 at least 6,000 copies of this work were sold. Another of Hatton's publications had smaller print runs. In his dedication to the 'Merchants And those Gentlemen who Instruct Youth in Their Accounts', of the eight impression of *The merchant's magazine* in 1726, Hatton claimed that their 'Approbation and Recommendation of this Book . . . hath encouraged the printing of about Twelve Thousand' copies.[21] How do print run figures relate to readership figures? It is usually assumed that periodical publications had multiple readers and so print run figures are inflated to obtain readership figures. As will be seen below some evidence of the readership of commercial manuals points in this direction. But other evidence also points in the other direction. That is, that print run figures should be deflated because some owners had multiple copies of the same texts, perhaps because they did indeed carry them in their pockets, and use them as heavily as authors hoped, or sought out the 'improved' and 'corrected' editions.

Some of the booksellers who published these very popular works were involved in the publication and sale of didactic literature more generally. Benjamin Billingsley in Cornhill, who published at least four editions of Vernon's *The compleat comptinghouse* (1678, 1683, 1698, 1703), and all four editions of Stephen Monteage's *Debtor and creditor made easie* (1675, 1682, 1690, 1708), first appears in the term catalogues in association with a didactic publication on husbandry.[22] George Conyers, who published *The*

---

[18] The 1721 third edition of Roger North's *The gentleman accomptant* was apparently the sheets of the 1715 second edition reissued by the publisher Edmund Curll with a new title-page: M. F. Bywater and B. S. Yamey, *Historic accounting literature: a companion guide*, London 1982, 148.

[19] Print runs are usually assumed to be 500 in this period.

[20] Edward Hatton, *Comes commercii*, 4th edn, London 1723, sig. A2v.

[21] Idem, *The merchant's magazine*, 8th edn, London 1726, sig. A2r.

[22] Plomer, *Dictionary, 1668 to 1725*, 35.

*merchant's ware-house laid open* (1696), specialised in instruction literature, and carried a stock which in the words of the bibliographer Henry Plomer was 'unique . . . hardly to be found in any other shop in London' and included titles on angling, cookery, dyeing, husbandry and perfumery.[23] Conyers, however, was an exception and most booksellers who published commercial manuals also published a wider variety of literature. Thomas Leigh and Daniel Midwinter, for example, were prominent competitors in the bookselling trade in this period and published, with Christopher Coningsby, the third edition of Hatton's *Merchant's magazine*.[24] Coningsby, as already mentioned, stocked commercial stationery as well as Hatton's books, and numerous handwriting manuals. Leigh and Midwinter were partners in a shop in St Paul's Churchyard which, in 1699, stocked devotional literature, Greek translations, an account of a voyage to the East Indies, histories of Poland and Ireland and an account of a remarkable cure after a viper bite, as well as Hatton's publication.[25] Some printers, like William Godbid, and booksellers, like Samuel Crouch, were involved in the production and sale of a number of commercial works.[26]

Robert and Thomas Horne, however, are perhaps the only booksellers who can be described as specialising in the genre of commercial manuals. As mentioned in chapter 1 Robert Horne had a shop at the south entrance to the Royal Exchange from the Restoration until 1686, when his son Thomas Horne took it over and remained there until 1711.[27] Their shop's stock, listed in various advertisements printed on endpapers, included commercial manuals by Browne, Collins, Dafforne, Liset, Marius, Malynes and Roberts, which were among the most substantial, and frequently republished, volumes in this genre, as well as John Locke's *Essay concerning human understanding*, volumes on gardening, surveying land, the Bible and common prayer book in Italian, and the works of Ben Jonson, Tillotson and Davenant.[28] The Hornes stocked, like Christopher Coningsby, both commercial stationery and mercantile manuals. Alongside the printed books they sold a wide range of

[23] J. F., *The merchant's ware-house laid open*, London 1696; Plomer, *Dictionary, 1668 to 1725*, 80.

[24] Plomer, *Dictionary, 1668 to 1725*, 204.

[25] Hatton, *Merchant's magazine*, 3rd edn, London 1699, final page.

[26] William Godbid printed Richard Dafforne, *The apprentices time-entertainer accomptantly*, 3rd edn, rev. John Dafforne, London 1670; Browne, *Accurate-Accomptant*; John Collins, *An introduction to merchants-accompts containing seven distinct questions or accompts*, London 1674, and other editions of the latter two publications. Furthermore, Samuel Crouch was listed on the imprint as a bookseller for J[ohn] Ayres, *Arithmetick*, London 1695, and *The trades-mans copy-book*, London [1688].

[27] Plomer, *Dictionary, 1641 to 1667*, 101; *Dictionary, 1668 to 1725*, 161. On Robert Horne see also Harris, 'Exchanging information', 195.

[28] Collins, *Introduction*, final page; Thomas Mun, *England's benefit and advantage by forein-trade*, London 1700, verso of p. 67; Richard Dafforne, *The young accomptants compasse*, London 1669, sigs Gg2v–Gg3r.

stationery for trade including some devised for international trade: 'Bills of Lading in English, Italian, Spanish, Portuguese, Dutch, and French'.[29] So mercantile manuals were available in specialist bookshops in the heart of the City as well as more generally across the capital.

Books were also sold at auction in this period. London booksellers sold their own stock this way and catalogues produced by Benjamin Walford, John Bullard, Adiel Mill and Edward Millington listed commercial didactic titles.[30] Auctions of individuals' libraries might also contain such texts. Book buyers who did not live in the capital could order books directly from London booksellers, or through their London correspondents. The *Term catalogues*, issued quarterly for much of this period, and on four occasions cumulatively, listed books available for purchase 'particularly to customers with no direct access to the London bookshops'.[31] Commercial manuals could also be bought directly from provincial booksellers, at least in some centres like Hereford (according to the 1695 inventory of the stock of the bookseller, Roger Williams who was based there).[32]

The explosion of print culture in this period affected, and was fuelled by, other developments in strategies for the promotion, and in some cases the marketing, of books. Advertisements for merchant manuals were placed in newspapers and periodicals to promote sales. In the early eighteenth century John Castaing, Sr, advertised his book of tables of interest payments in his own specialist commercial newspaper, *The Course of the Exchange*.[33] John Houghton's periodical, *A Collection for Improvement of Husbandry and Trade*, carried advertisements for Hatton's *Merchant's magazine* (1695), William

---

[29] Mun, *England's benefit*, verso of p. 67.

[30] Benj[amin] Walford, *Catalogue variorum & insignium tam antiquorum quam recentium librorum*, London 1691, and *Catalogus variorum & insignium librorum ex diversis europæ partibus advectorum*, London 1691. On these booksellers and their auctions see J. Lawler, *Book auctions in England in the seventeenth century (1676–1700)*, London 1898, chs ii, iii, and G. Pollard and A. Ehrman, *The distribution of books by catalogue from the invention of printing to A.D. 1800 based on material in the Broxbourne Library*, Cambridge 1965, 96–7. More generally on this subject see G. Walters, 'Early sale catalogues: problems and perspectives', in R. Myers and M. Harris (eds), *Sale and distribution of books from 1700*, Oxford 1982, 106–25.

[31] J. Feather, *The provincial book trade in eighteenth-century England*, Cambridge 1995, 45. The term catalogues were issued quarterly from 1668 to 1709 and cumulatively in 1673, 1675, 1680 and 1696.

[32] F. C. Morgan, 'A Hereford bookseller's catalogue of 1695', *Transactions of the Woolhope Naturalist's Field Club* xxxi (1942–5), 22–36. In the eighteenth century a number of accounting texts were in circulation on both sides of the Atlantic, as Terry Sheldahl's analysis of double-entry bookkeeping works in eighteenth-century American directories reveals: 'A bookseller directory of double entry works available in eighteenth-century America', *Accounting, Business and Financial History* iv (1994), 203–35.

[33] The book advertised was John Castaing, *An interest-book at 4, 5, 6, 7, 8 per c.*, London 1700. The advert first appeared in the *Course of the Exchange*, 28 May 1700. This edition and later ones were advertised in the newspaper at least until the middle of the eighteenth century.

Leybourn's *Panarithmologia* (1693) and other merchant manuals, alongside advertisements for numerous other books some of which were personally endorsed by Houghton.[34] Books had dominated newspaper advertisements since they were first placed in 1626 but the late seventeenth century saw the more thorough-going development of reviewing, in small ways like Houghton's brief comments, but also in the publication of periodicals devoted to reviewing.[35] Hatton's publications, in particular, were widely promoted with two of them being reviewed in periodicals. The booksellers saw the potential of the review of the first edition of the *Merchant's magazine* in 1695 to advance book sales and so reproduced it in a prefatory piece to the third edition in 1699. The reviewer commented on the general popularity of such a book 'seeing the general Current of Education amongst the midling sort of People, and not a few of the Gentry, does in our days run towards Trade and Merchandize, we cannot but conceive that this Book, if once known, will meet with a general Acceptation by all Men of business'. The review judged that the book 'deserves Encouragement from the Publick, as being calculated for the Improvement of Trade and Commerce, to which our English Nation is so much indebted for their Fame and Grandeur, and that great Figure they make in the World'.[36] Hatton's *Comes commercii* was also favourably received in 1699 by the author of the first issue of a publication devoted to reviewing, *The History of the Works of the Learned*. In an account bracketed between reviews of *A collection of the English muses* and *The certainty of the Christian revelation* the reviewer could not resist also praising the improved third edition of the *Merchant's magazine*.[37]

These texts were produced in a variety of formats. Indeed the size of the text could be used as a selling point. The booksellers of Hatton's *Comes commercii*, which was a long octavo, observed to the reader that the proposal for a rival publication revealed 'that the said Book will be too bulky for any Merchant, or Gentleman's Pocket'.[38] On the whole, works like *An useful companion* (1709), and *England's golden treasury* (1691), which contained tables and lists of commercial information, were octavo size.[39] Some books in this sub-genre were even smaller. John Castaing's book of tables of interest payments went through four editions in the first two decades of the eighteenth century and was advertised to be 'very exact, and convenient, not much bigger than a Spectacle-Case'.[40] Broadsides were also produced, like

34 *CIHT*, 14 Dec. 1694, 22 Sept. 1693.

35 Feather, *Provincial book trade*, 44, 47–8.

36 Hatton, *Merchant's magazine*, 1699, 'The booksellers to the Reader'. The review originally appeared in *Miscellaneous Letters, Giving an Account of the Works of the Learned* (Feb. 1695), 263–4.

37 *The History of the Works of the Learned*, I, no. 1 (Feb. 1699), 106–11.

38 Hatton, *Comes commercii*, 4th edn, sig. A2v.

39 *An useful companion*, London 1709; *Englands golden treasury*.

40 *Course of the Exchange*, 2 Jan. 1702.

the one by Thomas Mercer which was a 'Remembrancer', in the form of a chart, to help 'Young Accomptants' enter transactions correctly in double entry books; another, *An exact table of the weight of gold and silver*, was produced by Edward Hatton in the year of the recoinage which 'may (at this time) by usefull for the whole Nation to set up their Studies, Shops, Ware-houses, or Compting-houses'.[41] However, most of the books concerned with the details of merchant accounts and trading practices were folios, and a few were quartos, clearly books that were not easily carried in a pocket. Books advising on a variety of different areas of trade were sometimes sold bound together. The title page of the 1636 edition of Gerard Malynes's folio legal text, *Lex mercatoria*, announced that it was sold bound with Richard Dafforne's bookkeeping manual, *The merchants mirror*. By the third edition of 1686, Malynes's and Dafforne's books were bound together with seven other works on marine law, bookkeeping and bills of exchange.[42] Even some of the large works might have been used for quick reference. Many had clearly labelled divisions between topics, detailed contents pages, and thorough indexes. *The merchants map of commerce*, a folio text of more than 400 pages in which Roberts surveyed in detail the commercial conditions in each area of the commercial world, had a twelve-page index.[43] This genre, therefore, extended across the most common early modern formats, from miniature books for ready reference, to heavy volumes in which several works were bound, from broadsides to be displayed for easy consultation to deliberately pocket-sized publications. In the next section these tentative remarks about reading contexts are pursued in more depth.

## 'to learn good hands and accounts': manuals and commercial education

'The purposes', as Elizabeth Eisenstein has written, 'whether intended or actual, served by some early printed handbooks offer puzzles that permit no easy solution.'[44] In this section some attempts will be made to offer partial solutions, some more speculative than others. What were the opportunities then for a formal commercial education in this period and how might these books feature in it? Without a doubt, apprenticeship was the principal route

41 T[homas] M[ercer], *The young accomptants remembrancer*, London 1692; Edward Hatton, *An exact table of the weight of gold and silver*, London 1696. See also Ralph Handson, *Analysis or resolution of merchants accompts*, 4th edn, London 1669, and William Leybourne, *Four tables of accompts ready cast up*, London 1695?

42 Gerard Malynes, *Consuetudo, vel lex mercatoria*, London 1636, title page, and *Consuetudo, vel lex mercatoria*, London 1686, title page.

43 Lewes Roberts, *The merchants map of commerce*, 2nd edn, London 1671, [433–44].

44 E. L. Eisenstein, *The printing press as an agent of change: communications and cultural transformations in early-modern Europe*, Cambridge 1979, i. 65.

to a career as a merchant or trader. There were however, other opportunities to learn commercial skills and knowledge.

Many would-be merchants received some training at a writing school or from a private tutor (perhaps abroad), sometimes in anticipation of an apprenticeship or during the apprenticeship.[45] The Kendal mercer, Joseph Symson, apprenticed his son, Benjamin, to Edmund Neild, a yarn dealer and tick manufacturer in Manchester. Symson was aware that his son was not properly qualified to undertake the sort of arithmetic required in these trades and negotiated for Benjamin to be trained during his apprenticeship. He wrote to Neild: 'I perceive my son is short in arithmetic in your way of trade though what he learned here would have done in mine . . . that he may be rightly qualified for your service I desire that you'll allow him time in summers when you can best spare him to go learn what he wants (at my charge) of the most proper master you think fit to qualify him effectually for your business'.[46] Dudley North, who according to his brother was considered to have 'learning enough for a merchant but not phlegm enough for any sedentary profession', was placed in a London writing school 'to learn good hands and accounts', as the first step in his merchant career before his apprenticeship.[47] Similarly, John Verney learned accounting and arithmetic at Mr Rich's school before being apprenticed to a Turkey merchant.[48] As will be seen below, individual accountants also offered tuition in merchants' accounts alone.

Few grammar schools taught commercial subjects but private academies, some of which grew out of writing schools, did offer a formal commercial education.[49] However, it was not until the second half of the eighteenth century that these academies flourished; in this period there were only two substantial academies: Soho Academy, founded by Martin Clare, and Little Tower Street, formerly a writing school in Abchurch Lane, where 'Young Gentlemen are taught the several Parts of the Mathematicks, and Qualify'd for Trades, Merchandize, the Publick Offices, Clerkships, Stewardships, or any other Parts of Business.'[50]

---

45 Grassby, *Business community*, 189–92.

46 Joseph Symson to Edmund Neild, 3 Jan. 1718, in S. D. Smith (ed.) '*An exact and industrious tradesman*': *the letter book of Joseph Symson of Kendal, 1711–1720*, Oxford 2002, 557; see also p. cxiii. It seems that much of Benjamin Symson's arithmetic training was undertaken under the watchful eye of his father while he was absent from his master's house due to an outbreak of fever there. See the letters from Joseph Symson to Edmund Neild for the period 11 Sept.–13 Oct. 1718, 608–14.

47 North, *Dudley North*, ii. 3. On Dudley North see Grassby, *English gentleman*.

48 Whyman, *Sociability and power*, 41.

49 Grassby, *Business community*, 190–1; N. Hans, *New trends in education in the eighteenth century*, London 1951, 64–5, 67; R. O'Day, *Education and society, 1500–1800: the social foundations of education in early modern Britain*, Harlow 1982, 208–9.

50 Thomas Watts, *An essay on the proper method for forming the man of business*, ed. A. H. Cole, Cambridge, Mass. 1946, reverse of final page; Hans, *Education*, 82–92.

According to the advertisements carried in newspapers published in some English market towns towards the end of the second decade of the eighteenth century, commercial skills were taught throughout the country as part of a variety of curricula. In 1717 George Powell advertised in the *Worcester Post-Man* that he taught 'Merchants Accompts after the Italian Manner' as well as 'Writing in all the usual Hands of Great Britain' and 'Arithmetick in all its Parts'.[51] Likewise John Peter Verhasseld 'Speedily Taught' writing, arithmetic, 'Merchants Accompts in its Theory and Practice' and also 'Foreign Exchanges, Weights and Measures' in York in 1717.[52] John Dougharty (1677–1755) and his son taught 'Writing, Arithmetick, Book-keeping (in the most exact and Merchant-like Manner now us'd) Geometry, Trigonometry, Surveying, Gauging, &c.' at a school in Worcester 'where Youth may be commendably Boarded'.[53] For other instructors in the provinces commercial skills might be part of a different sort of curriculum: Abraham Birch, who taught at the Grammar School at Selby, offered to 'undertake to teach Young Gentlemen or others, that design of Travelling, Merchant's Business, &c. to speak Latine, and read the easier Latine/Classicks in about one Year'.[54] Book-keeping might also be part of a broader mathematical curriculum; the nonconformist preacher Adam Martindale offered training in an extensive range of mathematical skills which included 'balancing accounts' as well as other types of 'vulgar' arithmetic, and artificial arithmetic, geometry, astronomy, navigation and dialling from his house in Cheshire.[55] Although commercial skills might be part of a purportedly more 'gentle' education, like that proposed by Birch, or accounting might be part of a specialist mathematical education, it was most common for commercial skills to be taught in London and the provinces, as part of the writing school curriculum of writing, arithmetic and accounts.[56]

A substantial proportion of the commercial manuals was intended to be used, or at least to complement, the instruction received at a writing or mathematical school. Hatton wrote that his extensive guide to trade, *The merchant's magazine* (1695), could be used in schools 'both for the ease of the

---

51  *WPM*, 20 Dec. 1717.

52  *WC*, 25 July 1717.

53  *WPM*, 1 Apr. 1720. On Dougharty see E. G. R. Taylor, *The mathematical practitioners of Hanoverian England, 1714–1840*, Cambridge 1966, 117. John Dougharty was the author of *The general-gauger*, London 1707, and *Mathematical digests*, London [1747?].

54  *WC*, 26 Jan. 1716. G. A. Cranfield notes in his study of advertisements in the *Northampton Mercury* over the years 1723–60 that there were more than 120 advertisements concerned with education: 'The most popular subjects advertised were writing, reading and arithmetic, followed by Latin and Greek, and, significantly, book-keeping and accounts': *The development of the provincial newspaper, 1700–1760*, Oxford 1962, 125–6.

55  Adam Martindale, *The country survey book*, London 1702, reverse of p. 195.

56  V. H. Crellin, 'The teaching of writing and the use of the copy book in schools: the influences of the writing schoolmaster, with special reference to the period c. 1700–1873', unpubl. MPhil. thesis, London 1976.

Master, and improvement of the Scholar', and, according to Hatton, in the dedication to the eighth edition quoted above, these masters had supported this book.[57] Perhaps in a similar move to advance sales, Dafforne dedicated the 1670 edition of his *The apprentices time-entertainer accomptantly* 'To my loving Friends, The School-Masters, that are Lovers and Teachers of this Famous and never-dying Art of Accomptantship.'[58] Among the many copy-books produced by John Ayres, was *Youth's introduction to trade* (1700), designed as 'an Exercise-Book to employ Youth at the Writing-School, out of School-time as well as in it'.[59] This book illustrates the general emphasis in commercial education on using exercises 'such as generally occurr in real Business'.[60] It contained samples of bills which were intended for readers to copy in an appropriate hand and calculate the total, so combining the three components – writing, arithmetic and accounts – of an education at a writing school. Likewise, Thomas Browne recommended his text on accounting, *The accurate-accomptant*, as 'useful for all such as either desire to Learn or Teach the most exact Method of keeping Merchants Accompts, by way of Debitor and Creditor'.[61] In his dedication to the governors of Christ's Hospital he wrote that 'it hath been, and ever shall be my Study according to the Talent that God hath lent me, to attempt something which may conduce to the benefit of Your Foster-Children's Education, and render them more expert and dextrous in Accompts for Merchants'.[62] In fact, one of the places where the 1669 edition of Browne's text was sold was at the writing school at Christ's Hospital.[63] Browne's *Accurate-accomptant* may have been the text that John Collins recommended to James Gregory, then professor of math-ematics at Edinburgh: 'if an easy Journall and Leidger be desired there is one lately published by one Browne as a worke of his owne, whereas it was in truth none of his, but a worke commonly for many yeares past taught in Writing Schooles here'.[64] A number of authors in fact hint that their works had already been circulating in manuscript before their decision to go into print.[65] E. G. R. Taylor claims that a 'teacher distributed manuscript notes (at a price) among his pupils, as copied by a scrivener, and in old age published

57 Hatton, *Merchant's magazine*, 1695, sig. A3v.
58 Dafforne, *Apprentices time-entertainer*, sig. A2r.
59 John Ayres, *The accomplish'd clerk regraved*, London 1700, preface.
60 Watts, *Essay*, 20.
61 Browne, *Accurate-accomptant*, title page.
62 Ibid. dedication.
63 Thomas Browne, *The accurate-accomptant*, London 1669, title page.
64 John Collins to [James] Gregory, 19 Oct. 1675, in James Gregory, *James Gregory: tercen-tenary memorial volume, containing his correspondence with John Collins and his hitherto unpub-lished mathematical manuscripts, together with addresses and essays communicated to the Royal Society of Edinburgh, July 4th, 1938*, ed. H. W. Turnbull, Edinburgh 1939, 343. My thanks to Clare Jackson for the reference to the letter from Collins to Gregory.
65 William Leybourn, *Panarithmologia*, London 1693, sig. A2r; Collins, *Introduction*, sig. B1r.

them as a book'.[66] Manuscripts of mercantile manuals do indeed survive which very closely resemble print-published texts which suggests manuscript circulation at least at one time.[67]

Of the authors who can be identified, most were writing masters or accountants. The prolific author of writing manuals and arithmetics, John Ayres, ran a writing school at the sign of the 'hand and the pen' in St Paul's Churchyard.[68] Webster, the author of the popular bookkeeping manual *An essay on book-keeping*, was a writing master in 'Orange-Street, near Leicester Fields'.[69] On the title page of his book *Clavis commercii: or, the key of commerce* (1689), John Hawkins, described himself as 'Schoolmaster at St. George's Church in Southwark'. Declaring such a qualification on the title page may have boosted the sales of the book. At his school Hawkins taught 'all the usual Hands of this Kingdom; Merchants Accompts after the Italian manner', and also a number of mathematical subjects.[70] Similarly, Charles Snell (1670–1733), author of both bookkeeping texts and writing manuals, who, as the 'Master of the Free-Writing-School, in Foster-Lane', offered to teach writing, arithmetic and 'Merchants Accounts'.[71] He specifically targeted the apprentice in offering evening classes: 'and for the convenience of Merchants and Tradesmen, who are desirous their Apprentices should improve themselves in the abovesaid Arts; he is willing to continue at his School for that End every Monday, Wednesday, and Friday in the Evenings, from Six till Nine of the Clock'.[72] On the penultimate page of his 'introduction to merchant accounts', published in 1711, Abraham Nicholas advertised his writing school in 'Cusheon-Court' where 'Youth are Boarded, and Taught Writing in all the Useful Hands, Arithmetick Vulgar and Decimal. Book-keeping, after the present Practice of the most eminent Trades. The Italian Method of Merchants-Accounts, With Foreign Coins, Weights, Measures and Exchanges.' His programme 'Whereby Youth may be Fitted for Trade, Clerkshipe or Merchandize' was designed with a range of careers beyond trade in prospect.[73] Those clerks who were to form the backbone of the expanding state administration, as well as employees of the large

---

[66] Taylor, *Mathematical practitioners of Hanoverian England*, 117.

[67] Columbia University Library, Montgomery collection, MS 95, appears to be a copy of Alexander Malcolm, *A new treatise of arithmetick and book-keeping*, Edinburgh 1718.

[68] Such was Ayres's prominence and status that other writing masters advertised that they had served him; *WC*, 25 July 1717; John Hawkins, *Clavis commercii*, London 1718.

[69] William Webster, *An essay on book-keeping*, London 1719, title page.

[70] John Hawkins, *Clavis commercii*, London 1689, sig. a4v. In later editions of Hawkins's books, which were corrected by John Rayner, he was described as a merchant.

[71] On Snell see Bywater and Yamey, *Historic accounting literature*, 137–41. Snell examined the South Sea Company accounts in relation to accusations of bribery after the Bubble and published his findings.

[72] Charles Snell, *Rules for book-keeping*, London 1701, title page and final page.

[73] Abraham Nicholas, *The young accomptant's debitor and creditor*, London 1711, penultimate page.

trading companies, might launch their careers with this sort of schooling.[74] Charles Snell more explicitly addressed this sector in offering the fitting of 'Persons for Publick Offices' among his services.[75] As was the case in many other early modern instruction texts, books advertised the services of their authors, in this case their schools, and were perhaps principally a vehicle for such self-promotion.[76]

Some authors were accountants and also used their publications to advertise their accounting services, as well as their availability to teach. On the last page of *The accurate-accomptant* (1670), Thomas Browne wrote: 'If any Person desires to Learn the most exact method of keeping Merchants-Accompts, or to make use of the Author for the Auditing, Stating, or Drawing up any Reports of Accompts, he is willing to take the pains to Instruct, and ready to serve such as shall apply themselves to him to any of those intents and purposes.'[77] Such texts might continue to serve to promote business even after the death of their authors. Monteage died in 1687 and the fourth edition of his accounting manual published under his name in 1708 ended with an advertisement for Mr. Randolph, School-Master 'If any Persons desire the Assistance of a Master to hasten them in this Learning'.[78]

Authors advertised that those who required their services could contact the relevant bookseller. Thomas Browne as well as giving his street address advertised that readers could also 'enquire for him at Mr. John Hancocks Shop at the Corner of Popes-Head Alley Bookseller, at the Sign of the Three Bibles'.[79] Confirming the status of the Hornes as booksellers who specialised in this genre, John Collins (1624–83), in his advertisement for his accounting services in the preface to the 1674 edition of his *Introduction to merchants-accompts*, informed readers that he could be 'heard of at Mr. Robert Horn's the Stationer'.[80]

Not all authors were accountants or writing masters. A few authors styled themselves as merchants. N. H., the author of *The compleat tradesman* (1720), described himself as a merchant in the City of London.[81] Two authors whose

---

74 Brewer, *Sinews of power*, ch. iii.

75 Charles Snell, *Accompts for landed-men*, [London 1711], [31].

76 Eisenstein describes a similar situation a century earlier, 'Reckon masters and tutors found it profitable to turn out manuals and treatises which advertised their services and added luster to their names': *Printing press*, i. 383.

77 Thomas Browne, *An accompt partable between four partners upon two several designs*, London 1670, final page.

78 Stephen Monteage, *Debtor and creditor made easy*, 4th edn, London 1708, 36. Randolph also advertised his services when Monteage was still alive: [Stephen Monteage?], *Advice to the women and maidens of London*, London 1678, 36, which is bound with Stephen Monteage, *Debtor and creditor made easie*, 2nd edn, London 1682.

79 Browne, *Accompt partable*, final page. On Hancock see Plomer, *Dictionary, 1668 to 1725*, 141.

80 Collins, *Introduction*, sig. B1v.

81 N. H., *The compleat tradesman*, London 1684.

substantial works were first published earlier in the seventeenth century and were reprinted after the Restoration – Lewes Roberts (whose *Merchants map* was first published in 1638) and Gerard Malynes (whose *Lex mercatoria* was first published in 1622) – were both merchants.[82] The occupations of some authors cannot be identified but others, such as John Marius, author of *Advice concerning bills of exchange* (first published in 1651) were notaries.[83] The publication of Collins's bookkeeping manual in 1653 propelled him from teaching accounts to being employed in a succession of government departments. Only a few, like Monteage, Browne and Chamberlain as well as Collins were professional accountants; most were teachers, and only did accountancy part of the time.[84]

Some authors at times distanced themselves from the writing school context: Robert Chamberlain's *The accomptant's guide or merchant's book-keeper* (1679), was written 'chiefly for the unlearned and ignorant'.[85] Other authors gave specific instructions about how their books should be approached, sometimes with the student studying alone in mind. *Arithmetick* by John Ayres offered the rules of arithmetic 'made Plain and Intelligible to the meanest Capacities, for whose Sakes it is principally intended' including 'the plainest way of Division (for a Learner that wants the help of a Master)'.[86] John Mayne prefaced his 1674 *Socius mercatoris*, a book instructing on arithmetic, interest calculations and measuring solids, with the proposition: 'My Design in this Work is, to render the Rules of those excellent Arts . . . so plain and obvious, as that they may be easily apprehended without the Assistance of a living Master.'[87] Not all authors began their instruction from first principles but instead assumed that their readers had some background in the subject and intended that their books would be aides-memoires for those who had once been experts, or would build upon the basic understanding of others. William Webster in his *Essay on book-keeping* in fact criticised works in which the readers were assumed to be

---

[82] A brief biography of Malynes can be found in A. Finkelstein, *Harmony and the balance: an intellectual history of seventeenth-century English economic history*, Ann Arbor 2000, 26–8. She notes (p. 28) the doubts about his death date of 1641.

[83] John Marius notes in the preface to the second edition of his book that he 'do yet practice at the Royall Exchange in London both for Inland and Outland Instruments': *Advice concerning bills of exchange*, 2nd edn, London 1670, sig. A5r. See also Gresham repertory, 1669–76, pp. 24, 62.

[84] On Collins see W. Letwin, *The origins of scientific economics: English economic thought, 1660–1776*, London 1963, ch. iv; E. G. R. Taylor, *The mathematical practitioners of Tudor and Stuart England*, Cambridge 1954, 228; and Gregory, *James Gregory*, 16–18. On Monteage see B. S. Yamey, 'Stephen Monteage: a seventeenth century accountant', *Accountancy* lxx (1959), 594–5; and Bywater and Yamey, *Historic accounting literature*, 127–30. On the development of professional accountancy see D. Murray, *Chapters in the history of book-keeping accountancy and commercial arithmetic*, Glasgow 1930, 64.

[85] Robert Chamberlain, *The accomptants guide*, London 1679, to the reader.

[86] John Ayres, *Arithmetick*, London 1693, sigs A3r–v.

[87] John Mayne, *Socius mercatoris*, London 1674, preface.

completely ignorant, as 'the Reader, if prepar'd with some little general Knowledge, (as all shou'd be, who look into Books for Instruction in Science) is too long kept from the Purpose with needless Trifles'.[88] Most authors, however, as we will see in the next section, promoted their books to a very diverse range of readers.

### 'so useful for all sorts, sexes and degrees of persons': making claims for a readership

Most authors made claims about the sort of readers they expected to read their books. Many claimed that their books were designed for use in writing schools. According to Monteage, unlike most manuals on bookkeeping which were 'calculated for men of deep Capacities, that have seen or intend large Trade and Commerce', his manual was for 'Youths, young Scholars, men of Ordinary reach or employment, who have more need of such an A.B.C. or Primmer, to consult with'. His recommended method reduced the number of books to be kept to only two, and was 'principally intended' for 'the Accommodation of Merchants of lesser Trades, Retailers, Handicrafts-men, and the like' but not to the exclusion of 'Gentlemen, Noble-men and Princes' or 'the greatest Merchant'.[89] Likewise, Hatton pitched his *Merchant's magazine*, first published in 1695, to as wide an audience as possible: 'Accommodated chiefly to the Practice of Merchants and Tradesmen: But is likewise usefull for Schools, Bankers, Diversion of Gentlemen, the Business of Mechanicks, Land-waiters, and other Officers of Their Majesty's Customs and Excise.' With an eye for a new market, he also suggested that his instructions on interest calculations might be 'usefull for those concerned in the Bank of England'.[90] Liset adapted the usual accounting procedure by debtor and creditor in a 1660 publication 'Very useful and Convenient for Lords, Knights, Gentlemen, Commissioners, Treasurers, Comptrollers, Auditors, Farmers, Merchants, Factors, Stewards, and all degrees of Men.'[91] Although many works were directed at such ranges of readers a few were targeted at segments of the market.

Writing as an anonymous woman, one author wrote a short text specifically advising 'the Women and Maidens of London'. As the subtitle promised, women should 'apply themselves to the right Understanding and Practice of the method of keeping books of account: whereby, either single, or married, they may know their Estates, carry on their Trades, and avoid the

---

88  Webster, *Essay*, preface.
89  Monteage, *Debtor and creditor*, 1682, preface.
90  Hatton, *Merchant's magazine*, 1695, title page.
91  Abraham Liset, *Amphithalami, or, the accomptants closet*, London 1660, title page.

Danger of a helpless and forlorn Condition, incident to Widows'.[92] On the first page, the author argued that accounts were 'an Art so useful for all sorts, sexes and degrees of persons, especially for such as ever think to have to do in the world in any sort of Trade or Commerce' and went on to make the case for women in particular to undertake accounts. English families were placed in danger if a widow was ignorant of her estate, unlike women abroad who kept books for their trading husbands and were therefore secure on being widowed.[93] The author argued that doing accounts would not make women proud and that they were certainly capable of undertaking them, for according to the author's own experience 'I never found this Masculine Art harder or more difficult then the effeminate achievements of Lace-making, gum-work or the like'.[94] Such practice would lead to tangible benefits: 'by gaining or saving an estate you shall never be out of capacity to store your selves more abundantly with those trifles, than your own industry in such matter could have ever blest ye'.[95] The instructions offered to the women and maidens of London including keeping accounts for a retailer as well as the keeping of petty household accounts.

Gentlemen, and their servants, were also singled out for their own sub-genre of publications on bookkeeping. One example is *The gentleman's auditor* (1707), dedicated to 'the most eminently Loyal Society The Gentlemen of the Roiston Club in Hertfordshire'.[96] Another is the London writing master, Charles Snell's *Accompts for landed-men* which contained specimen accounts for a fictional estate of Nattington.[97] By the mid-eighteenth century this type of publication had developed into a separate genre. Most prominent in the early eighteenth century was a book written by Roger North (1653–1734) and published in 1714. J. Martin commended it at the beginning of Thomas King's bookkeeping manual: how 'very serviceable' bookkeeping after the Italian Method 'would be to Gentlemen of Estates, and to Men of Business of all Ranks, has been excellently set forth in a late Essay, Intitl'd, *The gentleman accomptant*'.[98] Martin was less happy with the method than he was with the author's aims: 'Had the Author of that Treatise been as intelligible, in the Method he has taken to explain the Art, as he is polite in his Expressions, the Learner must have been exceedingly beholden to his

---

92 [Monteage], *Advice*, title page. The attribution of this pamphlet to Monteage will be discussed below.

93 Ibid. 1–2.

94 Ibid. 2.

95 Ibid. 2.

96 T[homas] R[ichards], *The gentlemans auditor*, London 1707, verso of title page. On the composition of the Royston Club see G. O. Rickword, 'Royston Club and its Essex members', *Essex Review* xlvii (1938), 145–9.

97 Snell, *Accompts*. The bookkeeping method recommended here for landed-men was not double-entry.

98 J. Martin, 'To the reader', in Thomas King, *An exact guide to book-keeping*, London 1717.

Labour, which notwithstanding has its deserved Praise.'[99] Even if North failed to realise his aims, he goes into quite a lengthy discussion of the advantages to the gentleman of having a knowledge of accounting and so his book is worth considering in some detail.

The first edition of the *Gentleman accomptant* was published anonymously under the epithet 'Done by a Person of Honour'. Although North's identity was not revealed until 1721, his status did not go unnoticed and was commented upon by Alexander Malcolm (1685–1763), the Edinburgh mathematics teacher, who wrote that the writer 'thought it not below him to be Author of a Treatise upon this Subject'.[100] On the first page of the text North recommended that the method of debtor and creditor 'is so comprehensive and perfect, as makes it worthy to be put among Sciences, and to be understood by all Virtuosi, whether they ever intend to make use of it or no, but even for pure Speculation, Curiosity, or rather Admiration'.[101] According to North, then, his readers could appreciate what they learned from his book without necessarily applying it.

North did suggest that there were some reasons why gentlemen might find knowing about 'merchants accounts' useful. When they are called out to 'Publick Business', he argued, 'it is down right Dulness and Stupidity . . . to want a Knowledge, so universally concerned in all great Affairs, without which they cannot understand the Language, much less the Subject-Matter, when it relates to large Accompts'. Furthermore, in his private business as trustee, guardian or executor, North recommended gentlemen to 'affect neat and clear Accompts, if it were only for the sake of conscious Honour, as also of Advantage to Posterity'. Accounting skills, even if not undertaken by the gentleman himself, were an aid in all affairs, and at the very least allowed the appropriate supervision of an accountant employed to preserve an estate.[102] Likewise John Locke had asked gentlemen to consider the value of 'Merchant's Accompts, though a Science not likely to help a Gentleman to get an Estate, yet possibly there is not any thing of more use and efficacy, to make him preserve the Estate he has.' According to Locke gentlemen had to be persuaded to bridge the gap that separated them from such mercantile activity: 'I would . . . advice all Gentlemen to learn perfectly Merchants Accompts, and not to think it is a Skill, that belongs not to them, because it has received its Name, and has been cheifly practised by men of Traffick.'[103]

99   Ibid.
100   R. Straus, *The unspeakable Curll: being some account of Edmund Curll, bookseller; to which is added a full list of his books*, London 1927, 225; Malcolm, *New treatise*, preface. On Malcolm see M. J. Mepham, 'The Scottish enlightenment and the development of accounting', in R. H. Parker and B. S. Yamey (eds), *Accounting history: some British contributions*, Oxford 1994, 270–1.
101   [Roger North], *The gentleman accomptant*, London 1714, [1].
102   Ibid. 8–10.
103   [John Locke], *Some thoughts concerning education*, London 1693, 250–1.

North tackled this gap in a rather different way. In the preface he admitted (rather disingenuously given his brother Dudley's career as a merchant) that he was himself 'an Alien in Merchandise (which the Style of the following Essay apparently betrays)'.[104] The gentleman's understanding of accounting was couched in terms of his being an outsider in the world of commerce, and even in his own sphere of dealing with estates, inheritances and the property of those entrusted to him, accounting was undertaken to maintain honour and for posterity. Even when North got closest to suggesting that keeping accounts might offer the gentleman financial advantage: it was 'a great Means of keeping out of Debt', it remained 'a Pleasure to such, as find that Benefit by it'.[105]

Are these all just strategies to keep the gentlemen and the merchant separate? As other authors listed a variety of occupational categories, are these texts which specifically address gentlemen making a sham claim that denies the reality of the overlap between the world of the merchant and the world of the gentleman? Whether you want to go as far as the historian Richard Grassby and say that the 'movement between town and country was so continuous that the distinctions of social terminology became blurred' it is hard to deny that the status of and spheres in which gentlemen and merchants operated were more compromised than the writers of these manuals were suggesting.[106] Were such writers trying to map a social order that was knowable, safe and secure?

### 'all the mysterious terms or words I could think of': vocabularies of mercantile terms

In these commercial manuals it was understood that there was a set of characteristics which those who wished to be recognised as merchants could aspire to demonstrate. Robert Colinson, for example, in *Idea rationaria* (1683), claimed that only those perfect in the art of accounting 'should in reason assume the name of Merchant . . . more then a man should call himself a Souldier, until at least, he can handle his Armes'.[107] For S. Ammonet it was only those who had the required knowledge 'who truly merit the generous, nay, I may say, the noble name of a Merchant'.[108] Underlying much of Vernon's writing in his guide, designed to give young merchant apprentices a head-start, was a clear sense of what 'made' a merchant. For example, in the dialogue between master and youth concerning how many accounting books

---

104 [North], *Gentleman accomptant*, p. i. North's book may have drawn on a manuscript written by his brother: Bywater and Yamey, *Historic accounting literature*, 148.
105 [North], *Gentleman accomptant*, 56.
106 Grassby, *Business community*, 386–7.
107 Robert Colinson, *Idea rationaria*, Edinburgh 1683, dedication.
108 [S. Ammonet], *Key of knowledge for all merchants*, Dublin 1696, sig. A4v.

various traders kept, the master concluded 'If you will be a Merchant, you must act as a Merchant'.[109] Authors agreed that a man required certain attributes before he could assume, or merit, the title of, become, or, as Vernon put it later in his text, 'pass for' a merchant.[110] Roberts and Hatton were two authors who went into immense detail as to what these attributes were. Roberts stressed knowledge of geography, accounts, exchange and commodities.[111] Hatton added a few subjects to this list but also addressed the 'natural parts' of a merchant; he should have, among other qualities, a quick apprehension, a good constitution, be prudent, just and punctual.[112]

The acquired attributes were what most concerned the writers of these merchant manuals. Knowledge of prescribed areas 'made' a man a merchant, and authors described in some depth the role of knowledge in commerce. Knowledge of commodities and currencies, seasons for trading, shipping routes and journey times gave a merchant an advantage over other traders.[113] Knowledge of almost any area of commerce, it was stressed, was a shield against the threats of being cheated and legal action. A good reputation was vital to success in business, and commercial knowledge could provide it with some protection. In a section on discounting, Vernon put the following words into the mouth of 'the Master' on the disadvantages of ignorance in this area:

> I daily meet with them that have been old Traders, and experienced Men, and yet are ignorant of it [discounting]; and I hate to think a Man should pretend to pass for a Merchant, and yet the Shop-keeper stand and laugh in his Sleeve to see his ignorance and folly; and not only cheat him of his Mony, but jeer him when he is gone.[114]

Commercial knowledge, then, was not always the product of age and experience; having it could help a merchant maintain his standing above that of other traders, avoid ridicule and hold on to his money. As for the gentlemen North addressed in his accounting manual, knowledge of accounting offered protection from a variety of hazards.

Knowledge of the vocabulary of commerce was one area that concerned the writers of these manuals, and is explored in more detail here. According to Webster, a reader of a text on accounting who was totally ignorant of the subject 'is too much bewilder'd in Words, and lost in Definitions and Explanations'.[115] Other writers also acknowledged that there was a specialist terminology associated with commerce, and accounting in particular. In the preface to *Debtor and creditor made easie* (1682), Stephen Monteage wrote:

---

109  Vernon, *Compleat comptinghouse*, 38.
110  Ibid. 134, 135.
111  Roberts, *Merchants map*, passim.
112  Edward Hatton, *The merchant's magazine*, 6th edn, London 1712, sigs b1r–b1v.
113  John Every, *Speculum mercativum*, London 1674, 1; Watts, *Essay*, 25.
114  Vernon, *Compleat comptinghouse*, 135.
115  Webster, *Essay*, preface.

I affect our Mother Tongue, and wish that every Word or Name in this Book were perfectly English, and not borrowed from other Languages, such as the words Leidger, Cash, Debtor, Creditor, and would have coyned English in their steads, but that I dare not arrogate being Author of new Terms of Art.[116]

At the beginning of his book he included a list of fifteen hard words 'used in these or other Merchants Accompts' accompanied by explanations.[117]

Two other writers in this genre also produced lists of commercial terms with definitions in this period. North, who contended 'it is down right Dulness and Stupidity' for gentlemen not to be able to understand 'the Language relating to large Accompts' ended his *The gentleman accomptant*, with 'A short and easy Vocabulary of Certain Words, that in the Language of Accompting take a Particular Meaning' with over one hundred entries.[118] Like other writers he complained about the perplexing terms used in accounting, and the inaccessibility of other accounting manuals:

> they enter so deep into the Penetralia of abstruse Mercantile Practise, that he must be a good and experienced Trader, who can well apprehend their Sense; or so much as their Language, either of which is so foreign to the Apprehension of ordinary Persons that the very Jargon diverts them, who might hearken well enough to a lower Instruction, if it were in a plain English dress.[119]

Edward Hatton also produced an extensive commercial vocabulary as chapter fourteen of the second edition of *The merchant's magazine* (1697). Three hundred and thirty entries appeared in 'A Dictionary, or Alphabetical Explanation of most difficult Terms commonly used in Merchandize and Trade'.[120] This 'Merchant's or Trader's Dictionary' explained, according to Hatton, 'all the mysterious Terms or Words I could think on, that relate to Merchandizing; many of which I am sure, are not to be found in any Expositor extant'.[121] By the sixth edition of the *Magazine* in 1712 there were nearly 450 entries, and the vocabulary was fully alphabetical, with many of the additional entries referring to measures and coins.[122] Unlike Monteage's glossary, Hatton's and North's vocabularies were not intended, explicitly at least, to explain the texts they accompanied. In this sense then, they anticipated Malachy Postlethwayt's *Universal dictionary of trade and commerce*, the first English commercial dictionary, published in 1751.

Although it is difficult to generalise about the nature of the entries in these lists, some patterns can be observed. In the entries in his list Monteage tended to mention the origin of the word in question, perhaps to hammer

---

116 Monteage, *Debtor and creditor*, 1682, preface.
117 Ibid.
118 [North], *Gentleman accomptant*, sigs a1r–b5v, pp. 8–10.
119 Ibid. 24.
120 Hatton, *Merchant's magazine*, 1699, 223–39.
121 Ibid. title page and sig. a1v.
122 Ibid. 219–43.

home the point that such words were not 'perfectly English', followed by a brief explanation of its meaning. Under the headword 'Leidger' for example: 'The word Leidger may come from the Italian Ledgireo, which signifieth easie, nimble, or swift, denoting the use of the Leidger Book for the easie and ready finding the State of all Accounts.'[123] North, in fairly lengthy entries, made reference to the usage of some of the accounting words: super, 'a Term in the Exchequer'; tariff, 'a Word of late use among the Statesmen in Europe'; valorem, 'a Word used at the Custom-House'.[124] The following is his entry for Ledger: 'is the methodized Accompt-Book, being a Digest or Index to the Journal; it comes from the Italians Leggiero, because the Entries are short and slight'.[125] Like Monteage, North considered the origins of some of the words in his vocabulary: 'Hypothecate, a Greek Word; in Latin it is supponere; in English, to subject to; and among Notaries, intends a plain Mortgage of Goods and Merchandizes'; 'A line, in common Talk of Merchants, refers to the Ledger, in which only one Line in an Accompt for one Business is wrote, as when they say, – There's a Line in your Accompt'; and 'Mount, is used for Encrease of Sums in Process, like the Flight of Bird, or of an Arrow.'[126]

North was far from impartial in his explanations of the terms, and, by claiming an awareness of the values attached to many of the words in his vocabulary, he perhaps added a degree of apparent authenticity. He used 'one of the dear bought Words of this Age' to describe circulate; 'an high prized Word', estimates; 'one of the costly Words of late Invention, and now sure grafted into the English Language', fund; 'one of the burning Words of this Age', par.[127] Other terms received fuller treatment which articulated the author's attitudes. In particular, the terms stocks and stockjobbing in the vocabulary were described in a short essay which began 'a Mystery born in this Age', and went on to deem stockjobbing as 'contrived after a Popish Model, for no purpose but Cheating, . . . Brokers . . . are to Knaves, as Pimps to Whores'.[128]

Hatton's vocabulary contained accounting terms, as well as terms that related to commerce more generally. His definitions were apparently dispassionate; and, compared to North, Hatton placed less emphasis on etymology. In the 'h' section for example, he explained, among other terms, Hairs-breadth, 'accounted among the Jews the forty eighth part of an Inch', Harping-Irons, 'Iron Instruments to strike Whales and other great fishes withall', and Hogshead.[129] A few of the entries did refer the reader to various sections of the text of the Magazine, his entry for Ledger, for example: 'A

123 Monteage, Debtor and creditor, 1682, sig. B3r.
124 [North], Gentleman accomptant, sigs b3r, b4v.
125 Ibid. sig. a6v.
126 Ibid. sigs a5v–a6r, a6v, a7r.
127 Ibid. sigs a3r, a4v, a5v, a7v.
128 Ibid. sig. b2r.
129 Hatton, Merchant's magazine, 1699, 231.

Book of Accompts, wherein every Man's Accompt, and also that of every sort of Goods bought and sold by a Merchant are placed each by themselves. See Chap. 10. §1. and 6.'[130] Both North and Hatton gave lengthy explanations for some terms. Although none were nearly as long as a number of the multi-page entries in Postlethwayt's dictionary, they were more developed than the typical entry in the hard-word dictionary and closer to, anachronistically speaking, encyclopaedia entries.[131]

Some idea of how these vocabularies were intended to be used can be inferred from the texts. Monteage's list was designed to refer to his text, and possibly others. In Hatton's vocabulary there were a few references to the text, and hence it could serve as an index to the book, and, like North's, it was a separate section. Both these longer lists were arranged alphabetically, but all three were potentially reference tools. The only clue found as to how readers actually used such lists is in a copy of Hatton's *Merchant's magazine*, published in 1734, held in the Baker Library, Harvard, where manuscript annotations direct the reader from a section on 'the Par in Foreign Coin in Sterling' to consult the 'Dictionary' for the value of coins.[132] It is also possible that these vocabularies were 'read' rather than used only as works of reference. If, as Robert DeMaria suggests in the context of Samuel Johnson, dictionary reading was not very unusual, then we should not be surprised if these far briefer vocabularies were read as a whole.[133]

What are we to make of these vocabularies? Studies of commercial dictionaries, most notably, Jacques Savary de Bruslons's French publication of 1723, *Le Dictionnaire universel de commerce*, do not offer much help in this direction for they have concentrated on using such sources for the gestures and words used in exchanging goods in French market places, for studying commercial neologisms, and for examining particular terms like *ratio* and *le compte*.[134] With varying degrees of caution the dictionaries have been interpreted on the assumption that they reflect language usage in contemporary conversation and writing. However, the larger questions about the motivations for the compilation of commercial dictionaries and what they reveal about attitudes to commerce need to be addressed before beginning to

---

[130]  Ibid. 233.
[131]  In this period a clear distinction was not made between encyclopedias and dictionaries: T. McArthur, *Worlds of reference: lexicography, learning and language from the clay tablet to the computer*, Cambridge 1986, 102.
[132]  Hatton, *Merchant's magazine*, 1734, 131, in the Baker Library, Harvard.
[133]  R. DeMaria, Jr, *Johnson's Dictionary and the language of learning*, Oxford 1986, 3–4, 19.
[134]  M. Aubain, 'Par-Dessus les marchés: gestes et paroles de la circulation des biens d'après Savary des Bruslons', *Annales* xxxix (1984), 820–30; M. M. Pittaluga, *L'Évolution de la langue commerciale: Le Parfait négociant et Le Dictionnarie universel de commerce*, Genoa 1983; P. A. Mills, 'Words and the study of accounting history', *Accounting Auditing and Accountability Journal* ii (1989), 21–35. I am grateful to Palmira Fontes da Costa for assistance with translating Pittaluga's book. On the compilation of Savary's dictionary see J.-C. Perrot, 'Les Dictionnaires de commerce au XVIIIe siècle', *RHMC* xxviii (1981), 39–40.

speculate about what can be learnt from these sources concerning more general language usage. Moreover, questions about the construction of compilations of commercial terms deserve attention in their own right. What role do dictionaries, and indeed glossaries and vocabularies, play in defining the boundaries between areas of knowledge? What is the significance of an attempt to compile a commercial vocabulary?

In trying to answer these questions I will consider the vocabularies in three related contexts. First, glossaries of the type presented in Monteage's book were a common addition to texts in the early modern period. Although glossaries attached to translations of Latin texts were the most prevalent in the years from the late fifteenth to the early seventeenth centuries, glossaries were also appended to many legal, herbal and scientific texts and, by the beginning of the eighteenth century, fictional tales.[135] Many didactic texts contained glossaries; as Lawrence Klein notes, 'alleged guides to "practices" often take on a lexicographical character'.[136] John Smith's *Sea-mans grammar and dictionary* (1692), for example, contained not only a couple of alphabetical tables of sea terms but in the margins were listed those terms which appeared in the main text in black-letter type.[137] In other fields, such as law, expositors of the specialist terms had been produced since the sixteenth century and were republished throughout this period and into the eighteenth century in enlarged and corrected editions, and formed part of a general introduction to studying the law.[138] Paul Hunter has written in his study of fiction that 'common to all tonal varieties of didacticism . . . is a faith in language to mean clearly', and the inclusion of glossaries in advice and instruction manuals indicates a thorough-going attachment to such a faith.[139]

Monteage's glossary, and the lists in the manuals by Hatton and North, can be situated in the more general history of the development of the hard-word dictionary. It has been argued that monolingual glossaries, as opposed to spelling lists and Latin–English dictionaries, were the 'true forerunners of the hard word dictionaries, both in their format and in their vocabulary'.[140] This relationship between glossaries and dictionaries still

---

135 J. Schäfer, *Early modern English lexicography*, I: *A survey of monolingual printed glossaries and dictionaries, 1475–1640*, Oxford 1989, 7; S. V. Larkey, 'Scientific glossaries in sixteenth-century English books', *Bulletin of the Institute of the History of Medicine* v (1937), 105–14. For an example of a glossary attached to a fictional work see *The Jamaica lady*, London 1720.

136 Klein, 'Politeness for plebes', 376.

137 John Smith, *The sea-mans grammar and dictionary*, London 1692.

138 For example, a version of John Rastell's, *Exposicio[n]es t[er]mi[n]o[rum] legu[m] anglo[rum]*, London 1523, was being published into the middle of the eighteenth century. See also Thomas Manley's late seventeenth- and early eighteenth-century expanded versions of John Cowell, *The interpreter*, Cambridge 1607, and D. Lemmings, *Professors of the law: barristers and English legal culture in the eighteenth century*, Oxford 2000, 137.

139 J. P. Hunter, *Before novels: the cultural contexts of eighteenth-century English fiction*, New York 1990, 233.

140 Schäfer, *English lexicography*, 8.

functioned in the late seventeenth and early eighteenth centuries. Some of the entries from Hatton's dictionary, for example, were included as a separate table in *Cockers English dictionary* (1704), as 'Trade being now likewise extraordinarily improved and enlarged . . . and Merchants making use of Words in Traffick not commonly apprehended.'[141] Although it is disputable whether this dictionary should be attributed to Edward Cocker, the schoolmaster and author of writing manuals and an arithmetic, or to John Hawkins who claimed to have published a revised form of Cocker's manuscript, it can be said with confidence that a number of other dictionaries in this period were compiled by school teachers, reinforcing the associations between the lexicographical elements of commercial didactic manuals and their use in schools.[142] By including glossaries in their manuals therefore, Monteage, North and Hatton were employing a well-established device common to the didactic genre.

Secondly, the idea that occupational groups employed specialist terms for which definitions could be compiled was also developed by those involved, both within and beyond the Royal Society, to write the 'history of trades', accounts of the techniques, skills and knowledge peculiar to each trade. Both Hatton's and North's books can be seen as part of these programmes. North claimed that merchants' accounts were 'worthy to be put among Sciences, and to be understood by all Virtuosi'; and with perhaps an eye for the more 'useful' part of the schemes Hatton's reviewer described his book 'as being calculated for the Improvement of Trade and Commerce'.[143] Furthermore, both North and Hatton themselves were interested in the lexical features of such programmes. Hatton was among the subscribers to the publication of the first two editions of the *Lexicon technicum* (1704 and 1710) by John Harris, a Fellow of the Royal Society, and Roger North, although he distanced himself from the Royal Society, had a keen interest in etymology.[144] Dictionary makers with natural philosophical interests also took note of commercial dictionaries: John Worlidge reproduced the entries

---

141 Edward Cocker, *Cockers English dictionary*, rev. John Hawkins, London 1704, 'to the reader'; D. W. T. Starnes and G. E. Noyes, *The English dictionary from Cawdrey to Johnson, 1604–1755*, Chapel Hill 1946, 81; J. Green, *Chasing the sun: dictionary-makers and the dictionaries they made*, London 1996, 208. In the first two editions the vocabulary appeared at the end of the main part of the dictionary. By the third edition of the dictionary in 1724 the entries were incorporated in the body of the dictionary. Hatton's vocabulary was also reproduced in Giles Jacob, *Lex mercatoria*, 2nd edn, London 1729, 384–404.

142 Green, *Chasing the sun*, 206–8. Elisha Coles and Nathaniel Bailey were both school teachers and compilers of dictionaries: ibid. 170, 192.

143 [North], *Gentleman accomptant*, [1]; Hatton, *Merchant's magazine*, 1699, 'The booksellers to the reader'.

144 R. V. Wallis, and J. Wallis, *Index of British mathematicians, III: 1701–1800*, Newcastle upon Tyne, 1993, 64; F. J. M. Korsten, *Roger North (1651–1734) virtuoso and essayist: a study of his life and ideas, followed by an annotated edition of a selection of his unpublished essays*, Amsterdam 1981, 27–8, 39. See also his essay 'Etimology, as other Criticall Studys, are very usefull In ye world'; a transcription appears ibid. 160–5.

in Hatton's dictionary in his *Dictionarium rusticum, urbanicum & botanicum* (1726).[145]

More significant than the compiling of dictionaries by Fellows of the Royal Society and others, however, the 'improvement' project and the compiling of definitions intersected in Joseph Moxon's serial publication, *Mechanick exercises* (1678–80).[146] This comprised a series of accounts of joinery, carpentry, turning and typography, among other topics.[147] Moxon aimed to collect and disseminate information about trades; as he wrote in the preface to the *Exercises*, he saw 'no reason why the sordidness of some Workmen should be the cause of contempt upon Manual Operations. . . . And though the Mechanicks be by some accounted ignoble and scandalous. Yet it is very well known, that many Gentlemen in this Nation of good Rank and high Quality are conversant in Handy-Works'.[148] Moxon provided the readers of his serial with alphabetical glossaries to each of his accounts.[149] So the glossaries that Monteage, and perhaps more particularly North and Hatton, compiled, could be read as part of an attempt to write the history of trades, with its heavy emphasis on lexical dimensions. However, it is important not to overlook the overlap between the emphasis on trading terms and their definitions in the projects undertaken by Royal Society members and the tradition of including glossaries in manuals and advice literature, nor to neglect the fact that the projects were aimed not only at gentlemen. The history of trades did have a didactic element; in the words of its chronicler, Thomas Sprat, the Royal Society was designed that 'the worst Artificers will be well instructed, by considering the Methods, and Tools of the best'.[150]

Thirdly, it is worthwhile examining these vocabularies in the context of the concerns of the authors of commercial manuals for ways of communicating.[151] They advocated learning to write well, 'and that you may do it, you must learn to make the 24 Letters very plain', wrote Vernon.[152] Writing masters, like John Ayres, promoted the skills they taught. Ayres wrote a book

---

145 [John Worlidge], *Dictionarium rusticum, urbanicum & botanicum*, 3rd edn, London 1726, i. sig. A8v. The attribution of this dictionary has been disputed. Although it has been associated with Nathaniel Bailey, it is usually attributed to John Worlidge: J. Kennedy, W. A. Smith and A. F. Johnson (eds), *Dictionary of anonymous and pseudonymous English literature (Samuel Halkett and John Laing)*, Edinburgh 1926–56, ii. 60.

146 Green, *Chasing the sun*, 175, 205.

147 Joseph Moxon, *Mechanick exercises*, London 1677–80. On Moxon see G. Jagger, 'Joseph Moxon, F.R.S., and the Royal Society', *NRRS* xlix (1995), 193–208.

148 Moxon, *Mechanick exercises*, no. 1 (1 Jan. 1677), preface.

149 He later published a dictionary of mathematical terms, Joseph Moxon, *Mathematicks made easie*, London 1679. Michael Hunter notes that a glossary was included in the third edition of John Evelyn's *Sylva*, the previous editions of which had received criticism, partly for their difficult vocabulary: *Science and society*, 100–1.

150 Tho[mas] Sprat, *History of the Royal-Society of London*, London 1667, 310.

151 T. K. Sheldahl (ed.), *Education for the mercantile counting house: critical and constructive essays by nine British writers, 1716–1794*, New York 1989, p. xxii.

152 Vernon, *Compleat comptinghouse*, 12.

'to promote a Neat, Free and Graceful way of Writing amongst Tradesmen' in which he presented 'nimble Hands as are properly adapted for dispatch of Affairs in Trade and Merchandize'.[153] A 'good Style' as well as 'a fair and legible Hand' to satisfy foreigners, judges and magistrates were necessary skills to be acquired by the merchant Hatton envisaged.[154]

Other writers pursued the theme of communication between merchants by appealing to notions of polite conversation. Conversation was a central part of attempts to define the 'polite' in this period. Periodical writers were crucial to this project, and for them, in particular, conversation and commerce had overlapping meanings.[155] In his *Essay on the proper method for forming the man of business* (1716), John Watts wrote at length on the nature of polite style both in writing and conversation. The most successful businessman was the one who 'expresses himself without Ambiguity or Affectation'.[156] He noted that there were different kinds of style peculiar to the pulpit, the bar and common conversation:

> 'Tis this last that can alone suit Commerce; which, tho' like other Arts and Sciences, it has proper Rules and Terms belonging to it, yet delights in a Short and Familiar, but withal a Neat and Significant Way of Expression. So that the Merchant must converse with his distant Correspondent with no more Stiffness, than if he met him on the Exchange. He must not detain him an Hour for the Business of a Minute, nor put him to Pains to understand him, nor express himself to be understood to his Damage. This would render a Correspondent less agreeable to his Friend, and consequently less beneficial to himself. Majesty and Grandeur are a Stop to Dispatch, whereby Business lives, and thrives, and flourishes. So that the Style for Commerce must be Concise, Perspicuous and Natural; not lin'd with swelling impertinent Epithets, but purely Epistolary, and Expresing the Thoughts with the same Facility, as if the Correspondent were Face to Face.[157]

North, too, drew a stark contrast when it came to writing between merchants and gentlemen which emphasised an almost fanatical concern amongst merchants for transparency. In a paragraph on the correction of errors in entries in accounts, he noted that 'in Case of small Errors of Figures or Words', a Gentleman 'may be allowed to use his Penknife and Pounce. For perhaps his Books will go no further than his Cabinet, and the use of them terminates only in himself and Family.' Employing the word nice to mean exact, however, North wrote that, 'Merchants are so nice, that if a Word, nay

---

153  Ayres, *Trades-mans copy-book*, 3–4.

154  Hatton, *Merchant's magazine*, 1712, sig. B2r.

155  S. Copley, 'Commerce, conversation and politeness in the early eighteenth-century periodical', *British Journal for Eighteenth-Century Studies* xviii (1995), 64, 66. On conversation and politeness see also L. E. Klein, *Shaftesbury and the culture of politeness: moral discourse and cultural politics in early eighteenth-century England*, Cambridge 1994, 96–101.

156  Watts, *Essay*, 25.

157  Ibid. 25–6.

a Sentence be wrote a-miss, they will not raze or cancel, but set down the Right with a Dico . . . which I mention only to shew their extream Affect-ation of pure and fair Writing'.[158]

The calls for a straightforward style in commercial communication made by some of these authors can be related to movements in other areas for a simplification of language, as well as politeness. Plain styles were advocated for use in the pulpit, but they also take us back to the Royal Society's concerns for language and vocabulary.[159] Indeed, for Thomas Sprat, merchants were exemplars for the Royal Society which had 'exacted from all their members, a close, naked, natural way of speaking; positive expressions; clear senses; a native easiness: bringing all things as near the Mathematical plainness, as they can: and preferring the language of Artizans, Countrymen, and Merchants, before that, of Wits, or Scholars'.[160] If the style of communi-cation was plain then, terms should also be made plain by definitions.

Compiling vocabularies and recommending a particular style of communi-cation all served to demarcate commerce as a field of knowledge, particularly in the terms of reference set out by natural philosophy but also by the over-lapping conventions of didactic literature. Commerce then, was an area worthy of study. The language of commerce was portrayed as one that gentlemen and others did not know, one that provided access to a specialised area of knowledge, and one that it was in all their interests to know, in a context where merchant ways were the benchmark. The very fact that commercial language had to be 'explained' to non-commercial audiences, or was at least presented as though it was unknown to these audiences, contrib-uted to the process of distinguishing commerce as an area of knowledge. Success in commerce depended, according to these writers, on knowing this language and using it correctly, and it was among the commercial skills to be mastered in either the writing school or the gentleman's library.

Might such vocabularies also have offered reassurance? Some scholars suggest that these manuals can be read as rhetorical defences of trade.[161] If in

---

158 [North], Gentleman accomptant, 60.

159 B. Vickers, 'The Royal Society and English prose style: a reassessment', in B. Vickers and N. S. Struever (eds), Rhetoric and the pursuit of truth: language change in the seventeenth and eighteenth centuries, Los Angeles 1985, 1–76; R. F. Jones, 'The attack on pulpit eloquence in the Restoration: an episode in the development of the neo-classical standard for prose', Journal of English and Germanic Philology xxx (1931), 188–217. The numerous proposals for universal language schemes also signal the trend towards a preference for unambiguous and direct communication: J. Knowlson, Universal language schemes in England and France, 1600–1800, Toronto 1975.

160 Sprat, History, 113.

161 James Aho makes this argument in relation to late medieval double-entry book-keeping, as espoused by Pacioli: 'Rhetoric and the invention of double entry bookkeeping', Rhetorica iii (1985), 22. See also B. G. Carruthers and W. N. Espeland, 'Accounting for rationality: double-entry bookkeeping and the rhetoric of economic rationality', American Journal of Sociology lxlvii (1991), 31–69. For an opposing view see G. Thompson, 'Is

defending commerce one of the hurdles that had to be overcome was the fear that language itself was undermined by late seventeenth-century developments in commerce then readers might be reassured by these vocabularies. It could be argued that terms were 'pinned down' through straightforward definitions, which distanced commerce from instability and so sought to provide a legitimate basis for its operation. However obscure or specialist the terms employed by traders, definitions were readily available, and indeed were worthy of study, partly for the pleasure they offered. Like other lists in these manuals – of commodities, currencies, ports, fairs, coins – might the vocabularies have served to contain commerce?[162] Could the vocabularies, as a single image of the Royal Exchange did, capture the trading world?

But did such lists shed light on 'mysterious terms' as Hatton hoped? I wonder if they did not serve, for some readers at least, to do the opposite: to create mystery around the area of commerce but at the same time to offer the promise of experiencing the mystery of the merchant's world; to give readers a sense (perhaps an artificial sense) of expertise, of belonging to this world of commerce. In the same way that Steele gained a vicarious pleasure from rubbing shoulders with the merchants in the Exchange, were readers taken on imaginary journeys by reading merchant manuals?

### 'or if I be a Retailer': taking the imaginary journey

I want to probe a little further this particular context of reading such commercial manuals – that of giving readers an experience of the merchant's world – alongside the question of the delight reading such texts might offer. Hatton claimed that his *Merchant's magazine* offered 'Diversion' for gentlemen.[163] How might such texts be diverting? Some authors thought that bookkeeping itself offered satisfaction. Browne hoped that his improved method of accounting would make the practice of it 'more delightful' as well as 'in the end more facile and useful'.[164] Might there be more to it than that? North, at least, imagined that virtuosi might be curious about double-entry bookkeeping.[165] It is worth considering the possibility that others also read out of curiosity, and with a desire to find out about another world, and to experience vicariously another way of life. As Klein posits, didactic texts 'may have been read . . . by people wishing only to make imaginary visits to the social worlds of others'.[166] It is in this vein that Defoe, for example,

accounting rhetorical? Methodology, Luca Pacioli and printing', *Accounting, Organizations and Society* xvi (1991), 572–99.

162 Daniel A. Rabuzzi makes a similar argument for such lists in German handbooks: 'Commercial mentalities', 180–2.

163 Hatton, *Merchant's magazine*, 1695, title page.

164 Browne, *Accurate-accomptant*, dedication.

165 [North], *Gentleman accomptant*, [1].

166 Klein, 'Politeness for plebes', 376.

suggested that through books the 'Compleat English Gentleman' could experience the grand tour:

> If he has not travell'd in his youth, has not made the grand tour of Italy and France, he may make the tour of the world in books, he may make himself master of the geography of the Universe in the maps, attlasses, and measurements of our mathematicians. He may travell by land with the historian, by sea with the navigators. . . . He may make all distant places near to him in his reviewing the voiages of those that saw them, and all the past and remote accounts present to him by the historians that have written of them.[167]

As London guide-books could lead their readers on a virtual tour of the Royal Exchange, so too could commercial manuals offer their readers tours of the commercial world.

The different strategies that manual writers drew upon to instruct their readers gave readers different points of entry into this world. John Vernon's *Compleat comptinghouse* was a dialogue between a master and a young lad. Such a device allowed Vernon not only to work through a list of topics relevant to a prospective apprentice but also to invite the reader, particularly the young scholar, to assume the role of the inquisitive lad.[168] Many manuals instructed their readers to work through sample account books, tracing the transactions, and ideally reproducing the set of account books. William Webster, in his *Essay on book-keeping*, followed general instructions with sample pages from a waste book, journal and ledger. He directed his readers to read carefully the general section first, and then, after considering the particular examples, to trace the entries in the waste book through the journal and ledger and then to look at the earlier directions on the finding and correction of mistakes.[169] These instructions indicate that this sort of instruction manual was not designed to be followed in a linear fashion – to be read properly and effectively the reader must move from one part of the book to another repeatedly. Many readers of similar texts were instructed to reproduce systematically the set of sample books provided by the author. Collins wrote to a reader: 'let me advise him to write out the Journals of some of these Accompts . . . but if this be thought to laborious, he may prick and examin over' the relevant sections'.[170] Authors promised that such attentive studying would bring rewards. Like Collins, Monteage recommended that the reader of his book either 'prick the summs both Debtor and Creditor' in the sample ledger, or 'if instead of pricking over, he write over this Leidger by degrees, as he reads the Transactions herein contained, he would not fail of a good

---

[167] Daniel Defoe, *The compleat English gentleman*, ed. K. D. Bülbring, London 1890, 225.
[168] Richard Dafforne used a similar device of a dialogue between a schoolmaster (Philo-Mathy) and a pupil (School-Partner) in *The merchant's mirrour*, repr. of 3rd edition, London 1684.
[169] Webster, *Essay*, preface.
[170] Collins, *Introduction*, sig. B1v.

income and increase of knowledge in these matters'.[171] Readers were expected to become quite actively involved with these texts, to mark them up as an accountant would, or to compile the books an accountant might keep.[172]

Some writers took this further and quite explicitly suggested that their readers 'try on' different hats. Monteage intended his accounting manual, *Debtor and creditor made easie*, for a diverse audience. The title page listed six occupations: 'The Youth or Young Scholar, The Husband-man, or Farmer, The Country-Gentle-man, The Retailing Shop-keeper, The Handicrafts-man, The Merchant.'[173] This occupational division was preserved in his explanation of his bookkeeping methods and the sample accounts that Monteage provided for readers to follow. The method began with taking an inventory under the main heading 'The Inventory of my Estate, taken 10th April, 1675', which listed the values of assets of each of the six *personae* in turn. For example, under the subheading 'As a Youth I have in Stock', school books, pigeons, rabbits and cash were listed, and under the subheading 'As a Handicraft or mix Tradesman, to instance an Upholster, I have' were listed carpets, tapestries and feather beds. At the same time as drawing such distinctions between the different types of trade Monteage, 'for brevity sake', took 'all the said Persons or Callings beforenamed, to be but one only single person, dealing in all the fore-mentioned wayes' and added the value of the different estates together.[174] Having compiled this inventory, the next stage was 'to put forth our selves in Action, To buy and sell, Receive and pay'; Monteage again proposed to consider 'the dealing of the several Persons or qualities before-mentioned, one by one, in their several wayes' but in order that the text did not become 'too Volumnous', 'you are to take the whole work together collectively, as the Trade or Dealing of one single Person'. As the accounts unfolded consecutively over time, so too did a first-person narrative of the dealings of each *persona*. The youth bought counters and having played with his 'fellows' took home more than he began with, he bought food for his pigeons, sold some of them, bought apples, sold rabbits, bought books from his school fellow using cash and counters and received a gift of money from his uncle.[175] And so on through the *personae* in order, until the 'Merchants way of Trade, which alone and of it self contains all the rest, and much more variety than can be in all other Callings put

---

171 Monteage, *Debtor and creditor*, 1682, sig. D2.
172 Not all agreed on the benefits of such a method. Dafforne wrote in *Apprentices time-entertainer*, in which he included a specimen waste book, but no ledger or journal, that 'To the Arts-desirous Youth' that 'Here is no Copying of a Journal and Leager (as is too-too usual) making a Book full of Writing, and a Head void of Knowledge. Here each Practiser of these 313. Waste-book parcels must manifest his own apprehension, as divers by their Real practice can witness' (A3v).
173 Monteage, *Debtor and creditor*, 1682, title page.
174 Ibid. sig C1v.
175 Ibid. sigs C4v–D4r.

together' was dealt with last. The merchant engaged in an international trade in cloth, raisins, sugar, wine, writing paper; exchange between currencies was involved, insurance, bonds with interest, dealing with bankrupts, negotiating with ships' masters and company accounts 'in which branch there is the difficultest knots to untie'.[176] The second part of the book contained a sample ledger for all these transactions. The book ends with a description of the type of book Monteage used for his accounts, how he numbered the pages and divided the book up into sections. Part way through this description the reader is reminded that all this is just imaginary, for he wrote 'or if I be a Retailer' and went on to describe how he would then order his books.

Printed and bound with some editions of Stephen Monteage's *Debtor and creditor made easie*, was *Advice to the women and maidens of London* purportedly written 'By one of that Sex'. The pamphlet is usually attributed to Monteage and displays his characteristic style of presenting instruction in accounting. Having worked through the simple keeping of petty accounts, the author refers readers to *Debtor and creditor made easie* 'whence I derive all my small stock of Learning in Accounts', and then proceeds to explain the more complex accounts a retailer might undertake.[177] The first instruction is to 'Imagine an Exchange-Woman, Shop-keeper, or the like, newly entring upon Trade, is desirous to keep her Accounts in an exact Method'.[178] After the inventory of stock has been presented the transactions are detailed and it is clear that there is in fact only a colon between the imagined retailer and the reader: 'Having thus Posted your Account of Stock, and set open your shop, you begin your Trade after some such manner as this: And here I desire the Reader or Learner, as she reads these following Instructions, to cast her eye upon the Leiger where the Parcels are entred.'[179] After the transactions have been presented the instructions are altered slightly and 'the Practitioners' are directed 'not to satisfie themselves by looking in the Leiger; but as they understand each Parcel, to post it themselves in a Paper Book till the whole be finish'd'.[180] The reader here slips between being the pupil to be instructed and the retailer herself for she is to practise accounts by creating the ledger as if she were the retailer.

I'm not denying that these strategies – the dialogue, the reproducing of account books, or the developing of particular *personae* in the accounts – might be effective learning devices, or that indeed some youths, handicraftsmen or retail shopkeepers might find their section in Monteage's book particular useful, or find the answers to the young lad's questions in Vernon's book enlightening. What I am saying though is that it is perhaps through

176  Ibid. sigs G2r–K3r.
177  [Monteage], *Advice*, 18.
178  Ibid. 19.
179  Ibid. 20.
180  Ibid. 25.

such devices that readers might also take Lawrence Klein's 'imaginary visits to the social worlds of others'.

This may be too speculative a reading. Might readers really have engaged with the texts in these ways? Might they have imagined themselves into different capacities? Were there armchair retailing shopkeepers and handicraftsmen as Monteage styled himself to be? I'd like to put forward some slightly more substantive evidence that readers did at least engage with the 'characters' in these books, even if they did not go as far as identifying with them.

A copy of Thomas King's An *exact guide to book-keeping by way of debtor and creditor* (1717) in the Goldsmiths Collection held at the University of London Library offers such evidence.[181] In the sample account books King included characters who were labelled by their initials – Sister A., Mr B. D., C. S., Esq., Mrs M. M. and so on. The copy of the book in the Goldsmiths Collection contains some manuscript markings in the main text suggesting that one reader followed through at least some of the calculations.[182] What is far more significant, however, is the additional manuscript material on the endpapers of this copy. One unknown reader decoded the initials of the characters in the account books, and provided a key to their identity in a list written out on the blank sheets at the end of the book.[183] C. S. Esquire is identified as C. Searle Esquire, Ald. R. C. is identified as Robt Cowley Aldm. Mrs M. as M. Moses, and so on. Most initials are in accordance with the names given, a few however, are not. P. Q. is identified as Willm Layton. In total twenty-five names are given in the key. Whoever compiled this key, and perhaps it was King himself, and for whatever particular reason, it can be argued that this demonstrates an engagement with the characters in the text, rather than a concentration on the mechanics of the accounting methods alone.

### 'his hand and pen': owning and reading merchant manuals

Some of the contexts in which readers might have read and used commercial manuals have already been touched upon above. Here I wish to explore in more detail the evidence of ownership and reading practices. Margaret Spufford suggests that trade, in urban centres, was a greater motivation to literacy than religion.[184] Did traders, amongst whom literacy and presumably

---

181  King, *Exact guide*, Goldsmiths Collection, University of London Library, no. 5379.1.
182  Ibid, 2–3, 6.
183  There is also one 'decoding' in 'The Alphabet to Leidger B' where PQ is identified as Willm Dayton. And in fact this is the first entry in the listing on the endpapers.
184  M. Spufford, 'Literacy, trade and religion in the commercial centres of Europe', in K. Davids and J. Lucassen (eds), *A miracle mirrored: the Dutch Republic in European perspective*, Cambridge 1995, 229–83. I am grateful to Adam Fox for drawing my attention to this article.

numeracy rates were high, own these manuals, read them and make use of their reference material and follow their advice?[185] Although evidence is sparse, some scholars like Louis B. Wright, in a study of middle-class culture in the late sixteenth and early seventeenth centuries, assume that commercial manuals were read by merchants and their apprentices.[186] In eighteenth-century Germany, Daniel Rabuzzi suggests that there was an eagerness to read business handbooks: 'apprentices and ambitious retailers . . . who hungered for the knowledge that would secure or advance them at precisely a time when European expansion meant scarce information on foreign goods and markets became ever more crucial to success'.[187]

In relation to the books under consideration here there is piecemeal evidence that commercial manuals were owned by merchants. We know from inventories of merchants' moveable goods at their death that merchants owned books. The inventory of Sir Henry Creswicke, once Master of the Merchant Venturers in Bristol, for example, drawn up after his death in 1668, tantalisingly recorded 'Bookes of all Sorts' in the 'little New Parlour', valued at £10 but, like many other inventories, specific titles were not listed.[188] Auction catalogues are more promising. The auction catalogue of the library of a deceased 'Eminent Merchant . . . in the City of London', for example, which included Roberts's *The merchants map of commerce*, Malynes's *Lex mercatoria*, and John Marius's book on bills of exchange, was to be auctioned in November 1697 at Roll's Auction House in St Paul's Church Yard.[189] Similarly, the merchant Peter Hushar's library, sold at auction in 1685, also included Marius's book, alongside some arithmetics.[190] Those who have studied particular groups of merchants later in the eighteenth century have found that they owned commercial texts. David Hancock describes the possession of trade books 'concerned with everyday matters of practical import', amongst a group of eighteenth-century international traders.[191] Jacob Price has found that of the subscribers to the three editions of John

185 P. C. Cohen, *A calculating people: the spread of numeracy in early America*, Chicago 1982, ch. i; K. Thomas, 'Numeracy in early modern England', *TRHS*, 5th ser. xxxvii (1987), 103–32.

186 L. B. Wright, *Middle-class culture in Elizabethan England*, Chapel Hill 1935, 160–3, and 'Language helps for the Elizabethan tradesman', *Journal of English and Germanic Philology* xxx (1931), 335–47.

187 Rabuzzi, 'Commercial mentalities', 173.

188 P. McGrath (ed.), *Merchants and merchandise in seventeenth-century Bristol*, Bristol 1955, 94. On Creswicke see H. E. Nott and E. Ralph (eds), *The deposition books of Bristol*, II: *1650–1654*, Bristol 1948, 204.

189 *Bibliotheca curiosa, or, a choice collection of books*, London 1697.

190 Edward Millington, *A catalogue of the library of books . . . of Mr Peter Hushar*, London 1685, 20–1.

191 Hancock, *Citizens*, 34. The 1748 inventory of the Aleppo factor, Lister Bigg, listed a number of manuals including those by Hatton and Roberts: Ambrose, 'English traders', 267 n. 3.

Wright's *American negotiator* (1761–5), a reference book which included details of coins in use in the American colonies, just under a third of more than 3,500 of those for whom occupational information was recorded were described as merchants.[192] John McCusker and Russell Menard suggest that many of the copies of commercial texts in North American collections were owned by colonial merchants.[193] Not all of those involved in commerce, however, owned manuals or even any books at all. In Carl Estabrook's study of patterns of book ownership in and around Bristol, based on inventories, half of those in the occupational category 'commerce' in the period 1660–99 had no books, and for the period 1700–40 the proportion had risen to more than three-quarters.[194] The richest individual in his study was a merchant whose wealth was valued at over £5,000. He owned no books at all.[195]

All sorts of people who were not merchants themselves but had commercial interests kept commercial manuals in their libraries. John Locke, Isaac Newton and Samuel Pepys, whose range of interests encompassed the recoinage, the mint and naval and trade affairs generally, all had commercial texts advising on merchanting and accounting in their libraries.[196] Bookplates indicate that commercial texts were owned by the elites: the bookplate of the second duke of Beaufort, Henry Somerset, can be found inside a copy of Edward Hattton's compendium of tables of interest payments, an *Index to interest* (1711).[197] Such books could also be found in institutional libraries; a copy of the same edition of Hatton's book and Robert Colinson's *Idea*

---

[192] J. M. Price, 'Who cared about the colonies? The impact of the thirteen colonies on British society and politics, circa 1714–1775', in B. Bailyn and P. D. Morgan (eds), *Strangers within the realm: cultural margins of the first British empire*, Chapel Hill 1991, 411.

[193] J. J. McCusker and R. R. Menard, *The economy of British America, 1607–1789*, Chapel Hill 1985, 345.

[194] In the first category there were thirty-six people and in the second sixty-one: C. B. Estabrook, *Urbane and rustic England: cultural ties and social spheres in the provinces, 1660–1780*, Manchester 1998, 175, 176.

[195] Ibid. 181.

[196] J. Harrison and P. Laslett, *The library of John Locke*, Oxford 1965, 113, 192, 258. John Locke's copy of Vernon's *Compleat comptinghouse* (1683) is pristine, except for his signature and library classification: copy in the Bodleian Library, shelfmark Locke 7.170d/2. See also John Harrison, *The library of Isaac Newton*, Cambridge 1978, 260, and N. A. Smith, assisted by H. M. Adams and D. Pepys Whiteley, *Catalogue of the Pepys Library at Magdalene College Cambridge*, I: *Printed books*, ed. R. Latham, Cambridge 1978, 117, 151. On Pepys's accounting practices see P. G. Boys, 'Samuel Pepys's personal accounts', *Accounting, Business and Financial History* v (1995), 308–20.

[197] Copy of Edward Hatton's, *Index to interest*, London 1711, copy in the Folger Shakespeare Library, Washington, DC, shelfmark 200–867q. On Somerset's bookplates see B. N. Lee, 'Gentlemen and their book-plates', in R. Myers and M. Harris (eds), *Property of a gentleman: the formation, organisation and dispersal of the private library, 1620–1920*, Winchester 1991, 50–1, 75 n. 19. The bookplate of the Right Honourable Lord Viscount Malden can be found inside a copy of John Spicer's *Tables of interest*, London 1693, now at the Institute of Chartered Accountants.

*rationaria* (1683) were both part of the collection of books in the Library of Advocates in Edinburgh in this period as the bookplates attest.[198]

Many recorded their names on the endpapers and title pages, sometimes with a date.[199] A. W. Bickford wrote his or her name in the front of a copy of John Vernon's *Compleat comptinghouse* (1683) and dated it 1713.[200] One owner of John Hill's *The exact dealer refined* (1698) also demonstrated the long life of some copies of these books when he wrote 'John Grimes his hand and pen 1719' on the front endpaper.[201] Some left those who might pick up their book in no doubt about the identity of its owner: a Christopher Dauntesey signed his name and dated it 1719 at the front of his copy of John Ayres, *Arithmetick made easie* (1718), and at the back he added a cautionary rhyme next to his name: 'Steal not this Booke for feare of Shame for here you see the Owners name'.[202] Although the majority of owners who left their names in books were men, a few women's names can be found. In the Folger Library's copy of the 1707 edition of Hatton's *Merchant's magazine* the name of Elizabeth Owen is written (as well as that of Samuel Tavenor dated 1708).[203] If signatures are a sign of ownership then the repetition of a surname in the names in a single book suggests that these books were passed from one family member to another. Another copy of Hatton's *Merchant's magazine*, discussed again below, contains the signatures of four men all with the last name Martin over at least a twenty-four-year span.[204] Some books, then, had multiple owners. Some owners had more than one copy of the same book. Alexander Campbell owned two copies of Hatton's, *Merchant's magazine* and John Lowther owned at least two copies of Morden's *Geography*.[205]

Not all readers purchased their own copies. Books were also given as gifts.

[198] Both books are now in the National Library of Scotland.

[199] Such practices are described more generally in D. Pearson, *Provenance research in book history: a handbook*, London 1994, 12–25.

[200] Vernon, *Compleat comptinghouse* (1683), copy in the Institute of Chartered Accountants, shelfmark 3034.

[201] John Hill, *The exact dealer refined*, London 1698, title page, copy in the Huntington Library, shelfmark 230119.

[202] John Ayres, *Arithmetick made easie for the use and benefit of trades-men*, London 1718, copy in the Institute of Chartered Accountants.

[203] Edward Hatton, *The merchant's magazine*, 5th edition, London 1707, copy in the Folger Shakespeare Library, shelfmark 191874. Margaret Hunt provides evidence of the accounting skills of women: *Middling sort*, 89.

[204] Hatton, *Merchant's magazine*, 1695, copy in Columbia University Library, shelfmark Montgomery 210 H2811. David, Edward and two with the name Thomas record their names in the book.

[205] Campbell's copies of Hatton, *Merchant's magazine*, 1699, are held at the Baker Library, Harvard, and in the Goldsmiths Collection at the University of London Library, shelfmark 3603; John Lowther to William Gilpin, 1 Feb. 1698, in D. R. Hainsworth (ed.), *The correspondence of Sir John Lowther of Whitehaven, 1693–1698: a provincial community in wartime*, Oxford 1983, 494.

William Heathcote recorded on the front endpaper of a 1698 edition of Vernon's *Compleat comptinghouse*: 'Wm Heathcote his Book September 30 1705 given me by my Father'.[206] Pepys recorded in his diary giving a merchant manual to Frank Turner who was in December 1668 'upon the point of . . . going to the East Indys'. The book was Gerard Malynes's, *Lex mercatoria*, which was in Pepys's words 'an excellent [book] for him'.[207] From the possession of such a book, however, we cannot assume that Turner, or any other owner read their book and other evidence needs to be considered.

To begin at one end of the spectrum, particular copies of books contain clues that they have not been used at all. A copy of an octavo volume of pre-calculated interest tables, compiled by Michael Dary and published in 1677, and now in the Huntington Library, still has its pages uncut.[208] Owners left other traces of their lack of use. Edward Hatton's three editions of his book of tables of interest payments, an *Index to interest*, all contained a device labelled 'the circle of time'. It was a volvelle for determining the number of days between two particular dates (vital for calculating the interest owed) and was constructed from a paper disc that was to be cut out of one page and attached with a little string, or a paper fastener, to the centre of a printed ring on another page. Out of the thirty copies consulted only three have the two sheets still intact rather than the wheel made up.[209] In a few, the relevant pages are missing and in the rest the 'circle of time' has been constructed.[210] As it is difficult to tell when the circle of time might have been made up, the three in which the circle has not been made up are in many ways more inter-

---

206 John Vernon, *The compleat comptinghouse*, London 1698, copy in the Institute of Chartered Accounts, shelfmark E3245.

207 *Pepys*, viii. 580.

208 Michael Dary, *Interest epitomized*, London 1677, copy in the Huntington Library, shelfmark 433561.

209 Unconstructed: National Library of Scotland, Edinburgh (1711); Bodleian Library (1711); Cambridge University Library (1711).

210 Missing: University of London Library (1711); St Edmund Hall Library, Oxford (1714). Constructed: British Library (1711); Birmingham University Library (1711); Christ Church Library, Oxford (1711); Williams Andrews Clark Memorial Library, University of California, Los Angeles (1711); Rivera Library, University of California, Riverside, California (1711); William R. Perkins Library, Duke University, Durham, NC (1711); University of Oklahoma Libraries, Norman, Oklahoma (1711); Harry Ransom Humanities Research Center, University of Texas, Austin, Texas (1711); Rare Book and Manuscript Library, Columbia University, New York (1711); Folger Shakespeare Library, Washington, DC (1711); British Library (1714); National Library of Ireland, Dublin (1714); Glasgow University Library (1714); Institute of Chartered Accountants in England and Wales (1714); University of London Library (1714); Nottingham University Library (1714); Huntington Library, San Marino, California (1714); Baker Library, Harvard (1714); Rutgers University Library, New Brunswick, NJ (1714); Rare Book and Manuscript Library, Columbia University (1714); Cambridge University Library (1717); Lincoln College Library, Oxford (1717); Columbia University (1717) two copies.

esting, as they demonstrate the absence of readers' interest in the period under consideration.

Corrected errata suggest at least some interest from a reader. These hand-set books contained many figures which opened up great possibilities for errors. Although in copies of early modern books more generally the incidence of corrected errata is low some examples of corrected errata in merchant manuals do survive. Alongside the errata in a copy of George Clerk's *The landed-man's assistant*, for example, held in the library of the Institute of Chartered Accountants, one satisfied reader recorded that they had made the corrections listed.[211] Some readers made all the corrections and underlined the errata (perhaps as they went), while others only got part of the way through the task of making corrections.[212] Some were assiduous like the reader of a copy of *The purchasers pattern* (1656), now in the Huntington Library, who not only made the corrections listed in the errata in the main text but also made corrections to the errata.[213] Such attention to detail is unusual and most errata went uncorrected.

Many books contain jottings, marks and pointing hands in margins and blank spaces that suggest that readers did follow instructions and attempted to work through examples in the text. In a copy of Robert Colinson's *Idea rationaria* consulted in the National Library of Scotland, marginal manuscript asterisks in the specimen waste book suggest that at least one reader responded to the author's encouragement to follow entries through the various sample accounting books.[214] When calculations were incomplete, as in the 'cutts' in Hatton's *Merchant's magazine*, some readers completed them with their pen.[215] Other readers, found these 'cutts' hard to understand. One of the Thomas Martins who wrote his name in the Columbia copy of the *Merchant's magazine* recorded his frustration on the back of the engraved sheet which gave such lists as fractional parts of pounds in shillings and pence as 'A short way of Casting up all sorts of Merchandise'. He wrote that 'What is on the other side of this Leafe I do not under stand it at All.'[216]

---

211 George Clerk, *The landed-man's assistant*, London 1715, 49, copy in the Institute of Chartered Accountants, shelfmark 3312.

212 Thomas Willsford, *The scales of commerce and trade*, London 1660, copy in the Institute of Chartered Accountants, shelfmark 3211; Hatton, *Merchant's magazine*, 1695, copy in the Institute of Chartered Accountants, shelfmark 2029.

213 Henry Phillipes, *The purchasers pattern*, London 1656, copy in the Huntington Library, shelfmark 322506–7. Two names can be found in the book, Nath. Thyston (?) who recorded the price of the book as 1s. 6d., and Jno Newport who dated his signature 1716.

214 Colinson, *Idea rationaria*, Edinburgh 1683, copy in the National Library of Scotland, shelfmark H.33.c.8.

215 Hatton *Merchant's magazine*, 1695, copy in the Institute of Chartered Accountants, shelfmark 2029.

216 Hatton, *Merchant's magazine*, 1695, copy in Columbia University Library, shelfmark Montgomery 210 H2811, opposite p. 86. Confusion is also noted on p. 35.

The most common sort of marginalia in these books are scribbled calculations; endpapers, and also margins, are often packed tight with workings out, some reproducing the calculations in the text. Occasionally the commercial manuals served to chronicle the very transactions they instructed their readers to record more methodically in waste books, ledgers and journals. The Martins' copy of Hatton's *Merchant's magazine*, contains a manuscript addition noting an occasion on which one of the Thomas Martins repaid debts, with the date, place and names of the creditors listed.[217] So the accounting instruction manual might itself become the book of accounts. Although it was not very unusual in this period to record the provenance and price of books in the opening pages of the book, if the book was an accounting manual such a record took on extra significance.[218] Moreover, in the most self referential way, the selling of the book itself might also be recorded in the margins of the book. On page 99 of the Martins' book, it was recorded that 'David Martin sould Thomas Martin thes Booke'. If this refers to the second Thomas Martin to own this book, who was, as he records elsewhere, sixteen when he owned the book, then perhaps this entry signals a new awareness of recording transactions stimulated by the book itself?[219]

Some readers supplemented the texts of their books with corrections, helpful hints, rhymes to remember rules and additional information.[220] To Lord Arundell's copy of Leybourn's *Panarithmologia*, held in the Huntington Library, one reader has added a manuscript index of the second part of the book which contained various 'ready Calculated' tables including those for calculating simple and compound interest and the purchase of annuities.[221] With no detailed list of contents for this section, and no printed index supplied, such a manuscript index would presumably make this book more convenient to use.[222] Some readers extended the scope of their books with more substantial additions. In David Rochfort's copy of the 1714 edition of Hatton's *Index to interest* in the University of London Library a reader has added 31 pages of manuscript tables 'Pertinent to the Subject of this Book' including calendars of fixed feasts, and term dates for thirty years from 1715 onwards thus extending the period for which the book contained up-to-date information.

---

[217] Ibid. 34.

[218] Pearson, *Provenance research*, 16.

[219] Hatton, *Merchant's magazine*, 1695, copy in Columbia University Library, shelfmark Montgomery 210 H2811, p. 15.

[220] See, for example, the extensively annotated copies of Hatton's *Merchant's magazine*, 1699, owned by Alexander Campbell. One is held at the Baker Library and the other in the Goldsmiths Collection at the University of London Library, shelfmark 3603.

[221] Leybourn, *Panarithmologia*, pt II, section i, title page.

[222] Ibid., copy in the Huntington Library, shelfmark 387694. The manuscript index can be found on the rear endpapers.

Jacobite sentiments written in a space on a page of a copy of *Cocker's arithmetick*, however, caution against treating the readers' involvement with these books as an engagement with their commercial didactic element alone.[223] And in the Martins' book the recording of the births of a cow and bull calf, and on another page a journey, in March 1723, suggest the range of accounting practices undertaken in such books.[224]

Evidence for at least one trader who read an accounting manual and embraced the method it expounded in the late seventeenth century can be found in the diary of the provincial merchant Samuel Jeake. The entry for 1 January 1690 reads: 'I began to keep my Accompts in a Liedger after the method set down in Chamberlain's Accomptants' Guide; which course I alwaies continued henceforward.'[225] However, Jeake, according to Grassby, is an exceptional case. Grassby's research supports the conclusion reached by B. S. Yamey that although double-entry bookkeeping was the standard practice elucidated in early modern texts, most traders actually used single-entry accounting methods.[226] Contrary to much of the prescriptive advice, accounts were rarely balanced to calculate profit and loss, rather they were used to keep track of those who owed money and those to whom money was owed. Phyllis Whitman Hunter has charted the interesting case of Timothy Orne (1717–67) who, while apprenticed to a Boston merchant, 'kept an immaculate set of records for what must have been a hypothetical business . . . balancing different cost bases against sales made at different times and prices'. But when Orne later entered his father's business the accounts he kept were rather different, 'the careful consideration of costs versus sales disappeared from his records'.[227] It might be that the reader who produced the double-side folio page of a waste book set out exactly like the sample waste book in *Idea rationaria*, now tucked into a copy held at the Folger, was conducting an exercise in an equally fictitious business set in Edinburgh in 1700 as part of his or her training.[228]

---

223 [Edward Cocker], *Cocker's arithmetick*, London 1694, 79, copy in the National Library of Scotland, shelfmark NC 312.g.2. Books were used in many ways that did not involve their being read: D. Cressy, 'Books as totems in seventeenth-century England and New England', *Journal of Library History* xxi (1986), 92–106.

224 Hatton, *Merchant's magazine*, 1695, 101, 86 in Columbia University Library, shelfmark Montgomery 210 H2811.

225 Jeake, *Diary*, 149. Jeake undertook more reading in times when trade was quiet: ibid. 41.

226 R. Grassby, 'The rate of profit in seventeenth-century England', *EHR* lxxxiv (1969), 748–9, and *Business community*, 184–9; B. S. Yamey, 'Scientific bookkeeping and the rise of capitalism', *EcHR*, 2nd ser. i (1949), 105. There were exceptions, particularly in international trade, for example the East India Company kept its accounts in double-entry form: K. N. Chaudhuri, *The trading world of Asia and the English East India Company, 1660–1760*, Cambridge 1978, 413.

227 P. W. Hunter, 'Containing the marvellous: instructions to buyers and sellers', in Glaisyer and Pennell, *Didactic literature*, 180.

228 Colinson, *Idea rationaria*, copy in the Folger Shakespeare Library, shelfmark 161328.

Even if many merchants did not adopt the complex bookkeeping methods advocated by authors, evidence makes it clear that the reference elements of many of these texts remained valuable to readers. John Lowther recommended Morden's *Geography rectified* to his steward, William Gilpin, in Whitehaven 'If you be at any loss touching forreign coins'; Gilpin replied that Malynes's *Lex mercatoria*, also, 'gives us an account of coyns, weights, etc'.[229]

Among the aims of this chapter have been attempts to understand who might have been the readers of these didactic texts, and the contexts in which they read. Although there is good reason to err on the side of caution when speculating about the composition of the readership of these texts, principally because the evidence of readership is so sparse, and so much must be inferred from the texts themselves, three important, but not necessarily mutually exclusive, contexts for interpreting these manuals have emerged.

First, a number of the texts were closely associated with writing schools. Written by writing schoolmasters, and teachers of accounting skills, partly as vehicles for promoting their own services, many of these texts can be considered as proto-type text books, as they appear, in most cases, to have been designed to be used by masters, and in at least one case, to consolidate the teaching in the schools. There is no evidence to suggest that these texts in any way replaced apprenticeship, although it may have been that they were used independently of the writing schools to prepare for, or during, an apprenticeship.

Secondly, experienced merchants may have read these texts to learn new skills, as an aid in performing calculations and for reference, perhaps even to look up the definition of an unusual term in a vocabulary. However, it is also important to consider that they may have read them to reacquaint themselves with old skills, and for 'comfort'.[230]

Thirdly, some of these texts may have been used as a way of vicariously experiencing the commercial world. Klein speculates that one group of readers of alleged guides to practices were 'people who just wanted to be oriented in a discursive and cultural world in which encounters with gentility were quite common'.[231] As has been seen above the importance of an introduction to the discursive world of commerce must not be underestimated. It is crucial to acknowledge gentlemen's supposed interest in encountering the mercantile world through these texts, and indeed a number of texts claimed to address such readers, partly in the context of natural philosophical

---

229 Lowther to Gilpin, 1 Feb. 1698, and Gilpin to Lowther, 9 Feb. 1698, in Hainsworth, *Sir John Lowther*, 494, 499. It is not clear which edition is referred to here. Robert Morden's *Geography rectified* was published in London in 1680, 1688, 1693 and 1700.
230 Rabuzzi, 'Commercial mentalities', 174; Hunter, *Before novels*, 235.
231 Klein, 'Politeness for plebes', 376.

concerns. This is not to deny that other readers, like those who looked down on the merchants at the Royal Exchange from the surrounding balconies, were 'armchair merchants'. Nor is it to underestimate that some gentlemen would have had a genuine need for commercial information and skills through their own commercial dealings. Although some texts claim that they were for 'diversion', and encouraged the interest of what, anachronistically, could be called amateurs, finding evidence for this type of reading is problematic.

It is tempting to suggest correspondences between types of commercial didactic texts, for example descriptive, technical and those containing reference information, and the contexts in which they were read. Although some texts did make claims for the ways in which they were used, what can be deduced on the basis of available evidence is that the various types of texts could each have been read in a variety of contexts. Hatton's an *Index to interest*, for example, may have been used by a merchant negotiating transactions at the Exchange, and equally by students practising their calculations, as well as by a gentleman imagining himself into the role of a trader in a coffee-house.

# 4

# 'Useful Observations on Trade':
# Metropolitan and Provincial Newspapers

The 1699 edition of Edward Hatton's *Merchant's magazine*, one of the most substantial and frequently republished manuals on commerce, included an explanation of the contents of a specialist business newspaper, in this case the 'Course of the Exchange'. This was a serial publication listing exchange rates between European currencies, and had probably only recently started publication; as Hatton told his readers, 'I find the Generality of Persons ignorant of the meaning thereof, which induced me to explain the same.'[1] In 1707 another book instructing on commerce, specifically money and exchange, written by the French Huguenot refugee Alexander Justice provided a twenty-page explanation of the 'Course of the Exchange'.[2] Justice skipped over the exchange rates, which were all Hatton had discussed, and instead explained the other listings (stock prices and the money advanced and paid off at the exchequer) given in the specimen issue of the 'Course of the Exchange' of 11 June 1706 which he reproduced. Such a specialist publication, as Hatton's and Justice's evidently felt need to explain indicates, was perhaps only familiar to a small number of readers. There were other business newspapers published in the late seventeenth and early eighteenth centuries which almost exclusively reported current prices, details about exports and imports: commodity price currents, bills of entry and shipping lists.[3] Although their readership was geographically diverse (many were sent overseas), their circulation, if the commodity price currents provide any indication, was relatively small.[4] These were all specialist publications largely catering to the needs of those involved in foreign trade.

Unlike the trajectory of much periodical publishing in this period, which was influenced by the lapsing of the Licensing Act in 1696, these develop-

---

[1]  Hatton, *Merchants magazine*, 1699, 129. On the development of the 'Course of the Exchange' see McCusker and Gravesteijn, *Journalism*, 312–17.

[2]  Alexander Justice, *A general treatise of monies and exchanges*, London 1707, 31–51. I am indebted to McCusker and Gravesteijn for this reference: *Journalism*, 315.

[3]  Ibid; McCusker, 'Business press'; 'European bills of entry'; and ' "Lloyd's List" '; Neal, 'Financial press'; Price, 'London price-currents'.

[4]  Proctor's and Robinson's weekly price currents in 1712, according to the quantity of stamped paper purchased, had a circulation in England of around seventy and sixty copies respectively. Numerous copies printed on unstamped paper were no doubt sent overseas: McCusker and Gravesteijn, *Journalism*, 297.

ments, argue John McCusker and Cora Gravesteijn, were stimulated more by the demands for commercial information which accompanied the commercial revolution. By 1716, they have calculated, a London reader could spend more than £6 a year on subscriptions to seven different weekly or bi-weekly business newspapers.[5] Other periodical publications published in this period also dealt almost exclusively with commerce. Controversy surrounding the treaty with France in 1713 was played out in extensive debate in print, much of it carried out in the periodical press, particularly the *Mercator* and the *British Merchant*. Such debate, Perry Gauci argues, was the first time that commerce became a national political issue.[6]

If the specialist business newspapers and the periodicals which were devoted to rehearsing arguments about commerce were at one end of the spectrum then at the other were newspapers in which commerce was far less central to the content. Even the paper, of which only eight issues survive from 1703, entitled the *Merchant's News-Letter*, might be placed in this latter category.[7] It reported the foreign news much as other papers did and included only the usual commercial prices – the prices of the stocks of Bank, East India Company and South Sea Company – that were a regular component in many papers in the period. Of course, much of the foreign news might be read for its significance for the development of English trade and so in this sense all papers which reported foreign news provided the merchant with intelligence. Commercial information might also be found in advertisements and announcements. The *London Gazette*, for example, specialised in notices from trading companies, but in the early eighteenth century other papers also carried such announcements especially items published at short notice when their urgency required a daily paper and could not wait for the next issue of the tri-weekly *Gazette*.[8] These papers may have reported on commerce in their columns and under the heading advertisements but they were not specialist business papers.

Between these two extremes – the general paper and the specialist paper – were a number of papers that set out to put commerce, and particularly the sorts of price information contained in the specialist papers, before a wider audience. It is two of these papers, in particular, that I concentrate upon in the first two sections of this chapter: the apothecary, John Houghton's turn of the century paper, *A Collection for Improvement of Husbandry and Trade*, which incorporated London and regional prices, as well as essays on trade, into a larger project that developed Baconian agendas to improve trade and husbandry in the nation; and, later in the period, the *British Mercury*, published by the Sun Fire Office largely for subscribers to its policies for

---

5    McCusker and Gravesteijn, *Journalism*, 291–2.
6    Gauci, *Politics of trade*, ch vi.
7    The earliest surviving issue is numbered '2' and dated 27 Mar. 1703, the last, the eighteenth issue, is dated 17 July 1703.
8    India Office Records, H/MISC/17.

insuring goods and houses. To thousands of readers in the 1710s it presented prices of goods and stocks, as well as foreign news and advertisements. In this chapter I examine these papers and explore how they packaged commercial information. Where did it originate and how was it presented to particular readers? In the third section of the chapter these questions are also asked of many of the papers established in the early eighteenth century in market towns across England which although not so specifically focused on trade as the *Collection* and the *Mercury* did contain much trade information not all of which was culled from London papers.

## 'the whole Kingdom made as one trading City': A Collection for Improvement of Husbandry and Trade

John Houghton's monthly, quarto-sized periodical, *A Collection of Letters for the Improvement of Husbandry & Trade*, addressed a range of agricultural and commercial topics from English coin, to curing woodcocks, through to malting. It was published just twenty-one times in the 1680s and varied in length from eight to forty pages.[9] Houghton claimed that he had 'been very often Solicited to revive' this publication, and in the early 1690s he decided that he was 'willing enough to undertake the trouble thereof in a much higher degree than ever' in another periodical publication.[10] It is this later work, *A Collection for Improvement of Husbandry and Trade*, first issued in March 1692, and published in 583 issues and nineteen volumes over a period of more than a decade, that is treated more fully here.

In his intention to improve husbandry and trade, Houghton extended and developed the Royal Society's programmes undertaken in Bacon's shadow. The agenda of the society's georgical committee and the history of trades programmes were incorporated in Houghton's periodical project into a broader scheme that embraced the new financial world of the late seventeenth century.[11] A single example will illustrate how Houghton emphasised the interdependence of trade, husbandry and stocks: having discussed the navigable rivers of Yorkshire, he suggested that he might undertake a study of all the navigable rivers of England and that such a study 'will be a ground for learning what Trade already is, and what may be improv'd upon these Rivers, particularly what may be given to any that will enquire after Mines of Coal, Lead, Tinn, Iron, Copper . . . also for the easie carriage of Wood'. Knowledge

---

[9] John Houghton, *A Collection of Letters for the Improvement of Husbandry & Trade* (Sept. 1681–June 1684).

[10] BL, MS Sloane 2903, fo. 167r.

[11] N. Glaisyer, 'Readers, correspondents and communities: John Houghton's *A Collection for Improvement of Husbandry and Trade* (1692–1703)', in A. Shepard and P. Withington (eds), *Communities in early modern England: networks, place, rhetoric*, Manchester 2000, 235–51.

about things such as rivers connected intimately to investment schemes: 'And without doubt, had we much more natural History of our Country, we should much more improve it; especially at this time, when Companies of Men are so eager to enter into Joint-Stocks for improvement of any thing that appears reasonable.'[12]

In his attempts both to disseminate existing natural, trade and financial knowledge and stimulate further investigations Houghton, who was a Fellow of the Royal Society, was supported by many other Fellows.[13] He not only extended the scope of the Royal Society's vision but he also elaborated on its method of information exchange.[14] Much early modern natural philosophy was undertaken in the context of correspondence with the society itself acting as a clearing house, and to compile his periodical Houghton relied quite heavily on contributions from letter writers. He framed much of the content of the periodical in the context of a correspondence with himself as its broker at the centre.[15]

The periodical was an enormously wide-ranging publication, the advertisements alone suggest that Houghton's brokering activities ranged from finding positions for the well-qualified unemployed and acting as an intermediary in the sales of advowsons, properties and investments, to finding marriage partners. In the leading essays that appeared on the first page of every issue he covered an enormous range of subjects. At the risk of privileging some aspects of the paper over others, and denying the importance Houghton placed on the relatedness of all parts of his project for improvement, here I concentrate on the prices given in the paper and his discussions of the stock market. How did he package such information? Where did it come from? Could it be trusted? And where did it fit into his scheme?

In a manuscript proposal probably written around the middle of 1691, before the publication of a similar printed proposal, Houghton outlined his intentions for an extensive coverage of subjects: 'the prices of Wheat, Rye, Mault, Oats, Pease, Coales, Hops, Hay, Tallow, Wool . . . the Value of the Actions of the East Indie, Guinny, Hudsons Bay, Linnan & paper companyes . . . . The Shipping into and out of the Port of London w[i]th the name of the place whether bound, and from whence', and other listings like 'Goods imported and Exported from the Customhouse of London, to draw the particulars into gross Summs, in order to Examine the Expence and foreigne vent of each Commodity' as well as accounts ranging from 'As good an Account as may be had of the Trade, strength and policy of other Nations' to the 'Arts of Fishing, Fowling, Hunting and destroying of Vermine'.[16]

---

12 *CIHT*, 3 Mar. 1693.
13 Glaisyer, 'Readers', 238–9.
14 Ibid. 240–6.
15 Ibid.
16 J. Houghton, 'A proposall for Improvement of Husbandry and Trade', BL, MS Sloane

Much of this proposal was realised in the periodical. In every issue there appeared a table of the prices of agricultural commodities – wheat, rye, barley, malt, oats, beans, peas, hops, hay, tallow, wool and also coal – from market towns all over England supplied by Houghton's correspondents. In the initial issues of the paper Houghton promised that 'Whoever are willing , from their Market to send my Prices, in good time, I'll return them in lieu one of my Collections.'[17] As the list of places covered lengthened Houghton made requests in the paper to receive prices from specific places: in May 1692 he wanted prices from 'Yarmouth, Woodbridge, Hull, Scarborough, Whitby, Sunderland, Harwich, London, Lewes, Shoreham, Arundel, Southampton'.[18] By the end of the first volume, after twenty-five issues, prices were listed from thirty-five different places.[19] When the periodical restarted after a delay of almost six months, very few prices were listed but Houghton reassured readers that 'In a little time the old Correspondency will be better fix't.'[20] By March 1693 prices from forty-six places were listed but he still continued to solicit further correspondents for this part of his project, as when he urged Ralph Thoresby, the Leeds antiquarian: 'if without too much trouble I could often hear how Corn goes I would put Leeds in my paper'.[21] He also included reports about specific markets: 'I hear from Reading that the Market was very short', and on a later occasion 'From Hitchin I hear that there was the biggest Market my Friend ever knew; yet all was bought up quickly at a rising Price.'[22]

How reliable were these prices? On occasion Houghton had to encourage his correspondents to send him 'frequently and exactly the Prices of every thing . . . assuring all that I chearfully pay the Charge of their Letters to me, and that if at any time the prices be wrong, 'tis not my Fault; I am as punctual as I can'.[23] He desired to be 'as exact as possible', and so asked 'all my Correspondents to look over all the Prizes of their Town mentioned in my Paper, when they write to me'.[24] Richard Saunders, the almanac maker, did so; in his letter to Houghton in March 1693 he not only listed the latest prices of various grains and beans at Melton Mowbray but also pointed out an error in the *Collection*: 'There was a mistake in the Prize of Malt in your last paper I writ [per] Bushel 3s 8d which [per] Quarter should have been 29s 04d'.[25]

2903, fos 167–8, and *A proposal for improvement of husbandry and trade*, London 1691. Much of this proposal was reproduced in the first issue of the paper (30 Mar. 1692).

17  *CIHT*, 6 Apr. 1692.

18  Ibid. 11 May 1692.

19  Ibid. 27 June 1692.

20  Ibid. 20 Jan. 1693.

21  J. Houghton to R. Thoresby, 8 Jan. 1702, Yorkshire Archaeological Society, Leeds, MS 15, item 110; *CIHT*, 31 Mar. 1693.

22  *CIHT*, 28 Apr. 1693, 18 May 1694.

23  Ibid. 15 Nov. 1695. See also *CIHT*, 14 May 1697: 'I desire all my Correspondents to send me the exact Prices; because of the Rise of Malt.'

24  Ibid. 20 Oct. 1693.

25  R. Saunders to J. Houghton, 20 Mar. 1692/3, BL, MS Stowe 747, fo. 14r. The price of

Despite such efforts and Houghton's pleas to be sent 'more frequently the Price of Corn, &c.' the prices quoted contain unusual uniformities, suggesting a failure to maintain the steady correspondence he desired.[26] Indeed the convention of repeating the previous week's prices when no new prices had been received was actually encouraged by some correspondents. The apothecary and botanist, Samuel Dale, wrote to Houghton from Braintree offering that 'If the prices of our market will be acceptable to you I shall send them every weeke . . . which when there is not any alteration in the Prizes shall not need be sent you every weeke, but may be continued until alteration of prizes of which I shall inform you.'[27] Braintree prices appeared regularly until April 1698.[28] Other slip-ups might also occur. Dale's letter is annotated, 'pray put in the Prices mentioned in L' (presumably an instruction from Houghton to the printer) but the prices of barley and rye mentioned in a PS did not appear in the paper for that week.[29] These surviving letters indicate how current, or out-of-date, the prices in the paper were. Dale's letter dated 8 March 1693 gave the prices from 'this days market' and were printed in the paper published on Friday 10 March.[30] Saunders's letter dated 20 March 1693 gave the prices from the previous Tuesday's market on 14 March and appeared over two weeks later in the paper on 31 March.[31]

These weekly accounts were, according to Houghton, writing in the first issue, 'for the Advantage of Tenant, Landlord, Corn-Merchant, Meal-man, Baker, Brewer, Feeder of Cattel, Farmer, Maulster, Grazier, Seller and Buyer of Coals, Hop-Merchant, Soap-Boyler, Tallow Chandler, Wool-Merchant, their Customers'.[32] In the second issue he spelt out the nature of the advantage: 'The Landlord and Tenant may know, upon good grounds, when 'tis fit to raise or abate Rent. The Corn Merchant, &c. mentiond in my last Paper, may, upon good grounds, foresee when 'tis best to buy or sell.' Good grounds meant not only prices but exact prices as Houghton endeavoured to achieve and readers well knew. The steward, William Gilpin, writing from an estate in Whitehaven to his employer in January 1698, for example, considered the

malt in Melton Mowbray had been listed in the *Collection* of 17 Mar. 1693 as 26s. 8d. Saunders's programmes for the development of trade and husbandry had a lot in common with Houghton's: B. Capp, *Astrology and the popular press: English almanacs*, London 1979, 104–5.

26 *CIHT*, 3 June 1698; J. A. Chartres, 'The marketing of agricultural produce', in J. Thirsk (ed.), *The agrarian history of England and Wales*, V: *1640–1750* II: *Agrarian change*, Cambridge 1985, 457.

27 S. Dale to J. Houghton, 8 Mar. 1693, BL, MS Stowe 747, fo. 13r. I mistakenly dated this letter to Mar. 1692 in Glaisyer, 'Readers', 242, 250 n. 41.

28 They are last listed in *CIHT*, 22 Apr. 1698.

29 Dale to Houghton, 8 Mar. 1693, BL, MS Stowe 747, fo. 13r.

30 Ibid.

31 R. Saunders to Houghton, 20 Mar. 1693, ibid. fo. 14r; *CIHT*, 31 Mar. 1693. The market prices listed in a letter sent to Houghton from Arthur Charlett in Oxford do not appear in the paper: A. Ch[arlet]t to Houghton, 28 Mar. 1694, BL, MS Add. 4275, fo. 101r.

32 *CIHT*, 30 Mar. 1692.

possibility that the prices may not have been accurate: 'Some of Haughton's weekly papers have of late given us such an account of the prices of coals at Falmouth and other places in that chanel that (if they be to be depended on) seem to give good encouragement to us to send coals thither.'[33]

For the gentlemen readers of Houghton's periodical, these prices were supposedly useful, but only indirectly: 'The Gentleman that sends to Market to buy Houshold-Necessaries, may nearly guess whether he is abused by the Ignorance or Dishonesty of his Servant.'[34] Over a decade later Roger North gave similar reasons for his gentlemen readers to understand bookkeeping.

For the first volume of the *Collection* the papers were published on Saturdays and on Wednesdays. On the reverse of the Wednesday issue appeared the table of agricultural prices. On the reverse of the Saturday issue appeared, as announced in the proposal, 'An Account of Goods imported and exported from the Custom-House of London, to draw the particulars into gross Sums, in order to examin the Expence and foreign Vent of each Commodity.'[35] Houghton described the alternation between the table of provincial prices and the import and export figures was so 'that the Country may be expert in the London-Trade, to make amends for what the City learns from it'.[36] The monthly summary of the custom house bills was compiled from the printed daily bills produced by the custom house which listed exported goods, imported goods and goods imported for re-export from the port of London and was reproduced in Houghton's paper over four Saturday issues. Although this part of Houghton's enterprise was not continued beyond the first volume of the paper Houghton did devote considerable attention to explaining what the bills were and how and why different people might find them and his summaries of them useful. His discussion reveals his attitude to the dissemination of commercial information as well as his aspirations in undertaking to promote it and is therefore worth considering in some detail.

Having explained the content of the bills: 'In them (beside the Quantity of Goods) is the Name of the Merchant, and of the Place from whence the Goods come, or are to go', and indicating that they were a specialist (and expensive at 40s.) publication largely for merchants, Houghton went on to consider their usefulness. 'The Uses of these Bills are very great, they tell every one the proper Market where to carry such Goods they abound with, or where to fetch the Goods they want.' Houghton noted that not all agreed with him that this sort of information should be so widely dispersed: 'Some are against these Bills; but by the same reason a Shop-keeper should keep his Shop shut, his Goods covered, be against having Lists of Catalogues, or scorn to tell his Customers what he has, unless it be asked for.' In Houghton's opinion, the bills offered valuable information to the whole population, more

---

[33] William Gilpin to John Lowther, 5 Jan. 1698, in Hainsworth, *Sir John Lowther*, 471.
[34] *CIHT*, 6 Apr. 1692.
[35] Ibid. 30 Mar. 1692.
[36] Ibid. 20 Apr. 1692.

people should know of their existence and this was one of the goals of his publishing enterprise:

> Surely the more Trade is known, the larger it will be, and a great Trade is better for a Nation than a small one; if so, 'tis pity the whole Nation is not better acquainted with these Bills; however I'll strive to make it so.
>
> And that these may be more bought and seen, that Trade may be better understood, and the whole Kingdom made as one trading City, is the Design of these my Papers.[37]

In the following Saturday's paper he worked his way through different segments of the population to argue for the universal advantage of knowing the custom house bills. The court could use the figures to calculate whether customs had been paid on the whole quantities of various goods imported, and whether a greater consumption ought to be encouraged. 'The Parliament, by knowing what goes out, may lay on or take off a Duty, and so increase or decrease the Trade.' For the 'Political-Arithmetician' the figures could be used to calculate the 'Wealth and Strength of the Nation', and the 'Philosopher or Naturalist' could enquire after each of the things traded and 'learn the Explanation of each particular'. The quantity of goods usually consumed would help 'the Merchant and other inquisitive Trader' to know 'whither 'tis best to bring in more, or there's too much already for their Advantage'. The value of these lists for the country shopkeeper, the farmer, the tenant and the housewife, who 'will know when to lay in their Store of Sugar, Plums, Rice, and other Necessaries, and the best time of buying Oranges and Limons', were also discussed.[38]

Overall Houghton may have been aiming to convince readers of the significance of the daily bills but much of his supporting evidence drew upon his compilation of the previous month's figures. In demonstrating the value of these export figures for parliament he noted: 'this last Month was shipt out 11 Ton of Beef and Pork; now I should Quære, Whither by giving some Allowance, as is done in Corn, it might not greatly increase the Exportation of that Commodity'. His comparatively cheap compilation of monthly figures he claimed might still be valuable for those who subscribed to the more expensive daily bills: 'And surely whoever shall think it worth while to pay 40s the Year for the Custom House Bills, will not grudge 2d the Week to have each particular cast up to his hand.' Not only would the compiled figures appeal to a wide range of occupations but also to the country as a whole for 'tho this be but one Port, yet 'twill give light to the knowledge of the Trade of the whole Kingdom, when 'tis known, that London pays about twice as much Custom as all the rest of the Ports of England'.[39] As he had written in the

---

37 Ibid. 27 Apr. 1692.
38 Ibid. 30 Apr. 1692.
39 Ibid.

second issue of the periodical, he hoped that there were 'few People in the Nation, who first or last may not be advantag'd by' the papers.[40]

As Houghton was concerned to give exact prices of corn and other agricultural goods from provincial markets, so he hoped the figures from the custom house bills were correct. He considered potential inaccuracies in the daily bills upon which his monthly summaries were based, and dismissed them as insignificant: 'Whether the Merchants, for their private Gain, enter to one Place, when they mean another, or, by favour, the mention of some Goods be left out, the Merchant must answer. But I presume, such doings, if any, are very trivial to the bulk of things; However the Bills must be my Rule.'[41]

Although the weekly instalments of the monthly summaries of the daily custom house bills compiled by Houghton were omitted when the paper was reconceived in its second volume, Houghton makes much use of yearly compilations of the daily bills for the year 1694.[42] Following on from his essays on the shipping trade to and from London in 1694 he gave in successive essays an account 'of all the Goods imported that Year, and mentioned in the Bills of Entry, with the Quantities imported from each Place' with 'Notes Natural and Political, striving to make it the best Account of Trade, upon the best and most sure Foot that ever has been yet publish'd and I could hear of' for the 'Benefit of my Country.'[43] For at least a year after the systematic listing of exports and imports ended, Houghton regularly listed brief details of some goods imported including the importer's name in the advertisement section of the paper.[44] In July 1695, for example, he gave a list titled 'Lately were Imported' which began 'Amber-Beads, by Phil. Grynes. / Candy'd Nutmegs, by De. / Lime- Juice, by Oliver Carr. / Oil of Mace, by John Pym.'[45]

By incorporating current information that in its original newspaper context was 'instantly ephemeral' into his history project, Houghton was transforming commerce into something worthy of study.[46] He told readers how in different ways the monthly summaries of the custom house bills might be useful, and he later demonstrated how a yearly summary of the imports and exports compiled from these bills was an integral part of a larger project to give an account of trade.

His agenda extended beyond trade and husbandry, to include the new financial world of the stock market. From the very first issue Houghton listed

---

[40] Ibid. 13 Apr. 1692.

[41] Ibid. 27 Apr. 1692.

[42] Whether Houghton compiled these figures himself is unclear. McCusker notes that from the mid-1690s annual data was compiled from the bills of entry in the office of the Inspector General of Imports and Exports: 'Business press', 209.

[43] *CIHT*, 25 Oct. 1695. The shipping trade was discussed in issues dating from 25 Oct. 1695 until 28 Feb. 1696. The imports were discussed from 6 Mar. 1696.

[44] This item appeared in the paper from Aug. 1694.

[45] *CIHT*, 26 July 1695.

[46] The phrase 'instantly ephemeral' is borrowed from McCusker: 'Business press', 206.

stock prices, which he termed 'actions'.[47] In the early issues the share prices of around a dozen companies were listed underneath the table of agricultural product prices on the reverse of the first page. In May 1694 the table was expanded to include a greater range of companies for 'A great many desire a List of Stocks'. However, prices were given for only about a dozen of the more than fifty companies listed, accompanied by an invitation for those that 'desire the Values' of all the stocks on the list may have them 'Published . . . on very reasonable Terms'.[48] Houghton realised that there was extra money to be made by segmenting the market. Most readers, he assumed, only wanted to know the prices of the principal stocks, but some would pay a premium for knowing the whole range he listed and presumably the additional figures could be added to the relevant copies by hand. Using a different typeface and asterisks Houghton made a distinction in his list between those companies that were established by charter and those by patent.[49] After the first five years of the periodical's publication prices were again quoted for only a handful of companies and the list was moved to the front page.[50] At times he supplemented the prices of the stocks with other announcements about relevant developments: 'Since I last week printed the List of Stocks, I am inform'd that there is great hope of Gain from a Spanish Wreck, as yet very little talk'd on; and I am desired to let the World know it.'[51]

When Houghton started his paper in April 1692 he claimed that those who wanted to know the prices of stocks could either visit Garraways or purchase his paper. There was probably no other published listing of stock prices until John Castaing, Sr's paper, the *Course of Exchange, and other things*, appeared in October 1696, or March 1697 at the latest when it was advertised in the *Collection*.[52] Presumably Houghton was getting his prices from Garraways, and continued to do so even after Castaing's paper was published.[53] Whatever his source, his reporting was not always reliable as the price he quoted for bank stock remained the same for the first fourteen weeks of 1701, suggesting a 'lapse of attention on the part of the editor of the *Collections*'.[54] A single price was given against each stock (other listings in the period sometimes gave a range) and they were rarely dated; only in some of the Friday issues of the first volume were dates given and here it was a Wednesday.[55]

[47] *CIHT*, 30 Mar. 1692.
[48] Ibid. 11 May 1694.
[49] 'Great Letters by Charter. (*) by Patent', ibid. 15 June 1694.
[50] *CIHT*, 4 Dec. 1696, 22 Jan. 1697.
[51] Ibid. 18 May 1694.
[52] McCusker and Gravesteijn, *Journalism*, 312–13.
[53] John Castaing, *The Course of Exchange*. The prices listed in the *Collection* do not match those that appeared in Castaing's paper.
[54] Scott, *Constitution and finance*, iii. 217.
[55] *CIHT*, 16 June 1693.

Houghton imagined that the price of actions would be useful for those who could not go to Garraway's coffee-house each day, and that by being

> satisfi'd once a Week how it is . . . the whole Kingdom may reap Advantage by those Trades; Also they may learn hence some of the Cunning of Merchandizing, and have this Advantage, by laying their Monies there, in one or two days time they may sell, and have their Money to supply their wants at any time. Without doubt, if those Trades were known, 'twould be a great Advantage to the Kingdom; only I must caution Beginners to be very wary, for there are many cunning Artists among them.[56]

Similarly, in his printed proposal for the periodical, Houghton had emphasised the importance of disseminating stock prices to the provinces: the *Collection* was 'design'd, for Incouragement of those at distance to turn Merchants, and to inform them how their Stock goes'.[57] Many readers were slower to grasp the opportunity 'to turn Merchants' than Houghton hoped and in March 1693 he felt he had to explain to readers what actions were:

> Actions signifie Shares in Companies: For instance, If ten Men raise 10l. a piece to carry on a Trade; each 10l. is called an Action or Share; if they have hopes of great Gain, they will not sell their Share for 10l. If they fear Loss, they'l sell for less; and so Actions rise or fall, according to hopes or fears. This buying and selling of Actions is one of the great Trades now on foot . . . I find a great many understand not this affair, therefore I write this.[58]

He included this explanation again a few months later.[59] The following year he wrote a far more detailed explanation of the stock market which included discussions of some of the sophisticated mechanisms employed by the dealers, which perhaps indicated that there were then fewer who 'understand not this affair'. Following reports on earth, water, air, fire, fermentation, wheat and kine, Houghton presented accounts of joint-stocks and stockjobbing in his leading essays, as 'a little Diversion from Natural History, and the usefulness of the thing it self', as part of his undertaking 'to impart to others some Misteries in Trade, and to rectifie Men's Judgments, whom I find running into Errors and Mistakes'. Citing Descartes in Latin, Houghton requested his readers to 'lay aside all Prejudice and Partiality' before considering this topic. He went on to defend the practice of stockjobbing as useful and lawful, and to condemn the abuses committed by some traders:

> I know many worthy Persons of great Honour and Probity, who deal in Stocks, that do abominate the least unjust Action, and would not for the World have got an ill gotten Penny among the rest of their Estates; and it is a great

---

56 Ibid. 6 Apr. 1692.
57 Houghton, *Proposal*, 1.
58 *CIHT*, 17 Mar. 1693.
59 Ibid. 7 July 1693.

hardship on such Gentlemen to undergo the Censures of Mankind, who inveigh against all Traders and Trading in Stock, tho' at the same time they know little or nothing of it.[60]

In six subsequent issues he explained the 'plain, honest Proceeding' of establishing a joint-stock company, the bargaining process (including evaluations of the risks involved and the potential rewards), specimen contracts for refuse of shares and putting stock, as well as 'the Advantages [that] may accrue to the Nation' by various companies.[61] Houghton later referred to these accounts (and defences) of the trade in stocks as 'the History of Stocks, and Stock-Jobbing' and as such they sat alongside his histories of husbandry and trade.[62] As Houghton had set out, and to a large extent realised, his goal of epitomising the writings of Fellows of the Royal Society for the 'Plain Man', he had also explained the complexities of the stock market.[63] He saw his role not only as a provider of current and useful information (in this case stock prices) but also as a teacher and defender of the market. He wanted to stimulate both investment in the stock market and the formation of joint-stock companies, all as part of his project for the improvement of trade and husbandry.

The *Collection* was rich in other materials relating to the financial and commercial revolutions. Beginning in 1694 it listed funds deposited in, and advanced by, the exchequer, and from January 1695 onwards included rates of exchange at a dozen foreign cities.[64] Houghton also listed the prices of goods (although sometimes only meat) in London until April 1697.[65] He considered including shipping information believing "twill be very useful for Merchants to have in their Counting-Houses an Account of Ships taking in Goods, and their designed time of Sayling'.[66] However, he never systematically included such listings, only occasionally listing cargoes of ships recently arrived in London.[67] Houghton, who operated his business from the heart of the City, in Bartholomew Lane behind the Royal Exchange and later in Grace Church Street, advertised his own investment brokering services in

60 Ibid. 8 June 1694.

61 Ibid. 15 June–20 July 1694.

62 Ibid. 27 July 1694. In 1697 he reiterated his support for joint-stock enterprises in his account of copper (25 June 1697).

63 Ibid. 30 Mar. 1692, 7 Nov. 1701, 28 July 1693.

64 Exchange rates were already listed in commodity price currents published in London and in Castaing, Sr's paper: McCusker and Gravesteijn, *Journalism*, 316.

65 Although the listing was similar to contemporary price currents, given their rarity, it is impossible to say whether Houghton was lifting his listings from other publications. However, comparing the goods listed in the few surviving copies of *Whiston's Weekly Remembrancer* with Houghton's prices in the relevant weeks, reveals a close correlation, but not an exact match.

66 *CIHT*, 19 Apr. 1695. Earlier Houghton had asked readers whether they wanted such information (28 July 1693).

67 For example ibid. 27 Oct., 24 Nov. 1693, 3 Aug., 30 Nov. 1694.

the periodical, offering, for example, that 'If any want Lutestring Shares, I can tell how they may be furnisht.'[68] For nearly eighteen months, beginning in November 1695, Houghton provided a directory service listing in rotation mostly London-based physicians, gardeners, lawyers, schools, public notaries, woodmongers, and also exchange brokers. The *Collection* also carried advertisements for meetings of the East India Company, for the services of John Castaing, Sr, who 'at Jonathan's Coffee-house, or Exchange, buys and sells all Blank and Benefit Tickets; and all other Stocks and Shares', and proposals and developments of numerous lotteries.[69] Amongst his many brokering services Houghton negotiated various commercial exchanges. He offered, for example, to help 'to Mortgages for Money, and Money for Morgages [sic] of considerable Values in several Parts of England'.[70] And for 'Any Gentleman that hath a Thousand Pounds to dispose of, if he pleases to come to me, I will inform him how he may be secured of Ten per Cent profit for his Money for Three Years.'[71]

At the foot of the reverse page many of the early issues referred readers to the previous issue: 'Whoever compares this with the former, will see the Rise and Fall of Markets.'[72] This was in part an explanation as he added 'it is easier than to make Marks' which was presumably a reference to Whiston's *Merchants Remembrancer*, a London commodity price current published at this time, in which alongside each commodity a symbol indicated whether the price was rising, falling, had reached its highest price or remained the same compared to the previous week's price.[73] Even if this instruction was only directed towards the listing of the prices of London commodities it might apply to all the prices given on this side of the paper – the agricultural prices in provincial centres and the share prices. Houghton was not only teaching his readers that it was the rise and the fall in prices that mattered but encouraging them to treat his periodical as a serial publication where much of the value was in considering each issue in the context of a growing set of volumes. As with his summaries of the monthly and yearly figures of goods imported into and exported out of London, it was the collecting, comparing and compiling of commercial information, and not simply the current figures, that were crucial to Houghton's project to improve husbandry and trade.

---

68  Ibid. 17 Mar. 1693, 27 Oct. 1699, 2 Feb. 1700, 17 Aug. 1694.
69  Ibid. 12 Jan. 1694, 4 Jan. 1695.
70  Ibid. 12 June 1696.
71  Ibid. 2 Feb. 1694.
72  The phrase first appeared ibid. 5 Apr. 1692 and for the last time on 28 July 1693.
73  McCusker and Gravesteijn, *Journalism*, 298, 304–5.

## 'of general use to the public': *The British Mercury, 1710–15*

Like Houghton's *Collection*, the *British Mercury*, which was published by the Sun Fire Office insurance company, was not a specialist trading newspaper but one that provided current trading information and aimed to promote trade to a wide range of readers. It was launched in 1710 when the Sun Fire Office took over Charles Povey's insurance business.[74] Povey had been publishing the *General Remark on Trade* as an integral part of his business since 1705 and so in some respects the *British Mercury* was the reincarnation of that paper. Povey's *General Remark* also had quite a lot in common with John Houghton's *Collection*, which had ceased publication in September 1703.[75] As will be seen in what follows there were many similarities, partly through the link provided by Povey, between the *Collection* and the *Mercury* both in the context of the agendas they pursued and their content.[76]

Charles Povey's *General Remark on Trade* in 1705 was initially an advertising sheet, apparently with a circulation of 3,500, which was delivered free to London's 'Places of publick resort' – shops, taverns, and coffee-houses – where it was to be left on display and then sent to the provinces in country parcels.[77] According to Povey's May 1706 proposals for a life insurance scheme the paper was 'look'd upon by all Judicious and Unprejudiced Persons to be of great Use and Advantage to the Publick, for the more effectual promoting of Trade and Business'. Those subscribers who took out his life insurance policies 'as are come to full Ripeness of Age, so as in some measure to understand Trade and Business' were to have the paper delivered to their houses three times a week, and others could buy it for a penny an issue.[78] Povey was optimistic about the paper's success, imagining that the paper would sell six times as well as the 'common News Papers and other Pamphlets, which only serve to amuse the People, and breed Animosities among Parties'. The profits from the papers went towards an almshouse and

---

[74] The best account of Povey's businesses and the paper is in Dickson, *Sun Insurance*, ch. ii. See also F. B. Relton, *An account of the fire insurance companies associations institutions projects and schemes established and projected in Great Britain and Ireland during the 17th and 18th centuries including the Sun Fire Office: also of Charles Povey the projector of that office his writings and schemes*, London 1893, 476–80.

[75] The last issue of Houghton's paper was numbered 583 and dated Friday 24 Sept. 1703. He gave the demands of his apothecary business, and his coffee, tea and chocolate selling business as the reasons why he 'cannot without great Inconvenience to my private Affairs, which must not be neglected, spare Time to carry on this History so well as I would do': *CIHT*, 24 Sept. 1703.

[76] It is difficult to say whether or not Povey's publication filled the gap left by the cessation of Houghton's, or even to establish any substantive like between them. However, I do like Perry Gauci's notion that Houghton's 'mantle as trade journalist' was taken up by Charles Povey (and Daniel Defoe): *Politics of trade*, 165.

[77] *The General Remark on Trade*, 20 Nov. 1705.

[78] Charles Povey, *Proposals for raising a fund of two thousand pounds*, London 1706.

providing education and clothing for orphans.[79] By July 1707 the paper included many of the features of Houghton's paper: the course of the exchange, the prices of stocks, the custom house bills, moneys advanced and paid off at the exchequer and numerous advertisements as well as an essay that reflected on commercial issues. Povey also included shipping news, substantial coverage of foreign news, descriptions of English counties (including the character of their trades) and summaries of trading regulations.[80] Povey was hoping for a wide audience and justified the inclusion of the foreign news so that the paper 'may be universally approved of, not only by those who are concern'd in Trade and Business, but likewise become acceptable to all Persons of whatsoever Rank or Degree'.[81]

When the Sun Fire Office Company (also known as the Company of London Insurers) took over Charles Povey's insurance business in April 1710 they also took over his publishing enterprise. Povey agreed not to publish another paper, and the company decided to publish a thrice-weekly paper, the British Mercury, instead of the General Remark on Trade, which would be distributed to its policy-holders.[82] Although it had a different layout, the Mercury had much in common with Povey's publication. It was a single sheet format and included listings of stock prices, the course of the exchange, commodity prices in London, moneys advanced and paid off at the exchequer, shipping news and advertisements on the reverse. On the front was usually a summary of foreign news. In August 1712, after the passing of the Stamp Act, it became a weekly newspaper published in a pamphlet format and it continued to be published until 1716 when it was replaced by a quarterly publication, the Historical Register, which was also distributed to policy-holders. For over a year a French version of the paper was also produced in London, Le Mercure Britannique, about which little is known largely because no copies survive. Producing the papers was a central part of the company's business in its first years over which it took much care. The paper was used to promote the company's insurance services and was a vehicle for announcements to be made to its customers but it was not a free sheet. Policy-holders paid an extra 6d. on top of their quarterly premiums for fire insurance on their goods or buildings to receive the newspapers; most chose to take the paper and it obtained a considerable circulation. We must therefore take the paper seriously in the wider context of publishing in this period.

The Mercury was delivered 'gratis' three times a week by the company's walkers who were also paid to issue policies, collect the quarterly payments and put up the fire marks.[83] Walkers were paid 8s. a week for delivering the

---

79 The General Remark on Trade, 7 July 1707.
80 Ibid.
81 Ibid.
82 Dickson, Sun Insurance, 30; Relton, Fire insurance, 301.
83 The British Apollo was also delivered in this way in the years 1708–11: W. F Belcher,

first issues of the paper but by November of the first year of publication this was lowered to 3s. a week with bonuses for those who sold policies. Following complaints from the walkers (two threatened to resign) and the 'Inconveniences' of administering such a system the company returned to a regular wage of 6s. a week.[84] The number of subscribers to the newspaper increased and by January 1712 some walkers 'had too many Customers to serve Which makes The Service too late'. Prompt service mattered so extra walkers were hired and existing walks were divided.[85] In July 1712, in anticipation of the paper becoming a weekly, the company renegotiated with the ten walkers then employed, half of whom agreed to the new rate of 2s. 6d. a week and the remainder were replaced.[86] Customers 'neglected' by the walkers were encouraged to report to the company and were promised 'due satisfaction'.[87] The company's minutes record the dismissing of the walker, Thomas Baker, for example, who 'did not serve the Customer with the Mercury constantly' and against whom there were complaints daily, including that from Mr Hamilton of Chelsea who had received only one issue in eight days.[88] Although historians have established that women had an important role in the sale and distribution of London papers in this period, all the walkers who delivered the British Mercury were men.[89]

Although the company was to claim in August 1712 that the Mercury was 'never . . . design'd for, nor expos'd to common Sale', those who did not have insurance policies with the company could subscribe.[90] In December 1710 the paper carried an announcement that the Mercury was being delivered to some in London without the company's knowledge and requested that those who would like to receive the paper without insurance inform the company.[91] In 1711 it was advertised that subscribers could pay an annual subscription of 10s. to receive the paper without having to take out a policy with the company.[92] For a very short period the paper was in fact 'expos'd to common

---

'The sale and distribution of the British Apollo', in R. P. Bond (ed.), Studies in the early English periodical, Chapel Hill 1957, 77–8.

[84] Sun Fire Office copy book of orders, 1710–15, GL, MS 11931/1, p. 3, fos 19v, 25r (the first part of this manuscript is paginated and the remainder is foliated). A bonus payment of 6d. for each policy procured was introduced on 24 Oct. 1711 (fo. 52v) but was not accompanied by a reduction in wages. Walkers were also often paid extra money having collected the quarterly subscriptions.

[85] GL, MS 11931/1, fos 65v–66r. Extra walkers were again hired in Aug. 1713 following complaints that 'the Papers are not delivered in a reasonable time' (fo. 111v).

[86] Ibid. fos 82v–83r.

[87] BM, 8, 31 Aug. 1711.

[88] GL, MS 11931/1, fo. 58r.

[89] Hunt, 'Hawkers, bawlers, and mercuries', 46; T. O'Malley, 'Religion and the newspaper press, 1660–1685: a study of the London Gazette', in M. Harris and A. Lee (eds), The press in English society from the seventeenth to nineteenth centuries, London 1986, 31.

[90] BM, 2 Aug. 1712.

[91] Ibid. 20 Dec 1710.

[92] Ibid. 15 Jan. 1711.

sale'; the company agreed in October 1711 to the selling of 'Mercurys . . . by publick or particular hawkers at the rate of Others papers of news' and in November it was advertised that the paper was sold by 'J. Baker, at the Black-Boy, in Pater-Noster-Row' for a penny.[93] By the end of the month however, the company decided (without recording their reasons) that this advertisement should no longer appear.[94]

Although figures do not survive few, if any, probably chose to subscribe to the paper alone, for aside from a one-off payment of a 1s. stamp duty on the insurance policy it cost as much per year to subscribe to the paper alone as it did to have a policy with the company and receive the paper.[95] Policy-holders paid 2s. 6d. a quarter for their policy and their subscription to the paper. Those who only wanted their goods or buildings insured and did not want the paper could make a saving of 6d. a quarter. Most of the company's customers, however, chose to take the paper with their policy: committee minutes dated 8 November 1710 record that less than eight months after the paper was established the company had 684 customers, 608 of whom took the paper.[96] Almost 90 per cent of the company's customers, then, took the paper. To put this figure in perspective, in June 1710 just under 6,500 copies of the *London Gazette* circulated each week of which less than 5,500 were sold; the remainder were given away.[97]

In the subsequent months the number of policy-holders the company had grew, and consequently so too did the number of subscribers to the paper. The company believed that they had a captive audience for their insurance policies and consequently also for the paper. The first issue of the *Mercury* published after the Stamp Act came into force foretold the demise of other papers but heralded its own survival: 'its Being does not so much depend on Chance, and the inconstant Humour of the Multitude. It is to be believ'd there will be insuring as long as there are Goods and Houses to insure, and this Office having met with sufficient Encouragement, not to question its Establishment, the Mercury, which stands upon the same Foundation, may well promise it self a Continuance.'[98]

The 'Continuance' can be charted in some detail using the available subscription figures. In the last four issues of the *British Mercury* in 1712 the company published a list of the names of policy-holders who also received the paper.[99] In total there were 2,450 names listed which was a dramatic increase

---

93 GL, MS 11931/1, fo. 51v; BM, 26, 28 Nov. 1711.
94 GL, MS 11931/1, fo. 57v.
95 BM, 15 Jan. 1711.
96 GL, MS 11931/1, fo. 20r. Although the figures given in the minutes are not transparent I have assumed that they can be interpreted in the same way as the figures presented in the minutes of 17 Mar. 1713.
97 J. R. Sutherland, 'The circulation of newspapers and literary periodicals, 1700–30', *The Library* 4th ser. xv (1934), 114.
98 BM, 2 Aug. 1712.
99 Ibid. 10, 17, 24, 31 Dec. 1712.

on the figures for November 1710. How does this compare to other papers? Generally little is known of the number of newspapers sold. Print-run figures for Houghton's *Collection*, for example, can only be guessed at, despite his claim that by July 1693 it was the 'first Handmaid' to the *Gazette*.[100] However, for twenty-five weeks in the period 1712–14 records of the purchases of stamped paper have survived from which circulation figures for stamped newspapers can be estimated.[101] The *Mercury*'s circulation in 1712 exceeded the estimated circulation of most of these stamped newspapers.[102] In the six weeks after 1 August 1712 (when the Stamp Act took effect) it appears that only four stamped papers maintained an average circulation per issue of over 2,500.[103] The semi-weekly *Evening Post* and the tri-weekly *Post-Boy* and *Post-Man* probably each had a circulation of 3,500–4,500 per issue.[104] The circulation of the twice-weekly *London Gazette* is harder to estimate from these records because not all issues were printed on stamped paper, but Henry Snyder suggests that circulation figures probably ranged from just under 2,500 to nearly 5,000.[105] The Sun Fire Office's business continued to grow and by the middle of March the following year the *Mercury*'s circulation was 2,535 and the company had an additional 189 policy-holders who did not take the paper.[106] In February 1714 a list of policy-holders was again printed in the paper: they numbered 3,295.[107] Assuming that the percentage of policy-holders who chose to opt out of also taking the paper was fairly similar to that in November 1710 and March 1713 this probably represented a circulation of around 3,000.[108] By April 1715 the company claimed that it had almost 6,000 policies 'being delivered' and if most continued also to

---

[100] *CIHT*, 28 July 1693.

[101] H. L. Snyder, 'The circulation of newspapers in the reign of Queen Anne', *The Library* 5th ser. xxiii (1969), 206–35, and 'A further note on the circulation of newspapers in the reign of Queen Anne', *The Library* 5th ser. xxxi (1976), 387–9; J. M. Price, 'A note on the circulation of the London press, 1704–1714', *Bulletin of the Institute of Historical Research* xxxi (1958), 215–24. As will be discussed below the *British Mercury* was not a stamped paper.

[102] This comparison admittedly does not compare like with like since the figures for the *Mercury* relate to Dec. 1712 and the stamp duty records relate to Aug. and Sept. 1712.

[103] The details of the Stamp Act and how it affected the *Mercury* will be discussed below.

[104] Price, 'Circulation', table I at p. 220. Note that Price's calculations are based on the erroneous assumptions that the *Evening Post* was published three times a week (in fact it was a semi-weekly) and that *The Spectator* was published only once a week (in fact it was a thrice-weekly). See also Snyder, 'Circulation', 211.

[105] Snyder, 'Circulation', 218.

[106] GL, MS 11931/1, fo. 99r.

[107] *BM*, 24 Feb., 3, 10, 24 Mar. 1714. Unlike the list printed in 1712 (which included only those policy-holders who also took the paper) the list printed in 1714 was apparently a list of 'the Persons insur'd by the Sun Fire-Office'.

[108] In Nov. 1710 and Mar. 1713 89% and 93% of the policy-holders, respectively, took the paper suggesting a range of between 2,933 and 3,064 policy-holders who took the paper in Feb. 1714.

subscribe to the paper then the *Mercury* may have had a larger circulation than all the stamped newspapers produced at this time.[109]

We know very little about the identities of readers of newspapers in this period. For Houghton's *Collection*, for example, only fragmentary evidence of a few readers survives and the rest can only be surmised from the range of advertisements placed in the paper which suggests that servants and apprentices had access to the paper, as well as members of more wealthy middling sorts and elites. As much more can be said about the readers of the *Mercury* it is worth pausing to analyse the list of subscribers given in the issues of December 1712 and the list of policy-holders given in February 1714. Amongst the 2,450 subscribers to the paper in December 1710, 138 women were listed, and 213 women amongst the 3,295 policy- holders in February 1714, suggesting that around 6 per cent of subscribers and policy-holders, respectively, were women. Both lists included titles and aside from a few listed as duke, countess, earl, more than 10 per cent of the 1714 list was described as gent. or esq. In the 1714 list, for those without titles an occupation was given for men and for those women who were not listed as spinsters or widows. The occupational categories are problematic as many refer to the company of which the person was a freeman and may have had little to do with their livelihood; but some categories did indicate an occupation rather than a company. Ninety were listed as merchants with another eighteen listed as coal, wine, timber, brandy, orange, Virginia, hop or hair merchants. Most were listed as traders of the middling sorts: cheesemongers, victuallers, linen drapers, mercers, weavers, bakers, carpenters, vintners, apothecaries, confectioners, and inn keepers.[110]

Of course, we cannot be sure that all those listed in 1714 took the paper as this was a list of those who insured their goods or buildings with the Sun Fire Office. However, some of these names also appeared in the 1712 list which we know was a list of those who subscribed to the paper as well as had a policy. Fifty-three of the ninety merchants listed in the 1714 list as policy-holders were listed in the 1712 list of subscribers to the paper.[111] If merchant in this case means overseas trader then the paper was useful not only to those middling sorts of traders but also to those who are usually

---

[109] BM, 23 Apr. 1715. As the latest figures for the sales of stamped paper in this period relate to the week 27 Apr.–3 May 1714 it is difficult to know the extent of the *Mercury's* dominance of the market in 1715. In the spring of 1714 possibly only the *Evening Post* had a circulation greater than 7,000. Taking the other sales figures for this paper into account however, its average circulation was probably considerably lower: Snyder, 'Circulation', 225.

[110] See also M. Harris, *London newspapers in the age of Walpole: a study of the origins of the modern English press*, London 1987, 192.

[111] We would not expect all the names that appeared in the 1714 list also to appear in the 1712 list partly because many new policies and subscriptions were issued in the intervening period (and if not all of the 1712 subscribers renewed their policies the difference in the number of policy-holders between 1712 and 1714 would be greater).

associated with the more specialist sort of commercial journalism. Likewise, those with strong associations with newspapers and information networks also appear to have subscribed to the paper. Of the twenty-eight coffee-sellers and coffee-men in the 1714 list at least fourteen appeared in the 1712 list, eight of the twenty-six booksellers, and seventeen of the thirty stationers. Perhaps the paper could have been found in some London coffee-houses and bookshops. If the newspaper was read in coffee-houses then there is good reason to believe that the readership extended beyond the policy-holders.[112] More persuasively for the argument that the paper's readership extended beyond subscribers and policy-holders was the fact that those policy-holders who held more than one policy were given the option of having additional papers delivered to 'any Friend's House, as desir'd, within any of the Walks or Divisions belonging to the Company'.[113] In 1712 there were fifty-eight policy-holders who held more than one policy, and in 1714 almost 150 policy-holders. Even if only some of these subscribers took the company up on its offer to have their extra papers delivered to a friend then it still represents a not insignificant number of readers who did not hold policies with the company.

Printing lists of subscribers and policy-holders followed the practices of the East India Company, the Bank of England, the land bank and the government, all of which had printed lists of investors, often including titles and sometimes sums invested, from the 1690s onwards. Like these the Sun Fire Office lists served as testimonials to the quality and value of both the insurance policy and the *British Mercury*. Probably in hopeful anticipation of the sway status might have with prospective investors in the 1714 listing, those with titles were placed first under each letter heading. The company recognised that printing 'the severall subscribers Names in the Mercury Alphabetically would be Advantagious to the Compa' and also ordered that 1,250 copies of the 1714 list be printed separately for their use, presumably to distribute to likely clients.[114] Copies of the paper were also used to promote the company: in the first weeks of publication issues were distributed to those who were not subscribers and later in 1710 company proposals were delivered with an issue of the *Mercury* to every member of the Commons and Lords.[115] The printed style of the *Mercury* was used to characterise other printed promotional material for the company, as in April 1711 when the Sun Fire Office ordered 'a Postscript to be published as occasion shall happen with the title of the Mercury & the usual Avertissements for policies' and in August

---

[112] Pincus, ' "Coffee politicians" ', 819, 833; Klein, 'Coffee-house civility', 36–7.

[113] Sun Fire Office, *Proposals set forth by the company of the Sun-Fire-Office*, London 1712. A similar provision can also be found in article four of the 1710 proposals: Sun Fire Office, *Proposals set forth by the company of London-insurers*, London (16 Aug.) 1710.

[114] GL, MS 11931/1, fo. 124r. No copy of the separate printed list has been found.

[115] Ibid. p. 6, fo. 21v.

that year 40,000 proposals were ordered to be printed 'in the Caracter of the British Mercury'.[116]

The Sun Fire Office's business was centred on London but from its first year there were policy-holders and subscribers in the other parts of the country. In June 1710 twenty-five copies of the *Mercury* were to be sent to Bristol three times a week and at about the same time papers were also being sent into the provinces by the 'Country Messengers'.[117] In August of that year proposals were issued concerning insuring 'in any Place of Great Britain'; the paper for these policy-holders was to be 'left at his or her Friend or Correspondent's House in London, within the Weekly Bills of Mortality'.[118] Towards the end of the first year of publication the company increased its metropolitan delivery to extend five miles beyond London and Westminster except it was decided that no policy was to be undertaken where 'no Walker Established, unless the Persons Insured shall bee Contented to have the Mercurys left at their friends house within the said Cities, or any places belonging to the Walks already sett up next adjacent to the said persons houses till there shall be fifty persons Insured at such distant places'.[119] Presumably the geographical spread of both policy-holders and subscribers to the paper increased, as by April 1715 it was claimed in the paper that it was 'dispers'd as far as the Weekly-Bills of Mortality, and in almost all Counties in England'.[120]

The minutes of the general court and committee of the Sun Fire Office reveal that the content of the paper was quite closely controlled by the company and record how the production of the paper was organised. Before turning to look more closely at the content of the paper, and how it was acquired, it is worth outlining the general development of the paper across the period and noting some brief details about the various writers and printers involved.

The paper was published three times a week on Mondays, Wednesdays and Fridays as the *British Mercury* from March 1710 until August 1712, when the Stamp Act came into force. The act, which levied a duty of 1*d*. per copy on newspapers printed on a single sheet, was widely opposed.[121] The Sun Fire Office Company spent a number of months preparing to present their case to parliament; they had 600 copies of a petition to the House of Commons printed and six members of the company attended the lobby during the relevant debates.[122] The company claimed that they should be exempted from

---

116 Ibid. fos 34v, 48r.
117 Ibid. pp. 10, 12.
118 Sun Fire Office, *Proposals set forth by the company of London insurers*, London (30 Aug.) 1710.
119 GL, MS 11931/1, fo. 30v.
120 BM, 23 Apr. 1715.
121 Harris, *London newspapers*, 19–20.
122 GL, MS 11931/1, fos 68r, 68r, 75r, 76, 77r.

paying the duty on the *Mercury*, partly because they made no 'Profit or Advantage of the said paper, other than for carrying on the said Insurance from Fire.'[123] The petition failed and the company took advantage of a loophole in the law: on publications longer than one sheet the duty levied was only 2s. per sheet on each edition, regardless of the regularity of publication or the size of the print run.[124] It was decided in June 1712 that from the beginning of August the paper would be published weekly 'in one sheet & half by Way of a pamphlete'.[125] From 2 August the weekly paper was published on a Saturday as six octavo pages but 'at the request of many persons' it was changed to Wednesday at the end of August.[126]

The first printer of the paper was Matthew Jenour near St Sepulchre's back gate in Giltspur Street, who had printed Povey's *General Remark*, and was one of the twenty-four founding members of the Sun Fire Office Company in London. When his accounts were examined in November 1710 it emerged that he was overcharging the company for printing and using paper delivered by the stationer and paid for by the company 'for his owne use'.[127] He transferred his stock and left the company.[128] The experienced newspaper printer Hugh Meere took over and in November 1712 bought stock in the company and immediately initiated a review of his payments as printer.[129]

The printers were closely involved with shaping the content of the paper as will be seen below but the company also employed an 'author' for the paper. In the first few months of the publication of the *British Mercury* there was a high turnover of writers: the playwright and projector Aaron Hill (who had written for the *British Apollo*) wrote the first three issues for which he was paid 40s.; a Stephen Whately was paid £6 for writing the issues from 5 April until 16 June 1710; David Jones, apparently the historical writer and translator, was paid 10s. for each issue he wrote from mid-June 1710 until Alexander Justice was employed at the beginning of October that year at the rate of 20s. a week.[130] Justice, the author of the manual mentioned at the beginning of the chapter that explained the publication, the 'Course of the

---

123 *The case of the members of the Sun-Fire-Office* [London 1712].

124 Harris, *London newspapers*, 20.

125 GL, MS 11931/1, fo. 79v. A sheet and a half could be used to make either a six-page octavo pamphlet or a twelve-page quarto pamphlet. It seems that the company believed that in taking advantage of the loophole they still risked prosecution as they resolved to cease publication if they were prosecuted for printing on unstamped paper (fo. 85r). Later that month they were prepared to print on two sheets (fo. 85v).

126 Ibid. fo. 85v. The paper was printed on a Wednesday until Jan. 1715 when it reverted to Saturdays and then in Aug. 1715 it went back to being printed on a Wednesday.

127 Ibid. fos 20v, 21r.

128 Jenour went on to print the *Daily Advertiser* and the *Flying Post*.

129 GL, MS 11931/1, fos 92v, 93r, 95r. In 1712 Meere began to print the *Weekly Packet* and he went on to print the *Daily Post* and the *British Journal*. On Meere see M. Treadwell, 'London printers and printing houses in 1705', *Publishing History* vii (1980), 29–30.

130 GL, MS 11931/1, pp. 1, 9, annexed to p. 17b; Dickson, *Sun Insurance*, 37.

Exchange', was perhaps particularly well qualified for the job of presenting specialist commercial information to an audience that included specialists as well as non-specialists. When Justice wished in December 1711 'to goe beyond Seas at the Congress under a foreign Ambassador' his offer to send his contribution by post was declined and the writer Charles Gildon was employed for £80 a year.[131] Gildon wrote until the paper became a weekly in August 1712 when John Stevens, the antiquary and translator, was employed for £40 a year.[132] Stevens wrote the paper for three years; he was replaced in August 1715 by an unidentified author.[133]

The proposals the company issued in 1710 set out the content of the *British Mercury*: 'all Foreign and Domestick News, an Account of rising and falling of Publick Stocks, Payments at the Exchequer, Course of the Exchange, Port-Letters, Price Courant of several Commodities, with whatever else shall be thought proper to entertain the Publick'.[134] Proposals issued a few days later, probably for the use of agents in the provinces, specified the 'Commodities' whose prices were to be listed 'Merchandizes, Corn, Hops, Coals, and other Commodities (as they are then sold in London)'.[135] On the whole the paper's content reflected these proposals. Although the foreign and domestic news was often crucial to the course of trade, and the (often serialised) essays inserted when foreign posts were delayed touched commercial nerves, here, at the risk of neglecting part of the paper, I wish to concentrate on the financial and commercial information initially printed on the verso of the paper, and later, when the newspaper took the form of a pamphlet, on the final pages.[136]

The author of the paper was responsible for compiling the foreign and domestic news sections of the paper, but often shared the responsibility for the other sections of the paper. A few months after the first issue was published, for example, the printer was asked to leave out the weekly bill of mortality in future issues.[137] The Sun Fire Office company not only instructed the printer what to include or omit but also how information was

---

[131] GL, MS 11931/1, fos 59r–v. On Gildon see P. Dottin, *Robinson Crusoe examin'd and criticis'd or a new edition of Charles Gildon's famous pamphlet now published with an introduction and explanatory notes together with an essay on Gildon's life*, London 1923. On Gildon's authorship of the *Mercury* see, J. Honoré, 'Charles Gildon rédacteur du *British Mercury* (1711–1712): les attaques contre Pope, Swift, et les wits', *Études anglaises* xv (1962), 347–64.

[132] GL, MS 11931/1, fos 82v–83r; *ODNB*.

[133] GL, MS 11931/2, fo. 7v.

[134] Sun Fire Office, *Proposals* (16 Aug.) 1710. Relton suggests that the proposals had been revised at least twice since 10 Apr.: Relton, *Fire insurance*, 319.

[135] Sun Fire Office, *Proposals* (30 Aug.) 1710.

[136] The most extensive discussion of the essay part of the newspaper (admittedly for only the six months when Gildon was its author) can be found in Honoré, 'Charles Gildon'. See also Harris, *London newspapers*, 167, 179–80.

[137] GL, MS 11931/1, p. 10.

to appear. In December 1710 they instructed the printer to include the price of bread for London, as in the 'Weekly bill', and the price of bread for Middlesex, as in 'the printed assessment of Wylde in Aldergate street', in the Friday papers, '& distinctly in two Columns'.[138] The two columns allowed prices of the different types of loaves (the penny, 2d. 6d. 1s. and 18d.) to be compared between London and Middlesex and appeared until October 1712.[139]

Although the assize of bread and the bills of mortality were taken from printed sources, not all the numerical data included in the paper was always obtained from other published sources. In June 1710 the detailed listings of the prices of goods that had been appearing in segments over fortnightly periods, presumably taken from published commodity price currents, were replaced by a far shorter listing of selected agricultural prices: Colchester Crown bays, wheat, hops from 1708 and 1709 and coal by the chaldron.[140] These prices were collected three times a week by John Price who was ordered by the Sun Fire Office to go to 'bear key Battlebridge and Inns in the Borrow of Southwark to Informe himself of the Prices of Corn & hops & given account of the Same to Mr Jenour Every Wesdays Thursday & Satur-days'.[141] Over the months the list of prices became longer as the range of goods increased. By January 1712, for example, the list comprised the prices of wheat for shipping, best wheat, rye, barley, malt, beans, pease, oats, hops, coal and Colchester Crown bays.[142]

As in Houghton's *Collection* the *Mercury* also included a listing in every issue of the 'Money's Advanced and Paid off at the Exchequer'. In January 1713 it is clear that this information came directly from the exchequer as one of the members of the committee was ordered to 'agree With one of the Exchequer to send Every Tuesday the publick occurrence & alterations of the Exchequer'.[143] A rate of a guinea and a half *per annum*, plus postage, for the information was agreed between the company and the clerk of the exchequer.[144] Later, as will be seen below, partly to save these costs, the infor-mation was taken from a printed source.

From at least the second issue of the paper prices of stocks were listed. The prices in the early issues do not agree with those given in the twice weekly *Course of the Exchange* produced by John Castaing, Jr, and a little later in the period it is apparent that these prices were also collected specifically for the *Mercury*. By January 1712 it seems that John Price's job of collecting the

138 Ibid. fo. 23r.
139 BM, 8 Oct. 1712.
140 BM, 30 June 1710.
141 GL, MS 11931/1, p. 10. The detailed table of the Bill of Mortality was briefly replaced by a summary table.
142 BM, 23 Jan. 1712.
143 GL, MS 11931/1, fo. 95v.
144 Ibid.

prices of agricultural goods and coal had been taken over by Anthony Sayer, who had been (and possibly still was) a walker for the paper.[145] Sayer was to be paid 2s. a week for going to Bear Key, Billingsgate and Exchange Alley to collect prices.[146] The prices were obtained directly from Exchange Alley until August that year when the company ordered the printer, Hugh Meere, to take John Castaing's paper every Friday.[147] According to the imprint of Castaing's *Course of the Exchange* it cost 12s. a year at this time but presumably because the company only wanted the Friday issues the minutes record that they were to pay 6s. a year. The stock prices that subsequently appeared in the *Mercury* were indeed those given by Castaing. In March 1714 Hugh Meere proposed that the company should take John Freke's paper, the *Prices of Stocks, &c*, instead, at the cost of 12s. year. Meere claimed that this would save both the cost of subscribing to Castaing's paper and paying the clerk, Mr Milward, at the exchequer.[148] This seems a rather surprising argument as the exchequer prices were listed also by Castaing in his paper which begs the question of why the company continued to pay the exchequer for information which was in the paper they were already receiving?[149] Whatever the answer to this is, at the rates recorded in the minutes it would have been cheaper for the company to pay 6s. a year for Castaing's Friday papers rather than 12s. for Freke's.[150] Meere's preference for promoting Freke's paper at this time can perhaps be explained by the fact that he may have been its printer.[151] He made the suggestion to the company only a few days after the first issue of the paper was printed on 26 March. The Sun Fire Office accepted Meere's proposal and, as the committee requested, 'all Freke's Paper of Stocks' was reproduced in the issue of the *British Mercury* published on 19 May 1714.[152] So, in addition to the price of stocks, the course of the exchange, the money advanced and paid off in the exchequer, and the year's

---

[145] Ibid. p. 3.

[146] Ibid. fo. 66v.

[147] Ibid. fo. 84v.

[148] Ibid. fo. 127v. McCusker and Gravesteijn note that the cost of Freke's paper was initially cheaper than Castaing's at 2s. 6d. a quarter. It is unclear why the company minutes record the price as 6d. more expensive: *Journalism*, 316. Dickson notes that Freke was the brother-in-law of the merchant Charles Blount: Dickson, *Financial revolution*, 495 n. 2.

[149] The company began subscribing to Castaing's paper in Aug. 1712 and according to Meere's proposal they were still paying the exchequer for the information in Mar. 1714 (having negotiated arrangements with the exchequer in Feb. 1712).

[150] Presumably the company may have been able to negotiate a cheaper rate for taking only the Friday issues of Freke's paper. McCusker and Gravesteijn note that although Freke's paper was initially 2s. cheaper than Castaing's, the latter reduced his price also to 10s. in 1715 where it remained until around the time that Freke stopped publishing (Jan. 1722): *Journalism*, 316.

[151] According to McCusker and Gravesteijn, the printer of Freke's paper in 1715 was Hugh Meere. No printer is listed in the imprint for the 1714 issues: ibid. 321.

[152] GL, MS 11931/1, fo. 131v; BM, 19 May 1714. The *Mercury* published the prices from *The Prices of Stocks, &c.*, 18 May 1714.

purchase on annuities, which had previously been gathered from Castaing's publication and from the contact at the exchequer, four tables were added listing the state of the funds on the 1711 and 1712 lottery and classis. Within the space of three issues the committee agreed that this was too much information and 'Ordered that some part of Mr Freek's paper of Stocks be left out or alterd in the Mercury' and the next issue to appear included the range of numerical data that had previously been printed without the details about the funds on the lottery and classis.[153] Such decision-making reveals what the company thought the nature of the gap was between their *Mercury* and the more specialist commercial papers like Freke's.

A lot of the information was presented in the *Mercury* in such a way as to invite comparisons. Bread prices could be compared between London and Middlesex. Stock prices were presented in ways that allowed comparisons across time. When the paper was printed three times a week Monday's paper gave stock prices for Friday and Saturday, Wednesday's paper for Monday and Tuesday, and Friday's paper for Wednesday and Thursday. The names of the stocks were listed in rows with the prices for each day given in columns. When the paper became a weekly in August 1712 only the prices of stock on the day before the paper was published were given, even though the source of the prices, Freke's twice-weekly paper, listed three days of prices in each issue. In July 1715 however, stock prices for the whole week began to be listed in a table with each day's prices listed in columns making it straightforward to compare the prices of one particular stock across the whole week.[154]

From the early issues the *Mercury* carried advertisements for books, houses and businesses for sale and to let, cricket matches, medicines, lotteries, missing items and other insurance companies, as well as notices concerning either the paper or policies for prospective or existing customers. As in other papers published in this period some advertisements appeared in an identical form over many months and the Sun Fire Office negotiated considerably reduced rates with those who wished to place advertisements long term. An advertisement for Templeman's coffee-house, for example, announcing its brokering services to landlords, tenants, purchasers and sellers of estates, employers and job-seekers, was placed at the considerably reduced rate of £2 12s. for a year.[155]

It was announced in the paper that advertisements were taken in by the printer.[156] As happened occasionally with the foreign and domestic news sections of the papers, items from the advertisements section might give offence to some readers.[157] An advertisement defending Francis Richardson's

[153] GL, MS 11931/1, fo. 133r.
[154] BM, 27 July 1715.
[155] GL, MS 11931/1, p. 11. Templeman's was also one of the places where policies could be undertaken: BM, 3, 12 May 1710.
[156] BM, 26 Apr. 1710.
[157] GL, MS 11931/1, fos 89r, 129v; GL, MS 11931/2, fo. 9v.

and Joseph Oake's enterprise to inform adventurers whether their lottery tickets had been drawn caused a controversy which led to both a printed apology and an order from the committee that Hugh Meere, the printer, should 'for the future to take care not to give offence to any body & to lett all private advertisements brought to be perused & approved by Mr Alexander Justice to avoid offence'.[158] The proprietors of the paper were very keen that their authors produced 'an acceptable Newspaper Without intermeddling With the Affairs of State to the damage of the Company' and that 'no party business shall be incerted'.[159]

In the eyes of the company the advertisements played a crucial role in encouraging trade, for themselves, their readers and the nation as a whole. Producing the paper was a core activity of the company and served to promote its insurance business both through giving away copies of the paper and using the paper's style in its insurance proposals. As well as advertising the company's services the range of advertisements was tailored on at least one occasion to attract new policy-holders and subscribers to the paper. In August 1711, as the quarter day approached (perhaps the most likely time for those interested to take out a subscription which was paid quarterly), the Sun Fire Office committee ordered the printer to 'take out of sd mercurys all unnecessary advertisements for the time & instead of it such other advertisement for the information of these who will take the policys & papers'.[160]

The company considered a number of proposals to capitalise on the opportunities presented by the advertising in the Mercury.[161] Although not executed, one in particular, gives some clues as to the sorts of services the company might offer their customers for mutual benefit. The committee of the general court of the company put forward a proposal in February 1715 that every person insured by the company could advertise in the paper for free once in every quarter, but the minutes of the subsequent general court meeting do not record such a proposal.[162] In April 1715 the most persuasive and articulate case was made in the Mercury for the usefulness of placing advertisements. Following the boast that by this time almost 6,000 policies had been issued across England, the paper announced the cost of advertisements of 1s. for up to twelve lines (which represented a lowering of cost) 'whereby this Paper will be of general use to the Publick, and will help to

---

[158] Ibid. fo. 47v. Richardson and Oake's scheme was advertised in the British Mercury (30 July 1711) and the defence against an attack by Andrew Bell was printed in the British Mercury (1 Aug. 1711). See also Andrew Bell, Advertisement. July 25. 1710 To morrow, being the 26th of July, will begin to be drawn the lottery-tickets at Guildhall, London 1711. Harris notes that controversies over newspaper advertising not infrequently led to legal action: Harris, London newspapers, 177.

[159] GL, MS 11931/1, fo. 17b.

[160] Ibid. fo. 49r. Two issues (BM, 3, 5 Sept. 1711) have fewer advertisements than usual but they do not contain particularly lengthy details about policies.

[161] Ibid. fo. 92r.

[162] Ibid. fo. 160v.

advance Trade, both in Town and Country, having a Weekly Account of what Houses, Lands, Goods, and Wares, are to be bought or sold, and what lost or stollen, and of all other Business of Moment in way of Traffick, provided that nothing be mention'd therein relating to the Government, or State-Affairs'.[163] The proprietors of the *Mercury* shared Houghton's interest in promoting trade but, as we've already seen, they were keen that their paper did not become embroiled in party politics.

The *British Mercury* was last published on 2 May 1716, apparently because 'the great and still increasing Number of News-Papers, that are publish'd every Day, had spoil'd the Design of Weekly Intelligences, and render'd them of little or no Use or Value'.[164] It was replaced by a quarterly publication, also published by Hugh Meere, *The Historical Register*, described as 'a full true, clear, disinterested, and impartial Account of all the memorable Transactions that happen in foreign Countries, from Quarter to Quarter' with a chronological listing of events attached.[165] The only substantial numerical commercial data included in the quarterly publication was a summary of the money paid into and out of the exchequer over the quarter. In 1721 the Sun Fire Office resigned its responsibilities for the publication but it continued to be produced until 1738.[166]

As well as producing the *British Mercury* the Sun Fire Office also produced a French version, *Le Mercure Britannique*. No copies of this paper have been traced and the only information about it has to be taken from the *Mercury* and the minutes of the Sun Fire Office Company. In an issue of the *Mercury* from January 1711 it was stated that the *Mercure* had then been published for 'some weeks past' and was 'taken in by several hundreds of French Inhabitants in this City and Suburbs, and also by divers English, for the easier acquiring of the French Tongue, and by others sent to the Country and beyond Sea'.[167] In April 1711 there are hints that the circulation was not quite so large. Alexander Justice, who in addition to his employment as author of the *Mercury* wrote the French paper and was in charge of its distribution as well as securing customers for the policies, required 100 printed receipts for insurance and claimed that there were 50 customers for the paper alone, suggesting a circulation of 150.[168] Walkers were employed to deliver

---

163 *BM*, 23 Apr. 1715.

164 *The Historical Register*, i, pt 1 (1716), p. i.

165 Hugh Meere printed the *Register* until his death in 1723. Relton suggests that 4,500 issues of the first *Register* were printed: *Fire insurance*, 312; *The Historical Register*, i, pt 1 (1716), p. i. In the first four volumes each volume included a chronological register. After the first year the chronology covered the whole year and was included in the last volume of the year.

166 Relton, *Fire insurance*, 314–15.

167 *BM*, 10 Jan. 1711. The paper is first mentioned in the minutes on 13 Dec. 1710: GL, MS 11931/1, fo. 21v.

168 GL, MS 11931/1, fo. 32v.

the paper: they were three women and a small boy.[169] Perhaps reflecting the high expectations the company had for the expansion of the readership of the paper in May 1711, Justice was paid 10s. a week to write it and promised 20s. when the number of customers reached 800.[170] In December 1711, possibly its last month of publication, 350 copies of the paper were printed.[171] It is not clear whether the paper was a translation of the *British Mercury* or not; it seems that it may at least have carried different advertisements.[172] The company articulated its right to stop publishing the paper in October 1711 and a few weeks later decided that the paper would cease to be published at the end of that year.[173] However, despite the additional problem of having to find a translator for the paper because Charles Gildon supposedly 'did not understand the French tongue so much as to make a perfect traduction of our Mercury' the minutes reveal that the paper was still being printed in December 1711 and still being distributed in the middle of January 1712.[174]

In the *British Mercury*, and perhaps also in the *Mercure Britannique*, Houghton's and Povey's project to supply commercial information about stock prices and imports and exports and at times other price information to a large audience that might include, but certainly extended well beyond, merchants, and beyond London, was continued. Although much of the information also appeared in specialist commercial newspapers, the Sun Fire Office drew the line at including all the information that at times was published in such publications. The paper may have been carried on the back of the company's insurance business, as they argued themselves, but most policy-holders chose to take the paper and it survived for over five years and achieved a very considerable circulation. The surviving minutes of the company, coupled with the paper itself, indicate how early modern prices made their way from specialist publications, contacts and people paid to collect them, into a publication that reached an extensive and diverse audience.

### 'Together with an account of trade': reporting commerce in provincial papers

John Houghton and the Sun Fire Office claimed a country-wide readership for their papers and there is evidence that these papers, and others published

---

[169] Ibid. fos 47r, 48r.
[170] Ibid. fo. 40r.
[171] Ibid. fo. 62r.
[172] Ibid. fo. 78v.
[173] Ibid. fos 50v, 53r.
[174] Ibid. fos 60r, 62r, 66r. It surprised Relton that Gildon was not capable of this translation work, given his education at Douay: *Fire insurance*, 304 n. 1.

in London, did circulate throughout the country.[175] Specialist commercial publications were sent out from London to provincial and overseas readers. One of the surviving sets of Freke's *Prices of Stocks &c.* in the British Library had been owned by the MP John Plumtre, for example. In the summer and early autumn of 1719 and 1721 the paper was sent to him in Nottingham: presumably during the other months he was in London and the paper was delivered to his house there.[176] Clerks in the office of the secretaries of state sent copies of many London papers, as well as French and Dutch papers, to provincial distributors, and individual readers via the Post Office.[177] In the early eighteenth century a number of papers were produced in London with provincial readers in mind. The *Post-Man*, *Post-Boy* and *Flying Post* tended to be published on the days that the mails left the capital: Tuesdays, Thursdays and Saturdays. The position these papers held in supplying news to the provinces was challenged in the second decade of the century by papers published in the evening which contained the news that arrived in the foreign posts on the day of publication and were sent out the evening of publication.[178] Some printers left a space for London writers to add extra news for their country correspondents. Copies survive in the British Library of the *Evening Post*, a paper 'chiefly design'd for the Country', in which Thomas Walter writes from London to his brother and father in Kent. In the blank space in a copy of the paper from 10 August 1710 Walter adds a note directing his brother to the price of Bank stock given in the paper and his resolutions to buy it at a certain price.[179] Later issues are emended with similar notes telling of the delay and ultimate success in making this purchase at the desired price.[180]

From the early eighteenth century newspapers were also produced outside the capital in market towns. The earliest surviving copy of a provincial paper is an issue of the *Bristol Post-Boy*, numbered 91, from August 1704 which suggests a start date of November 1702. It may have been only the second paper to have been established outside London if we calculate back from a numbered issue of the *Norwich Post* from 1708, which suggests a start date of September 1701.[181] By 1710 ten provincial papers had been established in six

---

[175] At first Houghton's paper was available from hawkers in London as well as booksellers. Customers in London could also have the paper delivered by the Penny Post and those beyond London by carriers. Later, provincial booksellers stocked single issues and also bound volumes of issues. Houghton claimed an extensive circulation that extended beyond Britain to the plantations: Glaisyer, 'Readers', 236–7.

[176] McCusker and Gravesteijn, *Journalism*, 347 n. 117.

[177] M. Harris, 'Newspaper distribution during Queen Anne's reign: Charles Delafaye and the secretary of state's office', in R. W. Hunt, I. G. Philip and R. J. Roberts (eds), *Studies in the book trade in honour of Graham Pollard*, Oxford 1975, 139–51.

[178] Harris, *London newspapers*, 33–4.

[179] *Evening Post*, 10 Aug. 1710. I am indebted to R. M. Wiles for this reference: *Freshest advices: early provincial newspapers in England*, [Columbus], Ohio 1965, 8.

[180] *Evening Post*, 12, 16 Aug. 1710.

[181] Cranfield, *Provincial newspaper*, 13–14; Wiles, *Freshest advices*, 14–16.

different towns.[182] Even if many papers were established in towns which were quite far from London they were often places with major roads connecting them to the capital.[183] Stamford, for example, was on the Great North Road, and the building in which Thomas Baily and William Thompson began printing the *Stamford Post* in 1710 was opposite a coaching inn.[184] In 1720 there were at least twenty provincial papers being published in England.

To make a profit on such a publishing enterprise undertakers had to ensure that their paper reached as large a number of readers as possible and consequently it needed to be circulated over a wide geographical area. The *Northampton Mercury* claimed in its fifth issue, published in 1720, that it 'goes further in length, than any other Country News-Paper in England, and takes weekly the Counties of Bedford, Berks, Buckingham, Cambridge, Derby, Essex, Glocester, Hertford, Huntingdon, Leicester, Lincoln, Norfolk, Northampton, Nottingham, Oxford, Rutland, Stafford, Suffolk and Warwick'.[185] Most papers were sold by the printer who printed them, and many papers provided an extensive list of booksellers or other agents in surrounding towns who also stocked the paper. The *York Mercury* in 1719 could be delivered to the houses of those 'willing to take this Book Quarterly' on a Monday morning 'before they are Cryed about the City by the Hawkers'.[186] The *New-castle Courant* was sold by hawkers in the evenings and the *Worcester Post-Man* by the printer and 'by a Woman every Saturday from 10 in the Morning till 4 in the Afternoon, near St. Martin's Church in the Corn-Market, where all Country People may be furnished'.[187] Freedom of the Corporation of Stamford was granted to the *Stamford Mercury's* proprietors, Baily and Thompson, on condition that they 'make use of and employ such poor people in their servisses to disperse Newspapers'.[188] The *Salisbury Post-Man* was delivered in 1715 to addresses in the town and 'any Persons in the Country may order it by the Post, Coach, Carriers, Market-People, to whom they shall be carefully deliver'd'.[189] Increasingly newspapers employed people specifically for the purposes of distributing the paper in the local region; in 1719, the *Ludlow Post-Man*, for example, 'was dispers'd 30 or 40 Miles round, by Men imploy'd for that Purpose'.[190] Attempts have been made

[182] Norwich, Bristol, Exeter, Yarmouth, Shrewsbury and Worcester.
[183] Wiles, *Freshest advices*, 23.
[184] D. Newton and M. Smith, *The* Stamford Mercury: *three centuries of newspaper publishing*, Stamford 1999, 15.
[185] NM, 31 May 1720.
[186] YM, 9 Mar. 1719.
[187] One of the sellers of the *New-castle Courant*, James Brown, was assaulted while he was selling the paper on the Tyne Bridge about eight o'clock one Tuesday evening in Feb.: *New-castle Courant*, 23 Feb. 1712; WPM, 24 June 1715.
[188] Newton and Smith, *The* Stamford Mercury, 27 (quotation from the Corporation of Stamford's minutes, 15 Jan. 1715).
[189] *Salisbury Post-Man*, 29 Sept. 1715, quoted in Cranfield, *Provincial newspaper*, 191.
[190] *Ludlow Post-Man*, 9 Oct 1719, quoted in Cranfield, *Provincial newspaper*, 192.

to estimate the circulation of provincial newspapers by plotting the geographical area referred to in advertisements.[191] Of course, such methods have their limitations as the proprietors of the *Northampton Mercury* stated in a reply to their competitors, the proprietors of the *Stamford Mercury* and *Suffolk Mercury*: 'The Stamford Mercurist has lately given himself an Air of notifying to the Publick how far his Paper circulates, by the remote Places from whence he sometimes (by chance) receives an Advertisement; But he might with as much Truth have exemplify'd this, by the different Parts, from whence his foreign Advices come.'[192]

Judging the size of the print runs, or the number of readers, is very difficult. The sales of stamped paper included a listing for a 'Bristol Post' in August and September 1712, with an estimated circulation of under 300.[193] Samuel Farley, who set up the *Salisbury Post-Man* in September 1715, suggested that 200 subscribers would make it a workable business.[194] David Newton and Martin Smith estimate that a paper like the *Stamford Mercury*, if it had a circulation of around 3–400, would make an annual profit of £2 if advertising revenue were included.[195]

Although the early provincial papers drew very heavily on London papers and newsletters sent from the capital for their coverage of foreign and London news, they did include some local content.[196] The *York Mercury*, for example, reported the local assizes and a number of papers reported local prices and shipping news.[197] Surprisingly local news might also be sourced from London; the *York Mercury* reported a severe storm in a village a few miles from the city based on an account taken from a London paper.[198] Adapting the point made about London papers by Michael Harris – that advertisements can themselves be categorised as news – provincial papers printed much of local relevance under the heading of advertisements.[199] We have to take care, however, in what we take 'provincial' to encompass; as Carl Estabrook cautions, papers published beyond London, and in his partic-

---

191 Cranfield, *Provincial newspaper*, figure 7 facing p. 204.

192 *NM*, 25 July 1720.

193 Snyder, 'Circulation', 222. This was probably William Bonny's *Bristol Post-Boy* but it is difficult to be sure: Wiles, *Freshest advices*, 383.

194 C. Y. Ferdinand, 'Selling it to the provinces: news and commerce round eighteenth-century Salisbury', in Brewer and Porter, *Consumption and the world*, 396; Wiles, *Freshest advices*, 71. In 1718 the break-even point may have been as high as 1,200 copies for a one-and-a-half-sheet London weekly paper that sold for 3*d*.: Sutherland, 'Circulation', 123.

195 Newton and Smith, *The Stamford Mercury*, 32.

196 Cranfield, *Provincial newspaper*, 31.

197 *YM*, 6 Apr. 1719.

198 Ibid. 20 July 1719.

199 M. Harris, 'Timely notices: the uses of advertising and its relationship to news during the late seventeenth century', *Prose Studies* xxi (1998), 141–56.

ular study, Bristol papers, 'hardly addressed a rural audience at all' as what little local content there was related to the town.[200]

In this section of the chapter I will examine the trading information included in provincial newspapers. Many papers gave such elements prominence in their titles. From its first issue the *York Mercury* was subtitled 'With Useful Observations on Trade', the *Northampton Mercury*, the *Suffolk Mercury or St Edmund's Bury Post* and the *Leeds Mercury* all announced on the front page 'Together with An Account of Trade'. Papers included details of import and exports in the capital, prices from London's Bear Key, as well as reporting stock prices. Although much of this information was drawn from London papers and contacts in London, many papers also reported local prices, at times quite extensively.

Listings of the goods imported and exported from the port of London, presumably taken from the custom house bills, were included in some provincial papers, as in the *Collection* and the *Mercury*. In the *Worcester Post-Man*, for example, the quantities of exports were listed on the final page, sometimes as a table and sometimes set out as a paragraph of continuous prose.[201] Some issues also included imports, but on at least one occasion coverage was limited 'For want of Room'. The paper was published on a Friday and these listings covered a period of a week beginning on a Thursday usually from the week before last, and less often the week before that.

Readers in Nottingham could choose between two papers in the second decade of the eighteenth century, both published on a Thursday: the *Weekly Courant* and the *Nottingham Mercury*. Both papers gave details about exports and imports at London but of different kinds. The *Mercury* gave details about the quantities of various goods imported and exported at the port of London over a period of a week which ended the Thursday before the paper was published. The *Courant* gave more details – it included the destination or origin of goods, as well as the quantities of the different goods – but the information was more out of date as it referred to a week ending on a Friday just under two weeks before the paper was published.[202] So readers in Nottingham could choose between less detailed but more current information, or less current but more detailed information. The type of information on imports and exports given in the *Courant* resembles that given in every issue of the *Northampton Mercury*.[203] As will be seen below, Robert Raikes and William

---

[200] Estabrook, *Urbane and rustic England*, 206.

[201] *WPM*, 1 Feb., 17 May 1717.

[202] The different days of the week to which the information referred suggests either that it came from different weekly sources or that it was compiled in different ways from daily listings. The *Weekly Courant* for 9 May 1717, for example, included prices for the week ending Tuesday 23 Apr., the *Nottingham Mercury* for 19 July 1716 included prices for the week ending Friday 6 July.

[203] The *Northampton Mercury* was issued on a Monday and the list covered the trade for the week ending eleven days before.

Dicey, the proprietors of this paper, took these listings from the custom house bills and, in giving the information organised by destination or origin of the goods, they imitated the format of surviving bills that were published in London.[204] The format of the information in the *Nottingham Mercury* is not the same as that in the surviving custom house bills however. Where did it come from? It may have been that it was compiled from the same sort of bills reproduced in the *Northampton Mercury* and the *Weekly Courant*. Another possibility is that there were various sorts of custom house bills available, as John Houghton hints, and it was one of these other sorts that was used here.[205]

Most papers made few comments about this import and export information. The weekly *Northampton Mercury* however did, and in doing so recalled the project John Houghton had undertaken in his periodical publications. Even the terminology Raikes and Dicey used to describe their newspaper – 'Weekly Collection' – invoked Houghton. They endeavoured 'to acknowledge and improve the Favour' shown by their readers 'by redoubling our Care, particularly in our Account of Goods imported and exported, where omitting all trivial Matters, we shall make choice of the most valuable Commodities, as Wines, Brandies, Tobacco; Gold, Corn, Woollen, Wrought Iron, &c. so that any Gentleman may at the Year's End see how much has been imported and exported in the Year'.[206] By prompting gentlemen to use the papers' accounts of imports and exports as a basis for their own calculations, Raikes and Dicey were asking readers to become political arithmeticians.[207] The balance of trade was at the heart of many debates about trade in this period and there was much discussion about its accurate calculation. The idea that the papers were to be saved over the weeks to undertake such calculations was reinforced in the discussion of the 'Foreign and Domestick Occurrences' which were 'to be continued in such regular Consequence and Order, that the Second Week's News shall illustrate the First, the Third the Second, and so on. It will be in short a kind of Political Chronicle, the Newsman's Diary, and, at a Twelvemonth's Growth, merit a Place in any Gentleman's Library who is dispose'd to keep a Set'.[208] Other devices were also used to reinforce the notion of collecting the issues to make a set. Like other papers, the *Mercury* used issue numbers with fifty-two issues making up each volume, but unlike others, the *Northampton Mercury* continued the pagination from issue

---

[204] Surviving custom house bills published in London also included the names of traders but neither the *Northampton Mercury* nor the *Nottingham Courant* reproduced these details.

[205] 'Notwithstanding these general Bills, there are lesser ones printed, mentioning only the Goods relating to some particular Trades': *CIHT*, 13 Mar. 1683.

[206] *NM*, 24 Apr. 1721.

[207] There was also a pledge here to include an exact version of the Bills of Mortality in every issue (as many other provincial papers did in some form). There is not space here to discuss the bills in any detail but demographic calculations were central to political arithmetic.

[208] *NM*, 24 Apr. 1721.

to issue. Although this paper was alone in instructing readers on what to do with the information on imports and exports it included in each issue, readers of other provincial papers might have collected issues for the same purpose.

Included in the listing of 'Exports of the Woollen Manufacture, &c. from the Port of London' in the *Worcester Post-Man* in February 1717 was a listing of the 'Price of English Corn' which included prices of new and old wheat, rye, barley, pease, oats for horses, beans, old and new Cheshire cheese, Warwickshire and Gloucestershire cheese, new and old fine hops. Often listed under the heading 'Prices from Bear Key', this was a typical addition to provincial papers after the Stamp Act was passed in 1712, as part of the 'Account of Trade'. The listing was included in the Worcester paper for some months and then disappeared. It was reintroduced at the beginning of 1720, initially appearing regularly, but by the end of the year only intermittently.[209] More consistent was the reporting of Bear Key prices in the *Leeds Mercury*: no listing appeared in the surviving issues of 1719 but from 5 January 1720 a listing of prices appeared in every issue throughout that year.

Not all listings of prices from Bear Key were dated. Where they are given, however, they allow us to see how current the prices were. The surviving issues of the *Plymouth Weekly-Journal* from 1720 list the Bear Key prices for the usual range of goods. The 25 November issue gives prices from Bear Key for 22 November, at seven in the evening, and the 2 December issue has Bear Key prices for 27 November. In other papers the listings were far more out of date. The eight Bear Key prices that appeared in two columns in the 20 April 1719 issue of the *York Mercury*, when the listing began in this paper, were dated 11 April. This nine-day lag remained constant. A few weeks later more current York prices for wheat, rye, barley, oats, beans, rape seed, butter and tallow were listed beneath the London prices for wheat, barley, malt, oats, horse beans, 'hogg-pease', old hops and new hops. The similar layout of the prices and the order in which the goods were listed invited comparisons to be made between the London prices dated 9 May and the York prices dated 16 May for the goods which appeared in both lists.[210] This pair of tables became a permanent feature of the second page of the *York Mercury*.[211]

The reporting of the prices of agricultural goods was less systematic in other papers. The *Nottingham Mercury* did not carry regular listings in this period but occasionally listed prices from various neighbouring markets. The 24 December 1719 issue, for example, carried a listing of corn prices from markets held at Lincoln, Grantham, Warwick, Northampton, Newark and Tamworth held 'a Fortnight since'.[212] Such intermittent reporting perhaps

---

[209] *WPM*, 8 Jan. 1720.

[210] *YM*, 18 May 1719.

[211] The tables appeared in all but one issue (22 Feb. 1720) in the period up until the end of 1720.

[212] *NottM*, 24 Dec. 1719. Occasionally market prices from Grantham, Leicester and Lincoln were listed in the paper.

indicates John Collyer's (and others') approach to such information. When it came his way he reproduced it in the paper but he did not secure a regular source for it. Other proprietors, like Raikes and Dicey of the *Northampton Mercury* must have secured such sources. From the second issue of the paper, in May 1720, Bear Key prices were listed and over subsequent months prices of goods from other local markets were included – Biggleswade, Cambridge, Northampton, Reading, Royston – with St Neots, Oxford and Peterborough prices appearing on a regular basis, often set out, however, as continuous prose rather than in columns.[213] Likewise, the *Northampton Mercury's* predecessor and competitor, the *Stamford Mercury*, listed agricultural prices from an extensive region.[214]

Stock prices were a staple of London papers in the early eighteenth century.[215] The latest price of Bank stock was usually listed and quite often the East India Company and the South Sea Company stock prices, and at times others too. Some provincial papers did not list any stock prices, like the *Exeter Post-Boy* from 1711 and 1715, which does not list any share prices, or indeed any commercial information except shipping news. Most provincial papers, however, at least occasionally, listed the Bank share price, and many listed the Bank, East India Company and South Sea Company prices on a semi-regular basis.[216] By the end of the period, when the share prices were making the news the coverage of the stock market was at times extensive and prices were given in every issue. The prices were not taken from John Castaing's *Course of the Exchange*, but probably came either from another London newspaper or newsletter, or from a London correspondent.

After the Stamp Act, when provincial papers became weekly publications, the papers were compiled in stages and printed over the course of the week.[217] The space allocated to each section of the paper tended to remain the same regardless of the number of newspapers or newsletters that arrived and needed to be excerpted, or the significance of their contents. On publication day the news from the latest post was printed on the final page. In most papers the stock prices were printed on the last line of the 'news' part of the paper in this final printing. If important news arrived in the last post the printer might set the final section in smaller type to fit in as much news as possible or cut some of the regular content. In the second half of 1719, for example, the *Nottingham Mercury* reported three stock prices in every issue, and occasionally they were squeezed in by being set in a smaller type font as

---

213 *NM*, 9 May 1720.
214 Newton and Smith, *The* Stamford Mercury, 36.
215 Harris, *London newspapers*, 176.
216 *NC*, in 1711–12, is an example of the first sort of paper, and the *Nottingham Courant* and *Nottingham Mercury* fall into the second category.
217 Cranfield, *Provincial newspaper*, 33–7; Wiles, *Freshest advices*, 72–3; Newton and Smith, *The* Stamford Mercury, 29.

on 10 September 1719. In other papers such information was not given quite such a high priority and did not always appear when space was tight.

Many of the listings, as with the other price information given in the paper, were dated and occasionally a specific time was listed. Presumably most people with interests in the stock price information would be keen to know the most up-to-date prices. In the *Worcester Post-Man* we can see an attempt to include the most recent prices. In 1713 this weekly paper was set and printed at intervals over the week, usually on five pages. Page 4 was probably set and printed before page 5 which was headed 'Thursday's post', and contained the last news received before the paper went on sale. In some issues stock prices appear on both page 4 and page 5: in the issue dated 16 July 1714, for example, page 4 contains a listing of share prices for South Sea Stock, Bank, India, African and Blank lottery tickets from the 1710 lottery for 10 July, and on page 5 the prices for these stocks are give for 13 July. The most up-to-date prices were therefore only three days old in this issue. Whether the slightly older prices were printed on page 4 in case Thursday's post brought no updated prices (in many issues of the paper no prices appeared on page 5) or whether the paper's proprietor, Stephan Bryan, printed whatever prices were available to him during the week to give his readers as much information as possible, is not clear. Next to knowing the most recent stock prices, interested readers must have wanted to know whether prices were going up or down and as well as being able to make comparisons between issues of the paper it must have been an advantage to make comparisons across the week.

At moments in the early eighteenth century such stock price fluctuations made the news and were reported in prose in the provincial papers. The *New-castle Courant* reported in October 1711 that the 'Bank, India and other Stocks advance every Day, on account of the Prospect of a sudden Treaty of Peace, and many are so Credulous of this Subject, that they offer to lay Wagers, That the Preliminaries are Signed'. In this issue the price of the Bank Stock was added in a post script.[218] In January 1714 the impact of news on stock prices was reported in the *Worcester Post-Man*: 'There has been a great Outcry about the Pretender's landing, which has lower'd the publick Stocks 5 per Cent, but the same proving only an Amusement, they are risen again to day 3 per Cent, and many who had sold off, have bought again at 3 per Cent Loss.'[219] It was in 1720, however, with the South Sea speculation, that the fluctuations in the stock prices attracted continuous and much closer attention, as the *Ipswich-Journal, or, the Weekly-Mercury* reported in its last issue of the year: 'Scarce any Thing is talked of but the Scheme for restoring Publick Credit'.[220]

---

[218] NC, 10 Oct. 1711. The *New-castle Courant* only ever listed the price of Bank stock and then not in every issue.

[219] WPM, 5 Feb. 1714.

[220] *Ipswich-Journal*, 31 Dec, 1720. As Julian Hoppit notes the provincial papers did not report on the effects of the Bubble beyond London: 'Myths', 154.

In the weekly paper the *Northampton Mercury* the prose reporting of the news directed readers to the price listings and instructed them to make the sorts of price comparisons across the week that readers of the *Worcester Post-Man* could sometimes have made. When tension in Exchange Alley was mounting in July 1710 an N.B. was printed in the *Northampton Mercury*: 'The Fluctuation of the Stocks, as by every Post, shall be particularly and exactly taken Notice of in ours.'[221] The price changes were to be printed as news of them arrived in each post even if they were not available to readers until Mondays. As the foreign and London news stories unfolded in the instalments brought together into the once-a-week publication so the episodic reports of the stock prices formed a narrative.

Under the date heading 27 September 1720, on page 271 of the 3 October 1720 issue of the *Northampton Mercury*, it was recorded that 'The South Sea Stock is fallen since Saturday 90 per Cent. Being now 300. The Bank 20 per Cent. Being now at 200. India 30 per Cent.'[222] The falls in African, Royal Exchange Assurance, York Buildings and rise in Temple Mills were also recorded. It was unusual for falls to be expressed in percentages rather than a simple reporting of the prices. In this particular issue readers were given further guidance on comparing stock prices: two pages later on page 273, the prices were listed again under the date 29 September: 'South Sea is now but 200. Bank but 190. India but 180.' At the end of the listing readers were instructed to make a comparison with the prices for two days earlier: 'So that they all have fallen considerably since Tuesday, as the Reader may see, if he is pleas'd to compare the Stocks in Page 271. with these.' In the last section of the same issue on page 275 the prices were listed for 1 October.[223] As Raikes and Dicey promised, they recorded the prices of stocks from every post, and sometimes also the fluctuation. For those readers who had ignored the simple listings of prices, this more extensive prose reporting of the stocks as news, and specific instructions on how to read the prices, had a didactic purpose: teaching readers about the market.

Like the *Northampton Mercury* other provincial newspapers responded to the dramatic stock market activities and fluctuations in 1720 by reporting a wider range of stock prices. The *Leeds Mercury* on 16 August, for example, rather than its usual listing of three or four stock prices, listed thirteen.[224] These were not regularly reported and some issues around this time listed no stock prices.[225] The *York Mercury*, from its tenth issue in April 1719, regularly reported six prices: South Sea, Bank, India, Bank Annuities, Million Bank and African, and at times up to fifteen prices were reported.[226] Unlike the

---

221  *NM*, 18 July 1720.
222  The newspaper was paginated continuously in each year-long volume.
223  *NM*, 3 Oct. 1720.
224  *Leeds Mercury*, 16 Aug. 1720; see also 12 July 1720.
225  Ibid. 2, 9 Aug. 1720.
226  *YM*, 27 Apr. 1719. Of the thirty-five issues published after this one in 1719, only ten

Bear Key prices, which were often printed in tabular form in the provincial papers, and indeed unlike the reporting of share prices in Castaing's and Freke's lists, the *British Mercury* and Houghton's *Collection*, prices were usually given in provincial papers on unbroken lines. Exceptionally, in a couple of issues of the *York Mercury* published in September 1720, stock prices were listed in a table which was much clearer for readers.[227] By October that year tabular reporting of the stock market in the *York Mercury* had become even more sophisticated. In the 3 October issue of the paper, a table of stock prices was included under the date 27 September in two columns, for yesterday and 'This day at noon', allowing readers to make direct comparisons of stock prices over two days.[228] Tables like this one became a regular feature of the paper for the rest of the year.[229] Using these tables readers of the *York Mercury*, then, could make the sorts of comparisons that the *Northampton Mercury* readers were invited to make by flicking through their paper.

Although many of the stock price listings were printed at the end of sections headed up with newspaper and newsletter titles, it is not always clear that these were the sources for the prices. The proprietors of the *Northampton Mercury*, however, did make it clear that their stock prices came directly from gentlemen in London, and also confirmed that their import and export figures were taken from the custom house bills. Following their pledge to include the fluctuation in stocks in their paper, quoted above, Raikes and Dicey also indicated that they would include 'a succinct Account . . . of what Commodities belonging to the Woollen Manufactury are exported weekly: Two Gentlemen in London, who are intimately concern'd in both, having assur'd us their best Intelligence therein; besides the printed Catalogues of Goods imported and exported, to and from His Majesty's Custom House'.[230]

A common item in papers published in London in this period was port news – the time of the arrival and departure of ships, their provenance and their destination, and sometimes their cargo – all listed under the heading of the relevant port town.[231] This sort of news was also reported in manuscript newsletters. Provincial papers reproduced port news from both these sources and also printed local news and took advantage of regional contacts. The 6 November 1719 issue of the *Plymouth Weekly-Journal*, for example, printed

did not list stock prices: YM, 18, 25 July, 22 Aug. 1720. Similarly in the *Worcester Post-Man* the number of prices reported increased over the summer of 1720.

[227] YM, 5, 12 Sept. 1720.

[228] Ibid. 3 Oct. 1720. This table did not contain the latest available prices however, for the latest news from London was taken from Peck's letter dated 29 Sept., and although it did contain some prices the whole range covered in the table was not included. The tables were probably taken directly from the *White-hall Evening Post*.

[229] YM, 10, 31 Oct., 21, 28 Nov., 5,12, 19 Dec. 1720.

[230] NM, 18 July 1720.

[231] Harris, *London newspapers*, 175.

details of the ships that had arrived in the local port on 30 and 31 October.[232] The *New-castle Courant* had an established source of shipping news relating to North Shields which it regularly included in the final section of the paper. In a request, reminiscent of Houghton's printed pleas, the paper's producer in 1712 asked its readers for further shipping intelligence. This is worth reproducing in its entirety:

> Whereas many persons, living in or near Newcastle upon Tine, receive Letters from their Friends or Relations, giving an Account of the Arrival of Ships in diverse Ports (and sometimes of other Occurrences that happen in their Voyage) the knowledge whereof would be very acceptable to others, who may have Concerns in the same Ships; The Printer therefore of this Courant gives Notice, that if any of his Acquaintance, or others, will be pleased to communicate such Intelligence, or a Copy of it to him so that it may be inserted in this Paper of the Benefit of the Publick, They may be sure of a kind Reception, and Acknowledgment of their Favour, with a suitable Return and Gratification for it.[233]

Apparently the proprietors of the paper were unsuccessful and only news from the already-established contact in North Shields appeared in the paper in subsequent months.[234]

Of course, printed materials were not the only source of commercial information available in the provinces. The Rye merchant, Samuel Jeake, for example, recorded his enthusiastic investment in various schemes including the Bank of England and the East India Company in the summer of 1694. Much of the trade was conducted through his London-based broker, Thomas Miller. Miller kept Jeake up to date with the price of the shares he had invested in, and those in which he was thinking of investing, in letters that took two days to reach Rye.[235]

As the publication of specialist business papers took off in this period so too did the publication of semi-specialist papers that presented much of the same types of numerical commercial information but to a wider audience. In his newspaper *A Collection for Improvement of Husbandry and Trade*, John Houghton gave regular listings of exchange rates and commodity prices, as well as stock prices. He defended and promoted the stock market as an integral part of a programme of improvement, much of which reinforced natural philosophical priorities. Moreover, many commercial serial publications were, in John McCusker's useful phrase, 'instantly ephemeral' although, as we have seen, Houghton, and the proprietors of at least one provincial paper,

232 *Plymouth Weekly-Journal*, 6 Nov. 1719. See also 25 Nov. 1720, which reported on ships that had arrived and left Bristol, Portsmouth and Deal.
233 *NC*, 12 Jan 1712.
234 Cargoes were also listed in provincial papers. See, for example, *NottM*, 16 July 1719; *NC*, 8 Aug. 1711.
235 Jeake, *Diary*, 238, 240, 243–9, 257.

encouraged their readers to collect their papers and compile figures as political arithmeticians did.

We do not know whether Houghton's paper reached the wide range of readers he hoped, but by the early 1710s it was possible for a paper that offered much of the same information, with some foreign news (rather than essays on trade and husbandry), to have a circulation in the thousands. Moreover, such are the records associated with the Sun Fire Office's *British Mercury* that it has been possible to construct a picture of how stock prices, commodity prices and exchequer data were gathered. It has also been possible to see the great variability in how up-to-date commercial information was across the country. Serial print clearly had explicitly didactic purposes: Houghton hoped to educate his readers about many aspects of trade and in particular about the stock market. Likewise, a quarter of a century later the proprietors of some provincial newspapers felt the need to direct their readers to how stock prices fluctuated.

# Conclusion

One of the threads that runs through much this book has been the circulation of knowledge. At the Royal Exchange we saw a great range of commercial knowledge being established, displayed, discussed and questioned. Not only was the Exchange a hub of specialist commercial knowledge networks it was also where all sorts of information (particularly foreign news) was exchanged orally and in print. As the credit of merchants was negotiated at the Exchange, so too was the status of the information exchanged there.

The stock prices and exchange rates established orally in and around the Exchange were reported in serial publications that circulated widely. These stock prices, as well as exchequer data and commodity prices, appeared in non-specialist business newspapers, and also in provincial newspapers. Such information was gathered for the papers by people who were employed to go and collect it, solicited from paid and unpaid correspondents and also taken from newsletters and specialist business newspapers. Some newspapers defended and promoted the stock market to their readers, others educated their readers in how to understand price fluctuations and a few suggested that readers might make compilations of import and export data.

One of the contexts in which to place some of these initiatives is within the framework of the Royal Society's various programmes for improvement. Commerce was situated by some writers, most notably John Houghton, at the centre of these programmes; Houghton also extended their scope to include the new world of the stock market. Such a context is also appropriate for interpreting some of the merchant manuals. Roger North, for example, argued that commercial know-how might be of interest to gentlemen virtuosi. Natural philosophy, and programmes for improvement in particular, were discursively oriented and the vocabularies of commercial terminology that appeared in some manuals can be read in this context, as well as in the overlapping, but distinctive, contexts of didactic writing, and of movements towards plain language.

As far as possible, in addition to establishing how commercial knowledge and know-how moved about, and the contexts in which they were both developed, an emphasis has been placed on how the culture of commerce might have been consumed, and by whom. Certainly the many merchants who traded noisily and busily in the quadrangle of the Royal Exchange offered a spectacle both to those who visited in person, and to those who were guided by authors. There were other ways in which the curiosity of those interested in commerce could be satisfied. Manuals were probably not always read for technical instruction but also because they might offer an imaginary journey into the world of commerce. Authors claimed that a wide spectrum of people should be interested in commerce. Houghton, for example, asserted that almost all should, for differing reasons, gain something from knowing import and export information; authors of bookkeeping instructions claimed that such skills were widely applicable to all sorts of traders, as well as to youths, women and gentlemen. Whether Houghton reached his desired audience is not that easy to establish but the Sun Fire Office's newspaper, the *British Mercury*, which had many features in common with Houghton's paper, was subscribed to by thousands of readers of the elites and middling sorts.

Evidence for how readers engaged with their texts is sparse. Marginalia in merchant manuals does suggest, however, that some readers used the blank areas in their books in ways that were pertinent to what the book aimed to teach: some recorded struggling with their studies, others scribbled calculations and jotted down accounts, and at least one reader apparently engaged more with the identities of the characters in the specimen accounts than with the details of their transactions.

We have also learned in this book much about the ways commerce was celebrated in the late seventeenth and early eighteenth centuries. Sermons preached before the Levant Company and one of Addison's essays about the Royal Exchange appealed to a model of international trade that imagined it was a 'mutual intercourse' involving the exchange of superfluities between one country and another. Merchants were honoured as heroes in such accounts of trade, and lent their glory not only to institutions like the Exchange, or the Levant Company, but also to London, the nation and the monarch. Merchants were judged by their own standards and not found wanting. The trading world could also be contained and ordered by other images. Representations of the Exchange described the range of luxury imported goods for sale in the shops above and the gathering of international merchants in the quadrangle below. These images captured in words, or a picture, the world of trade in miniature.

There were also detractors of commerce and merchants. Some who attacked merchants used strategies that were not new to this period. Merchants and traders were condemned and satirised for their cheating, cunning and covetous natures and, for some preachers, the wealthy trader always concealed a tormented soul. In its associations with the stock market, much of it conducted in the neighbouring alleys, the Royal Exchange was attacked for being a 'gaming table' offering only investments in insubstantial and ruinous credit.

Indeed, in the culture of commerce, it was the speculative activities of the 1690s that probably had the most impact. It is telling that that none of the newspapers examined in detail in chapter 4 date from the early part of the period. The 1690s witnessed not only the development of specialist business newspapers but also the establishment of newspapers for the more general reader which sought to explain specialist knowledge. Whether Houghton's goal of teaching readers about the stock market had been achieved in London by the beginning of the eighteenth century is difficult to say but certainly the

*British Mercury* felt able to omit explanations for its readers in 1710. In 1720, however, the proprietors of the even less specialist provincial papers, did provide directions for readers interested in that year's dramatic stock market fluctuations.

As the 1690s witnessed the take-off of business newspaper publishing it also saw the beginning of some alterations at the Exchange. As the centre of the city moved away from the Exchange the shops there began to close. They were replaced partly by warehouses but also by businesses related to the financial revolution, such as insurance. If *The Spectator* is to be believed, the quadrangle also declined at the beginning of the eighteenth century but no other evidence points this way. The chronology of the financial revolution can also be seen in the publication of manuals for trade. From the 1690s onwards some authors claimed to address the needs of the employees of the Bank of England, for example, and others provided guides to some of the new and specialist business newspapers. Perhaps one could also argue that the financial revolution, with its demands for a more substantial (and trained) bureaucracy, stimulated a demand for such manuals and the writing school education with which they were often associated.

We do have to be careful not to overemphasise change at the expense of neglecting continuities. Even this relative newcomer – the stock market – might be defended and promoted by being integrated within existing priorities as Houghton did by incorporating it into a Bacon-inspired programme of improvement. Other continuities with both before and after the period are more prominent: a preoccupation with the preservation of personal credit, especially for merchants; concerns about the identity of the merchant, and the continuation of the dispute about his gentle status; the ongoing debate about the relationship between piety and the acquisition of wealth; and the perpetuation of the association of the image of London with trade.

Finally, this book can be situated between, on the one hand, studies of merchant culture, and, on the other, studies of the commercialisation of society more generally, in particular studies of consumption. Much of the book has been concerned with how commerce was presented and packaged for a public composed of those not directly involved in trade. A picture has emerged of the consolidation of commerce as an area of knowledge. Partly through projects undertaken by contemporaries to define a commercial language, and, building on the Royal Society's history of trades agenda, programmes to chart merchants' activities, commerce was seen to be of interest to the scholar. Through the purchase of printed materials, such as manuals instructing in merchant skills, or newspapers giving commercial information, commerce could be consumed, both by the merchants on the Exchange, and by those who gazed down on them from the balconies, or observed their activities from an armchair.

# Bibliography

## Unpublished primary sources

**Cambridge University Library**
Add 1

**Leeds, Yorkshire Archaeological Association**
MS 15

**London, British Library**
MSS Add. 4275, 22910
MS Sloane 2903
MS Stowe 747
India Office Records, B/31; H/MISC/17

**London, Corporation of London Record Office**
Reps 76, 82, 108, 111

**London, Dr Williams's Library**
Roger Morrice's entring book, vol. Q

**London, Guildhall Library**
MS 330
MS 3441
MS 4069/2
MS 11931/1
MS 11931/2

**London, Mercers Company Archives**
Gresham Repertories, 1626–69, 1669–76, 1678–1722

**London Metropolitan Archives**
Consistory Court of London, deposition book, June 1679–June 1681, DL/C/239
Peter Briggins diary, 1706–8, ACC 1017/2

**The National Archives: Public Record Office**
CO 1/20; 1/21; 1/29; 1/30; 1/36; 1/38; 389/3; 391/1
HCA 31/1; 31/24
PROB 4/12879
SO 1/7; 1/8
SP 29/71; 29/143; 29/150; 29/174; 29/181; 29/245; 29/275; 29/291; 47/1; 63/300;

63/330; 63/331; 63/338; 105/113; 105/114; 105/152; 105/153; 105/154;
105/155; 105/156
T 29/27

**London, Royal Society**
Journal books of scientific meetings, vol. 8

**New York, Columbia University Library**
Montgomery collection, MS 95


### Published primary sources

*The allegations of the Turky Company and others against the East-India-Company*,
[London 1681]
[Ammonet, S.], *Key of knowledge for all merchants*, Dublin 1696
[Arderne, James], *Directions concerning the matter and stile of sermons*, London
1671
John Ayres, *The trades-mans copy-book*, London [1688]
———— *Arithmetick*, London 1693
———— *Arithmetick*, London 1695
———— *The accomplish'd clerk regraved*, London 1700
———— *Arithmetick made easie for the use and benefit of trades-men*, London 1718
[Beeverell, James], *Les Délices de la Grand' Bretagne et d'Irlande* [2nd edn], Leiden
1727
Bell, Andrew, *Advertisement. July 25. 1710 To morrow, being the 26th of July, will
begin to be drawn the lottery-tickets at Guildhall*, London 1711
*Bibliotheca curiosa, or, a choice collection of books*, London 1697
Bredberg, Sven, *Griefswald – Wittenberg – Leiden – London: Västgötamagistern Sven
Bredbergs resadagbok 1708–1710 med inledning utgiven*, ed. H. Sandblad,
Göteborg 1982
Brent, Charles, *Honour thy Lord with thy substance*, London 1708
Briscoe, J[ohn], *An explanatory dialogue of a late treatise, intituled, 'A discourse on
the late funds of the Million-Act, Lottery-Act, and Bank of England'*, London
1694
Brown, [Tom], *Amusements serious and comical*, London 1700
Browne, Thomas, *The accurate-accomptant*, London 1669
———— *An accompt partable between four partners upon two several designs*, London
1670
———— *The accurate-accomptant*, London 1670
Brydges, Henry, *A sermon preached at St. Mary Aldermanbury*, London 1701
Bullord, J., *Bibliopoli littleburiani pars quinta, & ultima*, London 1697
Burdett, Charles, *A sermon preach'd before the right worshipful the deputy-governour
and the company of merchants trading to the Levant Seas*, London 1724
Burnet, Gilbert, *A sermon preached at the funeral of Mr. James Houblon*, London
1682
*By the Maior, Whereas divers rude and disordered young-men, apprentices and others,
. . .* [An Order prohibiting the throwing about of squibs and fireworks in the
streets and public passages], London 1674

Campbell, Colen, *Vitruvius Britannicus*, London 1715–25

*The case of Robert Crosfeild*, [London 1696]

Castaing, John, *An interest-book at 4, 5, 6, 7, 8 per c.*, London 1700

Chamberlain, Robert, *The accomptants guide*, London 1679

[Chamberlayne, Edward] *Angliæ notitia*, London 1669

Chishull, Edm[und], *A sermon preach'd before the honourable company of merchants trading to the Levant-seas*, London 1698

——— *Travels in Turkey and back to England*, London 1747

Claypoole, James, *James Claypoole's letter book: London and Philadelphia, 1681–1684*, ed. M. Balderston, San Marino 1967

Clerk, George, *The landed-man's assistant*, London 1715

[Cocker, Edward], *Cocker's arithmetick*, London 1694

——— *Cockers English dictionary*, rev. John Hawkins, London 1704

Colinson, Robert, *Idea rationaria*, Edinburgh 1683

Collins, John, *An introduction to merchants-accompts containing seven distinct questions or accompts*, London 1674

Colsoni, F[rançois], *Le Guide de Londres pour les estrangers*, London 1693

——— *Le Guide de Londres pour les estrangers*, 3rd edn, London 1710

*Commune Concilium tentum in Camera Guild-Hall Civitatis London die Sabbati, vicesimo primo die Februarii, Annoque Domini, 1673* [An act for the regulation of the brokers upon the Royal Exchange], London 1673

*Comune Concil' tent' in Camera Guihald' Civitat' London* [An order appointing hours for meeting in the Royal Exchange], London 1703

*Considerations on the present state of the nation*, London 1720

*The country girl's policy*, [London 1701?]

*The country spy or a ramble thro' London*, London [1730?]

Covel, John, *Some account of the present Greek Church*, London 1722

Cowell, John, *The interpreter*, Cambridge 1607

Crosse, William, *The nature and office of good angels, set forth in a sermon, preach'd before the honourable company of merchants trading to the Levant-seas*, London 1713

[Crouch, Nathaniel] (pseudonym Richard Burton), *Historical remarques*, London 1681

Dafforne, Richard, *The young accomptants compasse*, London 1669

——— *The apprentices time-entertainer accomptantly*, 3rd edn, rev. John Dafforne, London 1670

——— *The merchant's mirrour*, repr. of 3rd edn, London 1684

Dary, Michael, *Interest epitomized*, London 1677

[Davenant, Charles], *An essay upon ways and means of supplying the war*, London 1695

——— *Discourses on the publick revenues*, London 1698

[Defoe, Daniel], *The villainy of stock-jobbers detected*, London 1701

——— *The free-holders plea against stock-jobbing elections of parliament men*, 2nd edn, London 1701

——— *The anatomy of Exchange-Alley*, London 1719

——— *A tour thro' the whole island of Great Britain*, London 1724

——— *The complete English tradesman*, London 1726

——— *The compleat English gentleman*, ed. K. D. Bülbring, London 1890

Delaune, Tho[mas], *The present state of London*, London 1681

Dougharty, John, *The general-gauger*, London 1707

––––––– *Mathematical digests*, London [1747?]

[Duke, Henry], Ehver Kynd, *Londons-nonsuch*, London 1668

––––––– DEHNKRVY, *A brief memorial wherein the present case of the antient leasees . . . [is] truely, and impartially stated*, London 1674

Dunton, John, *The he-strumpets*, 4th edn, in his *Athenianism*, London 1710, ii. 93–9.

D['Urfey], T[homas], *Collin's walk through London and Westminster*, London 1690

Earle, John, *Micro-cosmographie*, 9th edn, London 1669

Edler, William, *The modish pen-man*, London 1691

Elliott, George, *Great Brittain's beauty*, London 1671

*Englands golden treasury*, London 1691

Evelyn, John, *London revived: consideration for its rebuilding in 1666*, ed. E. S. De Beer, Oxford 1938

––––––– *The diary of John Evelyn*, ed. E. S. De Beer, London 1955

Every, John, *Speculum mercativum*, London 1674

F., J., *The merchant's ware-house laid open*, London 1696

Ferguson, Robert, *A letter to a person of honour concerning the black box*, London 1680.

[Ford, Simon], *London's resurrection*, London 1669

Frampton, Robert, *The life of Robert Frampton bishop of Gloucester deprived as a non-juror 1689*, ed. T. S. Evans, London 1876

Fryer Mayor, *Martis xxxi die Januarii, 1720* [Order of the Court of Aldermen in reference to persons acting as brokers within the City of London without having been legally admitted to do so], London 1720

Gailhard, J[ean], *The compleat gentleman*, London 1678

Giles, Jacob, *Lex mercatoria*, 2nd edn, London 1729

[Glanvill, Joseph], *An essay concerning preaching*, London 1678

*Glossographia angliana nova*, London 1707

Goldwin, William, *A poetical description of Bristol*, London 1712

––––––– *A poetical description of Bristol*, rev. I. Smart, London 1761

Gough, Richard, *British topography*, London 1780

Graunt, John, *Natural and political observations*, 2nd edn, London 1662

Gregory, James, *James Gregory: tercentenary memorial volume, containing his correspondence with John Collins and his hitherto unpublished mathematical manuscripts, together with addresses and essays communicated to the Royal Society of Edinburgh, July 4th, 1938*, ed. H. W. Turnbull, Edinburgh 1939

H., N., *The compleat tradesman*, London 1684

Hacket, Laurence, *A sermon preach'd at St. Bennet-Finct Church*, London 1707

Hainsworth, D. R. (ed.), *The correspondence of Sir John Lowther of Whitehaven, 1693–1698: a provincial community in wartime*, Oxford 1983

Halifax, William, 'A relation of a voyage from Aleppo to Palmyra in Syria; sent by the Reverend Mr. William Halifax to Dr. Edw. Bernard (late) Savilian Professor of Astronomy in Oxford, and by him communicated to Dr. Thomas Smith. Reg. Soc. C.', *PT* xix (1695–7), 83–110

––––––– *A letter to a clergyman in the City concerning the instructions lately given to the proctors*, London 1702

––––––– *A sermon preach'd at Old Swinford in Worcester-shire*, London 1702

Handson, Ralph, *Analysis or resolution of merchants accompts*, 4th edn, London 1669

Hardy, Nath[aniel], *Carduus Benedictus, the advantage of affliction, or the reward of patience: unfolded in a sermon preached at the funeralls of Mr Thomas Bowyer Merchant*, London 1659

Hatton, Edw[ard], *The merchant's magazine*, London 1695

———— *An exact table of the weight of gold and silver*, London 1696

———— *Comes commercii*, London 1699

———— *The merchant's magazine*, 3rd edn, London 1699

———— *The merchant's magazine*, 5th edn, London 1707

———— *A new view of London*, London 1708

———— *Index to interest*, London 1711

———— *The merchant's magazine*, 6th edn, London 1712

———— *Index to interest*, London 1714

———— *Index to interest*, London 1717

———— *Comes commercii*, 4th edn, London 1723

———— *The merchant's magazine*, 8th edn, London 1726

Hawkins, John, *Clavis commercii*, London 1689

———— *Clavis commercii*, London 1718.

Hayley, William, *A sermon preached before the right honourable George Berkeley governour, and the company of merchants of England trading into the Levant seas*, London 1687

Hearne, Thomas, *Remarks and collections of Thomas Hearne*, ed. C. E. Doble, Oxford 1885–1921

*Hickelty pickelty*, London 1708

Hickman, Charles, *A sermon preached before the right honourable George earl of Berkeley, governour, and the company of merchants of England trading into the Levant Seas*, London 1681

H[ill], J[ohn], *The exact dealer*, London 1688

———— *The exact dealer refined*, London 1698

Historic Manuscripts Commission, *Fifth report*, London 1876

———— *Seventh report*, London 1879

———— *Twelfth report, appendix VII, the manuscripts of S. H. Fleming, Esq., of Rydal Hall*, London 1890

———— *Thirteenth report: the manuscripts of his grace the duke of Portland*, London 1891–1931

———— *Calendar of the Stuart papers belonging to His Majesty the King, preserved at Windsor Castle*, London 1902–23

Houghton, John, *A proposal for improvement of husbandry and trade*, London 1691

Hughes, John, *A sermon preach'd before the right honourable George earl of Berkley, governour, and the company of merchants of England trading in the Levant Seas*, London 1683

Jacob, Giles, *Lex mercatoria*, 2nd edn, London 1729

*The Jamaica lady*, London 1720

Jeake, Samuel, *An astrological diary of the seventeenth century: Samuel Jeake of Rye, 1652–1699*, ed. M. Hunter and A. Gregory, Oxford 1988

*Jovis Primo die Decembr' 1692; Annoque Regni Regis & Regine, Willielmi & Mariæ, Angl'*, London 1692

Justice, Alexander, *A general treatise of monies and exchanges*, London 1707

King, Thomas, *An exact guide to book-keeping*, London 1717

Knight, Val[entine], *Proposals for a new modell for re-building the City of London*, London 1666

Lawrence, Edward, *Two funeral sermons of the use and happiness of humane bodies*, London 1690

Letsome, Sampson, *The preacher's assistant*, London [1753]

Levett Mayor, *Jovis Decimo die Octobris, 1700. Annoq; Regni Regis Willielmi Tertii Angliæ, &c.* [Order that none of the Exchange brokers do for the future agitate any business in open Alley, 10 Oct. 1700], London 1700

Leybourn, William, *Panarithmologia*, London 1693

——— *Four tables of accompts ready cast up*, London 1695?

Liset, Abraham, *Amphithalami, or, the accomptants closet*, London 1660

[Locke, John], *Some thoughts concerning education*, London 1693

——— *Two treatises of government*, ed. P. Laslett, 2nd edn, Cambridge 1967

*London almanack for the year of our Lord 1706*, London 1706

*The London and Westminster guide*, London 1768

Luke, John, *A sermon preached before the right worshipful company of the Levant merchants at St. Olav's Hart-street London*, London 1664

McGrath, P. (ed.), *Merchants and merchandise in seventeenth-century Bristol*, Bristol 1955

[Macky, John], *A journey through England*, London 1714

Maitland, William, *The history of London from its foundation by the Romans, to the present time*, London 1739

Malcolm, Alexander, *A new treatise of arithmetick and book-keeping*, Edinburgh 1718

Malynes, Gerard, *Consuetudo, vel lex mercatoria*, London 1622

——— *Consuetudo, vel lex mercatoria*, London 1636

——— *Consuetudo, vel lex mercatoria*, London 1686

Mandeville, Bernard, *The fable of the bees*, London 1714

Marius, John, *Advice concerning bills of exchange*, 2nd edn, London 1670

Martindale, Adam, *The country survey book*, London 1702

Matthews, A. G., *Calamy revised: being a revision of Edmund Calamy's account of the ministers and others ejected and silenced, 1660–2*, Oxford 1934, repr. 1988

Maundrell, Henry, *A sermon preach'd before the honourable company of merchants trading to the Levant-seas*, London 1696

——— *A journey from Aleppo to Jerusalem at Easter, A. D. 1697*, 2nd edn, Oxford 1727.

——— *A journey from Aleppo to Jerusalem in 1697*, Beirut 1963

Mayne, John, *Socius mercatoris*, London 1674

M[ercer], T[homas], *The young accomptants remembrancer*, London 1692

[Miège, Guy], *The new state of England*, 3rd edn, London 1699

Millington, Edward, *A catalogue of the library of books . . . of Mr Peter Hushar*, London 1685

Milward, John, *The diary of John Milward Esq*, ed. C. Robbins, Cambridge 1938

[Misson, Henri], *Mémoires et observations faites par un voyageur en Angleterre*, The Hague 1698

Moll, Herman, *A system of geography*, London 1701

[Monteage, Stephen?], *Advice to the women and maidens of London*, London 1678

Monteage, Stephen, *Debtor and creditor made easie*, 2nd edn, London 1682

——— *Debtor and creditor made easy*, 4th edn, London 1708

Mould, Bernard, *A sermon preach'd before the right worshipful the deputy governor and the company of merchants trading to the Levant-seas*, London 1717

Moxon, Joseph, *Mechanick exercises*, London 1677–80

——— *Mathematicks made easie*, London 1679

Mun, Thomas, *England's benefit and advantage by forein-trade*, London 1700

Muralt, [Béat Louis de], *Lettres sur les anglois et les françois*, Cologne 1725

——— *Letters describing the character and customs of the French and English nations*, 2nd edn, London 1726

Nicholas, Abraham, *The young accomptant's debitor and creditor*, London 1711

Nicolson, William, *The London diaries of William Nicolson bishop of Carlisle, 1702–1718*, ed. C. Jones and G. Holmes, Oxford 1985

[North, Roger], *The gentleman accomptant*, London 1714

——— *The gentleman accomptant*, 3rd edn, London 1721

——— *The lives of the Right Hon. Francis North, Baron Guildford; the Hon. Sir Dudley North; and the Hon. and Rev. Dr. John North*, ed. A. Jessopp, London 1890

——— 'Etimology, as other criticall studys, are very usefull In ye world', in Korsten, *Roger North*, 160–5.

Nott, H. E. and E. Ralph (eds), *The deposition books of Bristol, II: 1650–1654*, Bristol 1948

Ogilby, John, *The entertainment of His Most Excellent Majestie Charles II*, London 1662

——— and William Morgan, *London survey'd*, London 1677

Owen, Thomas, *A sermon preach'd before the honourable company of merchants trading to the Levant-seas*, London 1706

Payne, Thomas, *A sermon preach'd before the right worshipful the deputy governour and the company of merchants trading to the Levant seas*, London 1718

Pepys, Samuel, *Samuel Pepys's naval minutes*, ed. J. R. Tanner, London 1926

——— *The diary of Samuel Pepys*, ed. R. Latham and W. Mathews, London 1970–84

Peter Murray Hill Ltd, *Catalogue* lxxxii (1962)

Petty, William, *The Petty papers*, ed. the marquis of Landsdowne, London 1927

Philalethes, Theophilus, *Great Britain's glory*, London 1672

Phillipes, Henry, *The purchasers pattern*, London 1656

Pilkington Mayor, [Order enforcing rules for hackney coaches], [London, 1691]

*A poem upon the new marble statue of his present majesty*, London 1684

Povey, Charles, *Proposals for raising a fund of two thousand pounds*, London 1706

*A preamble to the books for taking a subscription of ten hundred thousand pounds for the use of the Bank of England*, London 1713

*The proceedings on the king's commission of the peace, and oyer and terminer, and gaol-delivery of Newgate, held for the City of London, and county of Middlesex, at justice-hall in the Old Bayly, on Wednesday, Thursday, Friday, and Saturday, being the 25th, 26th, 27th, and 28th of February*, 1718

[Ralph, James?], *A critical review of the publick buildings, statues and ornaments, in and about London and Westminster*, London 1734

Rastell, John, *Exposicio[n]es t[er]mi[n]o[rum] legu[m] anglo[rum]*, London 1523

R[ay], J[ohn], *A collection of English proverbs*, Cambridge 1670

R[ichards], T[homas], *The gentlemans auditor*, London 1707

Roberts, Lewes, *The merchants map of commerce*, 2nd edn, London 1671

Rolle, Samuel, *[Shlohavot] or, the burning of London in the year 1666*, London 1667

*A sad and deplorable, but true account of the dreadful hardships, and sufferings of Capt. John Dean, and his company*, London 1711

Schellinks, William, *The journal of William Schellinks' travels in England, 1661–1663*, ed. M. Exwood and H. L. Lehmann, London 1993

Scott, John, *A sermon preach'd at the funeral of Sir John Buckworth*, London 1688

Settle, Elkanah, *The triumphs of London, for the inauguration of the right honourable Sir William Gore*, London 1701

Smith, Edward, 'An account of a strange kind of earth, taken up near Smyrna, of which is made soap, together with the way of making it', *PT* xix (1695–7), 228–30

———— 'Of the use of opium among the Turks', *PT* xix (1695–7), 288–90

———— 'Extract from the minutes of Philosophical Society at Oxford, Feb. 8. 1684, concerning Rusma and Alcanna', *PT* xx (1698), 295

Smith, John, *The sea-mans grammar and dictionary*, London 1692

Smith, Joseph, *Nouveau Théâtre de la Grande Bretagne*, London 1724

Smith, S. D. (ed.) *'An exact and industrious tradesman': the letter book of Joseph Symson of Kendal, 1711–1720*, Oxford 2002

Smith, Thomas, *Diatriba de chaldaicis paraphrastis, eorúmque versionibus, ex utroque Talmude, ac scriptis rabbinorum concinnata*, Oxford 1662

———— *A sermon preached before the right worshipful company of merchants trading into the Levant*, London 1668.

———— *Remarks upon the manners, religion and government of the Turks*, London 1678

———— 'Historical observations relating to Constantinople', *PT* xiii (1683), 335–46

———— 'An account of the city of Prusa in Bithynia, and a continuation of the historical observations relating to Constantinople', *PT* xiv (1684), 432–54

———— 'Journal of a voyage from England to Constantinople, made in the year 1668', *PT* xix (1695–7), 597–619

———— *Admodum reverendi & doctissimi viri, D. Roberti Huntingtoni, S. theologiæ doctoris, et episcopi rapotensis, epistolæ*, London 1704

———— 'The life and travels of the right rev. and learned Dr Robert Huntington', *Gentleman's Magazine* xcv (1825), 11–15, 115–19, 218–21

Smyth, Edward, *A sermon preached before the right worshipful the deputy-governour, and the company of merchants trading to the Levant-Seas*, London 1689

Snell, Charles, *Rules for book-keeping*, London 1701

———— *Accompts for landed-men*, London [1711?]

Soley, Joseph, *A sermon preach'd before the right worshipful the deputy governour and the company of merchants trading to the Levant-seas*, London 1719

Sorbière, [Samuel], *Relation d'un voyage en Angleterre*, Paris 1664

———— *A voyage to England*, London 1709

Spicer, John, *Tables of interest*, London 1693

Sprat, Tho[mas], *History of the Royal-Society of London*, London 1667

Steele, Richard, *The trades-man's calling*, London 1684

Stow, John, *Survay of London*, London 1598

———— *A survey of the cities of London and Westminster*, rev. John Strype, London 1720

Sun Fire Office, *Proposals set forth by the company of London-insurers*, London (16 Aug.) 1710

———— *Proposals set forth by the company of London insurers*, London (30 Aug.) 1710

————*The case of the members of the Sun-Fire-Office*, [London 1712]

———— *Proposals set forth by the company of the Sun-Fire-Office*, London 1712

Taubman, M., *London's yearly jubilee*, London 1686

Temple, Sir Richard, *Some short remarks upon Mr Lock's book*, London 1696

Thoresby, Ralph, *The diary of Ralph Thoresby*, ed. J. Hunter, London 1830

Tisser, John, *A sermon preached . . . before the honourable company of merchants trading into the Levant-seas*, London 1702

'The Treasury and the City: a proposal to create an assistant (financial) secretary, 1710', in H. Roseveare, *The Treasury, 1660–1870: the foundations of control*, London 1973, 174–5

*Troia rediviva*, London 1674

*The tryal and conviction of several reputed sodomites*, London 1707

Turner Mayor, *Martis vicesimo sexto die Januarii, 1668. Annóque Regni Regis Caroli Secundi, Dei Grat', Angliæ, &c. vicesimo* [Order respecting the hours of meeting of the citizens, merchants and traders, frequenting the Burse or Royal Exchange, 26 January 1668], London 1668

Twells, Dr, *The lives of Dr Edward Pocock*, London 1816

*An useful companion*, London 1709

Vernon, John, *The compleat comptinghouse*, London 1678

———— *The compleat comptinghouse*, London 1698

Voltaire, *Letters concerning the English nation*, London 1733

Von Uffenbach, Zacharias Conrad, *London in 1710 from the travels of Zacharias Conrad Von Uffenbach*, ed. and trans. W. H. Quarrell and M. Mare, London n.d.

Waker, Nathanael, *A sermon preached at the funeral of Mr. Lucas Lucie*, London 1664

Walford, Benj[amin], *Catalogus variorum & insignium librorum ex diversis europæ partibus advectorum*, London 1691

———— *Catalogue variorum & insignium tam antiquorum quam recentium librorum*, London 1691

Wallis, Richard, *London's armory accuratly delineated*, London 1677

Ware, James, *The works of Sir James Ware concerning Ireland revised and improved*, I: *The history of the bishops of that kingdom*, Dublin 1739

Watts, Thomas, *An essay on the proper method for forming the man of business*, ed. A. H. Cole, Cambridge, Mass. 1946

Webster, William, *An essay on book-keeping*, London 1719

Willsford, Thomas, *The scales of commerce and trade*, London 1660

Wood, John, *A description of the Exchange of Bristol*, Bath 1743

[Worlidge, John], *Dictionarium rusticum, urbanicum & botanicum*, 3rd edn, London 1726

## Newspapers and periodicals

British Mercury
Castaing, John, *The Course of the Exchange, and other things*
*The Historical Register*
*The History of the Works of the Learned*
Houghton, John, *A Collection for Improvement of Husbandry and Trade*
────── *A Collection of Letters for the Improvement of Husbandry & Trade*
*Ipswich-Journal, or, the Weekly-Mercury*
*Leeds Mercury*
*London Gazette*
*London Journal*
*Merchant's News-Letter*
*Miscellaneous Letters, Giving an Account of the Works of the Learned*
*New-castle Courant*
*Northampton Mercury*
*Nottingham Mercury*
*Plymouth Weekly-Journal*
Povey, Charles, *The General Remark on Trade*
*The Spectator*
[Ward, Edward], *The London Spy*
*Weekly Courant* (Nottingham)
*Whiston's Weekly Remembrancer*
*White-hall Evening Post*
*Worcester Post-Man*
*Works of the Learned*
*York Mercury*

## Secondary sources

Adams, B., *London illustrated, 1604–1851: a survey and index of topographical books and their plates*, London 1983

Aho, J. A., 'Rhetoric and the invention of double entry bookkeeping', *Rhetorica* iii (1985), 21–43

Ambrose, G., 'English traders at Aleppo (1658–1756)', *EcHR* 1st ser. iii (1931), 246–67

Anderson, B. L., 'Provincial aspects of the financial revolution of the eighteenth century', *BH* xi (1969), 11–22

Anderson, J. S. M., *The history of the Church of England in the colonies and foreign dependencies of the British empire*, 2nd edn, London 1856

Anderson, S. P., *An English consul in Turkey: Paul Rycaut at Smyrna, 1667–1678*, Oxford 1989

Andrew, D. T., 'Aldermen and big bourgeoisie of London reconsidered', *SH* vi (1981), 359–64

Angell, S., *An historical sketch of the Royal Exchange*, London 1838

Appleby, J. O., *Economic thought and ideology in seventeenth-century England*, Princeton 1978

Ashton, J., *A history of English lotteries: now for the first time written*, London 1893

Ashton, R., *The crown and the money market, 1603–1640*, Oxford 1960

Aspinall, A. W., *Catalogue of the Pepys Library at Magdalene College Cambridge*, III: *Prints and drawings*, I: *General*, ed. R. Latham, Woodbridge 1980

Aubain, M., 'Par-Dessus les marchés: gestes et paroles de la circulation des biens d'après Savary des Bruslons', *Annales* xxxix (1984), 820–30

Beckett, J. V., 'Social mobility and English landed society', *Social History Society Newsletter* xii (1987), 3–5

Beier, A. L. and R. Finlay (eds), *The making of the metropolis: London, 1500–1700*, London 1986

Belcher, W. F., 'The sale and distribution of the *British Apollo*', in R. P. Bond (ed.), *Studies in the early English periodical*, Chapel Hill 1957, 75–101

Berg, M., *A woman in history: Eileen Power, 1889–1940*, Cambridge 1996

—— and H. Clifford (eds), *Consumers and luxury: consumer culture in Europe, 1650–1850*, Manchester 1999

—— and P. Hudson, 'Rehabilitating the industrial revolution', *EcHR* 2nd ser. xlv (1992), 24–50

Bermingham, A. and J. Brewer (eds), *The consumption of culture, 1600–1800: image, object, text*, London 1995

Berry, C. J., *The idea of luxury: a conceptual and historical investigation*, Cambridge 1994

Blagden, C., *The Stationers' Company: a history, 1403–1959*, London 1960

Blondel, M., 'French and English eighteenth-century guide-books to London: plagiarism and translations', *Notes and Queries* ccxxx (1985), 240–1

Borsay, P., *The English urban renaissance: culture and society in the provincial town, 1660–1770*, Oxford 1989

—— 'The London connection: cultural diffusion and the eighteenth-century provincial town', *LJ* xix (1994), 21–35

Bowen, H. V., ' "The pests of human society": stockbrokers, jobbers and speculators in mid-eighteenth-century Britain', *History* lxxviii (1993), 38–53

—— *Elites, enterprise and the making of the British overseas empire, 1688–1775*, Basingstoke 1996

Boys, P. G., 'Samuel Pepys's personal accounts', *Accounting, Business and Financial History* v (1995), 308–20

Braudel, F., *The wheels of commerce*, trans. S. Roberts, London 1982

Breen, T. H., 'An empire of goods: the Anglicization of colonial America, 1690–1776', *JBS* xxv (1986), 467–99

Brewer, J., *The sinews of power: war, money and the English state, 1688–1783*, Cambridge, Mass. 1990

—— and R. Porter (eds), *Consumption and the world of goods*, London 1993

Brooks, C., 'Public finance and political stability: the administration of the land tax, 1688–1720', *HJ* xvii (1974), 281–300

Buck, P., 'People who counted: political arithmetic in the eighteenth century', *Isis* lxxiii (1982), 28–45

Bywater, M. F., and B. S. Yamey, *Historic accounting literature: a companion guide*, London 1982

Cain, P. J. and A. G. Hopkins, 'Gentlemanly capitalism and British expansion overseas, I: The old colonial system, 1688–1850', *EcHR* 2nd ser. xxxix (1986), 501–25

—— *British imperialism: innovation and explansion, 1688–1914*, London 1993

Cairncross, A. K., 'In praise of economic history', *EcHR* 2nd ser. xlii (1989), 173–85

Cannadine, D., 'Economic history', in his *The pleasures of the past*, New York 1989

Capp, B., *Astrology and the popular press: English almanacs*, London 1979

Carlos, A. M. and S. Nicholas, 'Agency problems in early chartered companies: the case of the Hudson's Bay Company', *JEcH* i (1990), 853–75

Carruthers, B. G., *City of capital: politics and markets in the English financial revolution*, Princeton 1996

———— and W. N. Espeland, 'Accounting for rationality: double-entry bookkeeping and the rhetoric of economic rationality', *American Journal of Sociology* lxlvii (1991), 31–69

Carswell, J., *The South Sea Bubble*, London 1960

Caudle, J., 'Preaching in parliament: patronage, publicity and politics in Britain, 1701–1760', in Ferrell and McCullough, *English sermon revised*, 235–63

Chartres, J. A., 'The marketing of agricultural produce', in J. Thirsk (ed.), *The agrarian history of England and Wales, V: 1640–1750, II: Agrarian change*, Cambridge 1985, 406–502

Chatfield, M., *A history of accounting thought*, Hinsdale, Il. 1974

Chaudhuri, K. N., *The trading world of Asia and the English East India Company, 1660–1760*, Cambridge 1978

Cipolla, C. M., *Between history and economics: an introduction to economic history*, trans. C. Woodall, first published 1988, Oxford 1991

Clark, G., *Betting on lives: the culture of life insurance in England, 1695–1775*, Manchester 1999

Claydon, T., 'The sermon, the "public sphere" and the political culture of late seventeenth-century England', in Ferrell and McCullough, *English sermon revised*, 208–34

Clemens, P. G. E., 'The rise of Liverpool, 1665–1750', *EcHR* 2nd ser. xxix (1976), 211–25

Cochran, T. C., 'Cultural factors in economic growth', *JEcH* xx (1960), 515–30

Cockerell, H. A. L. and E. Green, *The British insurance business, 1547–1970: an introduction and guide to historical records in the United Kingdom*, London 1976

Cohen, P. C., *A calculating people: the spread of numeracy in early America*, Chicago 1982

Cole, A. H., 'Conspectus for a history of economic and business literature', *JEcH* xvii (1957), 333–88

Coleman, D. C., 'Early modern economic history', *EcHR* 2nd ser. xxv (1972), 690–6

———— *History and the economic past: an account of the rise and decline of economic history in Britain*, Oxford 1987

———— 'History, economic history and the numbers game', *HJ* xxviii (1995), 635–46

Colley, L., *Britons: forging the nation, 1707–1837*, London 1992

Copley, S., 'Commerce, conversation and politeness in the early eighteenth-century periodical', *British Journal for Eighteenth-Century Studies* xviii (1995), 63–77

Corfield, P. J., 'The rivals: landed and other gentlemen', in N. B. Harte and R. E. Quinault (eds), *Land and society in Britain, 1700–1914*, Manchester 1996, 1–33

Crafts, N. F. R., *British economic growth during the industrial revolution*, Oxford 1985

Cranfield, G. A., *The development of the provincial newspaper, 1700–1760*, Oxford 1962

Cressy, D., 'Books as totems in seventeenth-century England and New England', *Journal of Library History* xxi (1986), 92–106

Cust, R., 'News and politics in early seventeenth-century England', *P&P* cxii (1986), 60–90

Dabydeen, D., *Hogarth, Walpole and commercial Britain*, London 1987

Dallas, J., 'The City of London and its dragons', *Journal of the British Archaeological Association* xix (1913), 88–102

Daunton, M., 'What is economic history . . .?', in J. Gardiner (ed.), *What is history today . . .?*, Basingstoke 1988, 37–8

Davies, K. G., 'Joint-stock investment in the later seventeenth century', *EcHR* 2nd ser. iv (1952), 283–301

Davis, N. Z., 'Sixteenth-century French arithmetics of the business life', *Journal of the History of Ideas* xxi (1960), 18–48

Davis, R., 'English foreign trade, 1660–1700', *EcHR* 2nd ser. vii (1954–5), 150–66

———— 'English foreign trade, 1700–1774', *EcHR* 2nd ser. xv (1962–3), 285–303

De Beer, E. S., 'The development of the guide-book until the early nineteenth century', *Journal of the British Archaeological Association* 3rd ser. xv (1952), 35–46

de Krey, G. S., *A fractured society: the politics of London in the first age of party, 1688–1715*, Oxford 1985

Deane, P. and W. A. Cole, *British economic growth, 1688–1959: trends and structure*, 2nd edn, Cambridge 1967

DeMaria, Jr, R., *Johnson's* Dictionary *and the language of learning*, Oxford 1986

Desmond, R. (ed.), *Dictionary of British and Irish botanists and horticulturists: including plant collectors, flower painters and garden designers*, London 1994

Dickson, P. G. M., *The Sun Insurance Office, 1710–1960: the history of two and a half centuries of British insurance*, London 1960

———— *The financial revolution in England: a study of the development of public credit, 1688–1756*, Oxford 1967

Donald, D., ' "Mr Deputy Dumpling and family": satirical images of the city merchant in eighteenth-century England', *Burlington Magazine* cxxxi (1989), 755–63

Dottin, P., *Robinson Crusoe examin'd and criticis'd or a new edition of Charles Gildon's famous pamphlet now published with an introduction and explanatory notes together with an essay on Gildon's life*, London 1923

Dowling, S. W., *The Exchanges of London*, London 1929

Duguid, C., *The Stock Exchange*, rev. E. D. Kissan, 5th edn, London 1926

Earle, P., *The making of the English middle class: business, society and family life in London, 1660–1730*, London 1989

Edwards, J. R., *A history of financial accounting*, London 1989

Eisenstein, E. L., *The printing press as an agent of change: communications and cultural transformations in early-modern Europe*, Cambridge 1979

Estabrook, C. B., *Urbane and rustic England: cultural ties and social spheres in the provinces, 1660–1780*, Manchester 1998

Ewen, C. L'Estrange, *Lotteries and sweepstakes*, London 1932

Feather, J., *The provincial book trade in eighteenth-century England*, Cambridge 1995

Feavearyear, A., *The pound sterling: a history of English money*, Oxford 1963

Feingold, M., 'Oriental studies', in N. Tyacke (ed.), *The history of the University of Oxford*, IV: *Seventeenth-century Oxford*, Oxford 1997, 449–504

Ferdinand, C. Y., 'Selling it to the provinces: news and commerce round eighteenth-century Salisbury', in Brewer and Porter, *Consumption and the world of goods*, 393–411

Ferrell, L. A., and P. McCullough, 'Revising the study of the English sermon', in Ferrell and McCullough, *English sermon revised*, 2–21

——— (eds), *The English sermon revised: religion, literature and history, 1600–1750*, Manchester 2000

Finkelstein, A., *Harmony and the balance: an intellectual history of seventeenth-century English economic history*, Ann Arbor 2000

Fitzmaurice, A., ' "Every man, that prints, adventures": the rhetoric of the Virginia Company sermons', in Ferrell and McCullough, *English sermon revised*, 24–42

Foster, J., *Alumni oxonienses: the members of the University of Oxford, 1500–1714: their parentage, birthplace, and year of birth, with a record of their degrees*, Oxford 1891–2

Fox, A., *Oral and literate culture in England, 1500–1700*, Oxford 2000

Fox-Davies, A. C., 'Domine dirige nos', *The Genealogical Magazine* ii (1898–9), 249–56

Francis, J., *Chronicles and characters of the Stock Exchange*, London 1849

French, C. J., ' "Crowded with traders and a great commerce": London's domination of English overseas trade, 1700–1775', *LJ* xvii (1992), 27–35

Gauci, P., *The politics of trade: the overseas merchant in state and society, 1660–1720*, Oxford 2001

Gibson, K., ' "The kingdom's marble chronicle": the embellishment of the first and second buildings, 1600–1690', in Saunders, *Royal Exchange*, 138–73

Glaisyer, N., 'Merchants at the Royal Exchange, 1660–1720', in Saunders, *Royal Exchange*, 198–202

——— 'Readers, correspondents and communities: John Houghton's A Collection for Improvement of Husbandry and Trade (1692–1703)', in A. Shepard and P. Withington (eds), *Communities in early modern England: networks, place, rhetoric*, Manchester 2000, 235–51

——— 'Networking: trade and exchange in the eighteenth-century British empire', *HJ* xlvii (2004), 451–76

——— and S. Pennell (eds), *Didactic literature in England, 1500–1800: expertise constructed*, Aldershot 2003

Glennie, P., 'Consumption within historical studies', in D. Miller (ed.), *Acknowledging consumption: a review of new studies*, London 1995, 164–203

Goldgar, A., *Impolite learning: conduct and community in the republic of letters, 1680–1750*, New Haven 1995

Goldie, M., 'Roger Morrice and his entring book', *History Today*, Nov. 2001, 38–44

Grassby, R., 'The rate of profit in seventeenth-century England', *EHR* lxxxiv (1969), 721–51

——— 'The personal wealth of the business community in seventeenth-century England', *EcHR* 2nd ser. xxiii (1970), 220–34

—— 'Social mobility and business enterprise in seventeenth-century England', in D. Pennington and K. Thomas (eds), *Puritans and revolutionaries: essays in seventeenth-century history presented to Christopher Hill*, Oxford 1978

—— *The English gentleman in trade: the life and works of Sir Dudley North, 1641–1691*, Oxford 1994

—— *The business community of seventeenth-century England*, Cambridge 1995

Green, J., *Chasing the sun: dictionary-makers and the dictionaries they made*, London 1996

Grote, D., J. Hoock and W. Starke, 'Handbücher und Traktate für den Gebrauch des Kaufmanns, 1470–1820: Bibliographie und Analyse des Wandels einer literarischen Gattung', *Tijdschrift voor Geschiedenis* ciii (1990), 279–93

Gunn, J. A. W., *Politics and the public interest in the seventeenth century*, London 1969

Hallett, M., *The spectacle of difference: graphic satire in the age of Hogarth*, New Haven 1999

Halliday, S., 'Social mobility, demographic change and the landed elite of County Durham, 1610–1819: an open or shut case?', *Northern History* xxx (1994), 49–63

Hamilton, A., 'The English interest in the Arabic-speaking Christians', in Russell, *'Arabick' interest*, 30–53

Hancock, D., ' "Domestic bubbling": eighteenth-century London merchants and individual investment in the funds', *EcHR* 2nd ser. xlvii (1994), 679–702

—— *Citizens of the world: London merchants and the integration of the British Atlantic community, 1735–1785*, Cambridge 1995

Hans, N., *New trends in education in the eighteenth century*, London 1951

Hanson, J., 'Order and structure in urban design: the plans for the rebuilding of London after the Great Fire of 1666', *Ekistics* lvi (1989), 22–42

Harris, M., 'Newspaper distribution during Queen Anne's reign: Charles Delafaye and the secretary of state's office', in R. W. Hunt, I. G. Philip and R. J. Roberts (eds), *Studies in the book trade in honour of Graham Pollard*, Oxford 1975, 139–51

—— *London newspapers in the age of Walpole: a study of the origins of the modern English press*, London 1987

—— 'Exchanging information: print and business at the Royal Exchange in the late seventeenth century', in Saunders, *Royal Exchange*, 188–97

—— 'Timely notices: the uses of advertising and its relationship to news during the late seventeenth century', *Prose Studies* xxi (1998), 141–56

—— 'Shipwrecks in print; representations of maritime disaster in the late seventeenth century', in R. Myers and M. Harris (eds), *Journeys through the market: travel, travellers and the book trade*, Newcastle, Del. 1999, 39–63

Harris, R., 'The Bubble Act: its passage and its effects on business organization', *JEcH* liv (1994), 610–27

Harrison, J., *The library of Isaac Newton*, Cambridge 1978

—— and P. Laslett, *The library of John Locke*, Oxford 1965

Hartwell, R. M., 'Good old economic history', *JEcH* xxxiii (1973), 28–40

Heal, A., *London tradesmen's cards of the xviii century: an account of their origin and use*, London 1925

—— '17th-century booksellers' & stationers' trade-cards', *Alphabet and Image* viii (1948), 51–62

Helgerson, R., *Forms of nationhood: the Elizabethan writing of England*, Chicago 1992

Herbert, W., *The history of the twelve great livery companies of London*, London 1836–7

Hirschman, A. O., *The passions and the interests: political arguments for capitalism before its triumph*, Princeton 1977

Holmes, G., *Augustan England: professions, state and society, 1680–1730*, London 1982

Holt, P. M., 'The study of Arabic historians in seventeenth century England: the background and the work of Edward Pococke', *Bulletin of the School of Oriental and African Studies* xix (1957), 444–55

———— 'Background to Arabic studies in seventeenth-century England', in Russell, *'Arabick' interest*, 20–9

Honoré, J., 'Charles Gildon rédacteur du *British Mercury* (1711–1712): les attaques contre Pope, Swift, et les wits', *Études anglaises* xv (1962), 347–64

Hoock, J. and P. Jeannin, *Ars mercatoria: eine analytische Bibliographie*, II: *1600–1700*, Paderborn 1993

Hoppit, J., 'Financial crises in eighteenth-century England', *EcHR* 2nd ser. xxxix (1986), 39–58

———— 'The use and abuse of credit in eighteenth-century England', in McKendrick and Outhwaite, *Business life and public policy*, 64–78

———— *Risk and failure in English business, 1700–1800*, Cambridge 1987

———— 'Attitudes to credit in Britain, 1680–1790', *HJ* xiii (1990), 305–22

———— 'Political arithmetic in eighteenth-century England', *EcHR* 2nd ser. xlix (1996), 526–40

———— 'The myths of the South Sea Bubble', *TRHS* xii (2002), 141–65

Horsefield, J. K., *British monetary experiments, 1650–1710*, Cambridge, Mass. 1960

Horwitz, H., ' "The mess of the middle class" revisited: the case of the "big bourgeoisie" of Augustan London', *Continuity and Change* ii (1987), 263–96

Houghton, W. E., 'The history of trades: its relation to seventeenth-century thought', in P. P. Wiener and A. Noland (eds), *Roots of scientific thought: a cultural perspective*, New York 1957, 354–81

Howard, E., *The Eliot papers*, Gloucester 1893–4

Hunt, M., 'Hawkers, bawlers, and mercuries: women and the London press in the Early Enlightenment', in M. Hunt, M. Jacob, P. Mack and R. Perry, *Women and the Enlightenment*, New York 1984, 41–68

———— *The middling sort: commerce, gender, and the family in England, 1680–1780*, Berkeley 1996

Hunter, J. P., *Before novels: the cultural contexts of eighteenth-century English fiction*, New York 1990

Hunter, M., *Science and society in Restoration England*, Cambridge 1981, repr. Aldershot 1992

———— *Establishing the new science: the experience of the early Royal Society*, Woodbridge 1989

———— *The Royal Society and its Fellows, 1660–1720: the morphology of an early scientific institution*, 2nd edn, Oxford 1994

Hunter, P. W., 'Containing the marvellous: instructions to buyers and sellers', in Glaisyer and Pennell, *Didactic literature*, 169–85

Iliffe, R., 'Author-mongering: the "editor" between producer and consumer', in Bermingham and Brewer, *Consumption of culture*, 166–92

Imray, J., 'The origins of the Royal Exchange', in Saunders, *Royal Exchange*, 20–35

Innis, H. A., 'On the economic significance of culture', *JEcH*, supplement iv (1944), 80–97

Jagger, G., 'Joseph Moxon, F.R.S., and the Royal Society', *NRRS* xlix (1995), 193–208

Johns, A., *The nature of the book: print and knowledge in the making*, Chicago 1998

Jones, E., 'London in the early seventeenth century: an ecological approach', *LJ* vi (1980), 123–33

Jones, R. F., 'The attack on pulpit eloquence in the Restoration: an episode in the development of the neo-classical standard for prose', *Journal of English and Germanic Philology* xxx (1931), 188–217

Kadish, A., *Historians, economists, and economic history*, London 1989

Kennedy, J., W. A. Smith and A. F. Johnson (eds), *Dictionary of anonymous and pseudonymous English literature (Samuel Halkett and John Laing)*, Edinburgh 1926–56

Key, N. E., 'The political culture and political rhetoric of county feasts and feast sermons, 1654–1714', *JBS* xxxiii (1994), 223–56

Klein, J. T., 'Satirists and South-Sea baubles in the age of hope and golden mountains', *Southern Review* xiv (1981), 143–54

Klein, L. E., *Shaftesbury and the culture of politeness: moral discourse and cultural politics in early eighteenth-century England*, Cambridge 1994

——— 'Politeness for plebes: consumption and social identity in early eighteenth-century England', in Bermingham and Brewer, *Consumption of culture*, 362–82

——— 'Coffeehouse civility, 1660–1714: an aspect of post-courtly culture in England', *Huntington Library Quarterly* lix (1997), 30–51

Knowlson, J., *Universal language schemes in England and France, 1600–1800*, Toronto 1975

Koot, G. M., *English historical economics, 1870–1926: the rise of economic history and neomercantilism*, Cambridge 1987

——— 'Historians and economists: the study of economic history in Britain ca. 1920–1950', *History of Political Economy* xxv (1993), 641–75.

Korsten, F. J. M., *Roger North (1651–1734) virtuoso and essayist: a study of his life and ideas, followed by an annotated edition of a selection of his unpublished essays*, Amsterdam 1981

Lake, P., 'From Troynouvant to Heliogabulus's Rome and back: "order" and its others in the London of John Stow', in J. F. Merritt (ed.), *Imagining early modern London: perceptions and portrayals of the city from Stow to Strype, 1598–1720*, Cambridge 2001, 217–49

Landa, L. A., 'Pope's Belinda, the general emporie of the world, and the wondrous worm', *South Atlantic Quarterly* lxx (1971), 215–35

Lang, R. G., 'Social origins and social aspirations of Jacobean London merchants', *EcHR* 2nd ser. xxvii (1974), 28–47

Larkey, S. V., 'Scientific glossaries in sixteenth century English books', *Bulletin of the Institute of the History of Medicine* v (1937), 105–14

Latham, R. (ed.), *Catalogue of the Pepys Library at Magdalene College Cambridge,* IV: *Music maps and calligraphy,* Woodbridge 1989

Lawler, J., *Book auctions in England in the seventeenth century (1676–1700),* London 1898

Lee, B. N., 'Gentlemen and their book-plates', in R. Myers and M. Harris (eds), *Property of a gentleman: the formation, organisation and dispersal of the private library, 1620–1920,* Winchester 1991

Lemmings, D., *Professors of the law: barristers and English legal culture in the eighteenth century,* Oxford 2000

Lennard, R., 'English agriculture under Charles II: the evidence of the Royal Society's "enquiries" ', *EcHR* 1st ser. iv (1932–4), 23–45

Lessenich, R. P., *Elements of pulpit oratory in eighteenth-century England (1660–1800),* Cologne 1972

Letwin, W., *The origins of scientific economics: English economic thought, 1660–1776,* London 1963

Lewis, J., *Printed ephemera: the changing uses of type and letterforms in English and American printing,* Woodbridge 1962, repr. 1990

Li, M.-H., *The great recoinage of 1696 to 1699,* London 1963

Loftis, J., *Comedy and society from Congreve to Fielding,* Stanford 1959

Love, H., *Scribal publication in seventeenth-century England,* Oxford 1993

McArthur, T., *Worlds of reference: lexicography, learning and language from the clay tablet to the computer,* Cambridge 1986

McCusker, J. J., 'European bills of entry and marine lists: early commercial publications and the origins of the business press, I: Introduction, and British bills of entry; II: British marine lists and continental counterparts', *Harvard Library Bulletin* xxxi (1983), 209–55, 316–39

––––––– 'The business press in England before 1775', *The Library* 6th ser. viii (1986), 205–31

––––––– 'The early history of "Lloyd's List" ', *HR* lxiv (1991), 427–31

––––––– and C. Gravesteijn, *The beginnings of commercial and financial journalism: the commodity price currents, exchange rate currents, and money currents of early modern Europe,* Amsterdam 1991

––––––– and R. R. Menard, *The economy of British America, 1607–1789,* Chapel Hill 1985

McKendrick, N., ' "Gentleman and players" revisited: the gentlemanly ideal, the business ideal and the professional ideal in English literary culture', in McKendrick and Outhwaite, *Business life and public policy,* 98–136

––––––– J. Brewer and J. H. Plumb, *The birth of a consumer society: the commercialization of eighteenth-century society,* London 1982

––––––– and R. B. Outhwaite (eds), *Business life and public policy: essays in honour of D. C. Coleman,* Cambridge 1986

Macleod, C., 'The 1690s patents boom: invention or stock-jobbing?', *EcHR* 2nd ser. xxxix (1986), 549–71

McVeagh, J., *Tradefull merchants: the portrayal of the capitalist in literature,* London 1981

Manley, L., *Literature and culture in early modern London,* Cambridge 1995

Mascuch, M., 'Continuity and change in a patronage society: the social mobility of British autobiographers, 1600–1750', *Journal of Historical Sociology* vii (1994), 177–97

——— 'Social mobility and middling self-identity: the ethos of British autobiographers, 1600–1750', *SH* xx (1995), 45–61

Mason, A. E. W., *The Royal Exchange: a note on the bicentenary of the Royal Exchange Assurance*, London 1920

Matthew, H. C. G. and B. Harrison (eds), *Oxford dictionary of national biography*, Oxford 2004

Mayer, R., 'Nathaniel Crouch, bookseller and historian: popular historiography and cultural power in late seventeenth-century England', *ECS* xxvii (1994), 391–419

Mepham, M. J., 'The Scottish enlightenment and the development of accounting', in R. H. Parker and B. S. Yamey (eds), *Accounting history: some British contributions*, Oxford 1994, 268–93

Mills, P. A., 'Words and the study of accounting history', *Accounting Auditing and Accountability Journal* ii (1989), 21–35

Mitchell, W. F., *English pulpit oratory from Andrewes to Tillotson: a study of its literary aspects*, London 1932

Morgan, E. V. and W. A. Thomas, *The Stock Exchange: its history and functions*, London 1962

Morgan, F. C., 'A Hereford bookseller's catalogue of 1695', *Transactions of the Woolhope Naturalist's Field Club* xxxi (1942–5), 22–36

Morrison, J. J., 'Strype's Stow: the 1720 edition of A *survey of London*', *LJ* iii (1977), 40–54

Mukerji, C., *From graven images: patterns of modern materialism*, New York 1983

Muldrew, C., 'Interpreting the market: the ethics of credit and community relations in early modern England', *SH* xviii (1993), 163–83

——— *The economy of obligation: the culture of credit and social relations in early modern England*, Basingstoke 1998

Murphy, G., *A bibliography of English character-books, 1608–1700*, Cambridge 1925

Murray, D., *Chapters in the history of bookkeeping accountancy and commercial arithmetic*, Glasgow 1930

Neal, L., 'The integration and efficiency of the London and Amsterdam stock markets in the eighteenth century', *JEcH* xlvii (1987), 97–115

——— 'The rise of a financial press: London and Amsterdam, 1681–1810', *BH* xxx (1988), 163–78

Newman, K., 'City talk: women and commodification in Jonson's *Epicoene*', *English Literary History* lvi (1989), 503–18

Newton, D. and M. Smith, *The Stamford Mercury: three centuries of newspaper publishing*, Stamford 1999

Nicholson, C., *Writing and the rise of finance: capital satires in the early eighteenth century*, Cambridge 1994

North, D. C., 'Beyond the new economic history', *JEcH* xxxiv (1974), 1–7

Norton, R., *Mother Clap's molly house: the gay subculture in England, 1700–1830*, London 1992

O'Brien, P. and P. A. Hunt, 'The rise of a fiscal state in England, 1485–1815', *HR* lxvi (1993), 129–76

Ochs, K. H., 'The Royal Society of London's history of trades programme: an early episode in applied science', *NRRS* xxxix (1985), 129–58

O'Day, R., *Education and society, 1500–1800: the social foundations of education in early modern Britain*, Harlow 1982

Olson, A. G., 'The Virginia merchants of London: a study in eighteenth-century interest-group politics', *William and Mary Quarterly* 3rd ser. xl (1983), 363–88

O'Malley, T., 'Religion and the newspaper press, 1660–1685: a study of the *London Gazette*', in M. Harris and A. Lee (eds), *The press in English society from the seventeenth to nineteenth centuries*, London 1986, 25–46

Pearson, D., *Provenance research in book history: a handbook*, London 1994

Pearson, J. B., *A biographical sketch of the chaplains to the Levant Company, maintained at Constantinople, Aleppo and Smyrna, 1611–1706*, Cambridge 1883

Pennell, S., 'Consumption and consumerism in early modern England', *HJ* xlii (1999), 549–64

Perks, S., 'London town-planning schemes in 1666', *Journal of the Royal Institute of British Architects* xxvii (1919), 69–79

Perrot, J.-C., 'Les Dictionnaires de commerce au XVIIIe siècle', *RHMC* xxviii (1981), 36–67

Philip, I. G., *The Bodleian Library in the seventeenth and eighteenth centuries*, Oxford 1983

Pincus, S. C. A., '"Coffee politicians does create": coffeehouses and Restoration political culture', *Journal of Modern History* lxvii (1995), 807–34

———— *Protestantism and patriotism: ideologies and the making of English foreign policy, 1650–1668*, Cambridge 1996

Pittaluga, M. M., *L'Évolution de la langue commerciale:Le Parfait négociant et Le Dictionnarie universel de commerce*, Genoa 1983

Plomer, H. R., *A dictionary of the booksellers and printers who were at work in England, Scotland and Ireland from 1641 to 1667*, London 1907

———— *A dictionary of the printers and booksellers who were at work in England, Scotland and Ireland from 1668 to 1725*, ed. A. Esdaile, Oxford 1922

Pocock, J. G. A., *The Machiavellian moment: Florentine political thought and the Atlantic republican tradition*, Princeton 1975

———— *Virtue, commerce, and history: essays on political thought and history, chiefly in the eighteenth century*, Cambridge 1985

Pollard, G. and A. Ehrman, *The distribution of books by catalogue from the invention of printing to A.D. 1800 based on material in the Broxbourne Library*, Cambridge 1965

Poovey, M., *A history of the modern fact: problems of knowledge in the sciences of wealth and society*, Chicago 1998

Price, F. G. H., *A handbook of London bankers: with some account of their predecessors, the early goldsmiths*, London 1876

Price, J. M., 'Notes on some London price-currents, 1667–1715', *EcHR* 2nd ser. vii (1954–5), 240–50

———— 'A note on the circulation of the London press, 1704–1714', *Bulletin of the Institute of Historical Research* xxxi (1958), 215–24

———— 'What did merchants do? Reflections on British overseas trade, 1660–1790', *JEcH* xlix (1989), 267–84

———— 'Who cared about the colonies? The impact of the thirteen colonies on British society and politics, circa 1714–1775', in B. Bailyn and P. D. Morgan (eds), *Strangers within the realm: cultural margins of the first British empire*, Chapel Hill 1991, 395–436

Pruett, J. H., *The parish clergy under the later Stuarts: the Leicestershire experience*, Urbana 1978

Rabuzzi, D. A., 'Eighteenth-century commercial mentalities as reflected and projected in business handbooks', *ECS* xxix (1995–6), 169–89

Raven, J., 'The abolition of the English state lotteries', *HJ* xxxiv (1991), 371–89

———— 'Imprimés et transactions économiques: représéntation et interaction en Angleterre aux XVIIe et XVIIIe siècles', *RHMC* xliii (1996), 234–65

Raynes, H. E., *A history of British insurance*, rev. edn, London 1950

Reddaway, T. F., 'The rebuilding of London after the Fire', part I, *Town Planning Review* xvii (1937), 205–11

———— *The rebuilding of London after the Great Fire*, London 1951

Reedy, S. J. G., 'Mystical politics: the imagery of Charles II's coronation', in P. J. Korshin (ed.), *Studies in change and revolution: aspects of English intellectual history, 1640–1800*, Menston 1972, 19–42

Relton, F. B., *An account of the fire insurance companies associations institutions projects and schemes established and projected in Great Britain and Ireland during the 17th and 18th centuries including the Sun Fire Office: also of Charles Povey the projector of that office his writings and schemes*, London 1893

Richards, R. D., 'The lottery in the history of English government finance', *Economic History* iii (1934–7), 57–76

Rickword, G. O., 'Royston Club and its Essex members', *Essex Review* xlvii (1938), 145–9

Rivers, I., *Books and their readers in eighteenth-century England*, Leicester 1982.

Robertson, J., *The art of letter writing: an essay on the handbooks published in England during the sixteenth and seventeenth centuries*, London 1942

Rogers, J. S, *The early history of the law of bills and notes: a study of the origins of Anglo-Amercian commercial law*, Cambridge 1995

Rogers, N., 'Money, land and lineage: the big bourgeoisie of Hanoverian London', *SH* iv (1979), 437–54

———— 'A reply to Donna Andrew', *SH* vi (1981), 365–9

Roscoe, I., ' "The statues of the sovereigns of England": sculpture for the second building, 1695–1831', in Saunders, *Royal Exchange*, 174–87

Roseveare, H., *The financial revolution, 1660–1760*, London 1991

Rudolf, E. A. de M., 'Some notes on the building of the second Royal Exchange', *Home Counties Magazine* vi (1904), 293–8

Rupp, G., *Religion in England, 1688–1791*, Oxford 1986

Russell, G. A. (ed.), *The 'Arabick' interest of the natural philosophers in seventeenth-century England*, Leiden 1994

Sacks, D. H., *The widening gate: Bristol and the Atlantic economy, 1450–1700*, Berkeley 1991

Saunders, A., 'The second Exchange', in Saunders, *Royal Exchange*, 121–35

———— (ed.), *The Royal Exchange*, London 1997

Schäfer, J., *Early modern English lexicography*, I: *A survey of monolingual printed glossaries and dictionaries, 1475–1640*, Oxford 1989

Schaffer, S., 'Defoe's natural philosophy and the worlds of credit', in J. Christie and S. Shuttleworth (eds), *Nature transfigured: science and literature, 1700–1900*, Manchester 1989, 13–44

———— 'A social history of plausibility: country, city and calculation in Augustan

Britain', in A. Wilson (ed.), *Rethinking social history: English society, 1570–1920, and its interpretation*, Manchester 1993, 128–57

Schama, S., 'Perishable commodities: Dutch still-life painting and the "empire of things" ', in Brewer and Porter, *Consumption and the world*, 478–88

Schlatter, R. B., *The social ideas of religious leaders, 1660–1688*, London 1940

Schubert, E. S., 'Innovations, debts, and bubbles: international integration of financial markets in western Europe, 1688–1720', *JEcH* xlviii (1988), 299–306

Scott, W. R., *The constitution and finance of English, Scottish and Irish joint-stock companies to 1720*, Cambridge 1910–12

Sekora, J., *Luxury: the concept in western thought, Eden to Smollett*, Baltimore 1977

Shammas, C., *The pre-industrial consumer in England and America*, Oxford 1990

Shapin, S., *A social history of truth: civility and science in seventeenth-century England*, Chicago 1994

Sheldahl, T. K., 'A bookseller directory of double entry works available in eighteenth-century America', *Accounting, Business and Financial History* iv (1994), 203–35

———— (ed.), *Education for the mercantile counting house: critical and constructive essays by nine British writers, 1716–1794*, New York 1989

Skelton, R. A., *County atlases of the British Isles, 1579–1850: a bibliography*, London 1964–70, v (1970)

Slack, P., 'Perceptions of the metropolis in seventeenth-century England', in P. Burke, B. Harrison and P. Slack (eds), *Civil histories: essays presented to Sir Keith Thomas*, Oxford 2000, 161–80

Smail, J., 'Manufacturer or artisan? The relationship between economic and cultural change in the early stages of the eighteenth-century industrialization', *Journal of Social History* xxv (1992), 791–814

Smith, N. A., assisted by H. M. Adams and D. Pepys Whiteley, *Catalogue of the Pepys Library at Magdalene College Cambridge*, I: *Printed books*, ed. R. Latham, Cambridge 1978

Snyder, H. L., 'The circulation of newspapers in the reign of Queen Anne', *The Library* 5th ser. xxiii (1969), 206–35

———— 'A further note on the circulation of newspapers in the reign of Queen Anne', *The Library* 5th ser. xxxi (1976), 387–9

Sommerville, C. J., *Popular religion in Restoration England*, Gainesville, Fl. 1977

———— 'The anti-Puritan work ethic', *JBS* xx (1981), 70–81

Sperling, J., 'The international payments mechanism in the seventeenth and eighteenth centuries', *EcHR* 2nd ser. xiv (1961–2), 446–68

Spufford, M., 'Literacy, trade and religion in the commercial centres of Europe', in K. Davids and J. Lucassen (eds), *A miracle mirrored: the Dutch Republic in European perspective*, Cambridge 1995, 229–83

Starnes, D. W. T. and G. E. Noyes, *The English dictionary from Cawdrey to Johnson, 1604–1755*, Chapel Hill 1946

Stearns, R. P., 'Fellows of the Royal Society in North Africa and the Levant', *NRRS* xi (1954), 75–90

Stevenson, L. C., *Praise and paradox: merchants and craftsmen in Elizabethan popular literature*, Cambridge 1984

Stewart, L., *The rise of public science: rhetoric, technology, and natural philosophy in Newtonian Britain, 1660–1750*, Cambridge 1992

Stratton, A., 'The Royal Exchange, London, II: the second and third buildings', *Architectural Review* xlii (1917), 44–50

Straus, R., *The unspeakable Curll: being some account of Edmund Curll, bookseller; to which is added a full list of his books*, London 1927

Stone, L. and J. C. F. Stone, *An open elite? England, 1540–1880*, Oxford 1984

Stubbs, M., 'John Beale, philosophical gardener of Herefordshire, II: The improvement of agriculture and trade in the Royal Society (1663–1683)', *Annals of Science* xlvi (1989), 323–63

Supple, B. E., *The Royal Exchange Assurance: a history of British insurance, 1720–1970*, Cambridge 1970

—— 'Old problems and new directions', *JIH* xii (1981), 199–205

Sutherland, J. R., 'The circulation of newspapers and literary periodicals, 1700–30', *The Library* 4th ser. xv (1934), 110–24

Sutton, A. F., *I sing of a maiden: the story of the maiden of the Mercers' Company*, London 1998

Tanner, J. R. (ed), *A descriptive catalogue of the naval manuscripts in the Pepysian Library at Magdalene College, Cambridge*, London 1903–23

Taylor, E. G. R., *The mathematical practitioners of Tudor and Stuart England*, Cambridge 1954

—— *The mathematical practitioners of Hanoverian England, 1714–1840*, Cambridge 1966

Temin, P., 'The future of the new economic history', *JIH* xii (1981), 179–97

—— 'Is it kosher to talk about culture?', *JEcH* lvii (1997), 267–87

Thomas, K., 'Numeracy in early modern England', *TRHS* 5th ser. xxxvii (1987), 103–32

Thompson, G., 'Is accounting rhetorical? Methodology, Luca Pacioli and printing', *Accounting, Organizations and Society* xvi (1991), 572–99

Thompson, J., *Models of value: eighteenth-century political economy and the novel*, Durham, NC 1996

Thompson, R. H., 'Tokens of the Royal Exchange', in Saunders, *Royal Exchange*, 239–49

Tilly, C., L. A. Tilly and R. Tilly, 'European economic and social history in the 1990s', *Journal of European Economic History* xx (1991), 645–71.

Toomer, G. J., *Eastern wisedom and learning: the study of Arabic in seventeenth-century England*, Oxford 1996

Treadwell, M., 'London printers and printing houses in 1705', *Publishing History* vii (1980), 5–44

Turner, J. G., ' "News from the New Exchange": commodity, erotic fantasy, and the female entrepreneur', in Bermingham and Brewer, *Consumption of culture*, 419–39.

Tyacke, S., *London map-sellers, 1660–1720*, Tring 1978

Venn, J. and J. A. Venn, *Alumni cantabrigienses: a biographical list of all known students, graduates and holders of office at the University of Cambridge, from the earliest times to 1900*, Cambridge 1922–7

Verner, C., 'Engraved title plates for the folio atlases of John Seller', in H. Wallis and S. Tyacke (eds), *My head is a map: essays and memoirs in honour of R. V. Tooley*, London 1973, 21–54

—— 'John Seller and the chart trade in seventeenth-century England', in N. J. W. Thrower (ed.), *The compleat plattmaker: essays on chart, map, and globe making in England in the seventeenth and eighteenth centuries*, Berkeley 1978, 127–57

Vickers, B., 'The Royal Society and English prose style: a reassessment', in B. Vickers and N. S. Struever (eds), *Rhetoric and the pursuit of truth: language change in the seventeenth and eighteenth centuries*, Los Angeles 1985, 1–76

Viner, J., 'Satire and economics in the Augustan age of satire', in H. K. Miller, E. Rothstein and G. S. Rousseau (eds), *The Augustan milieu: essays presented to Louis A. Landa*, Oxford 1970, 77–101

Wahrman, D., 'National society, communal culture: an argument about the recent historiography of eighteenth-century Britain', *SH* xvii (1992), 43–72

Walcott, R., 'The East India interest in the general election of 1700–1701', *EHR* lxxi (1956), 223–39

Wallis, R. V. and J. Wallis, *Index of British mathematicians*, III: *1701–1800*, Newcastle upon Tyne 1993

Walsh, R., *An account of the Levant Company; with some notices of the benefits conferred upon society by its officers, in promoting the cause of humanity, literature, and the fine arts*, London 1825

Walters, G., 'Early sale catalogues: problems and perspectives', in R. Myers and M. Harris (eds), *Sale and distribution of books from 1700*, Oxford 1982, 106–25

Weatherill, L., *Consumer behaviour and material culture in Britain, 1660–1760*, London 1988

Webb, D., 'Guide books to London before 1800: a survey', *London Topographical Record* xxvi (1990), 138–52

Weber, M., *The Protestant ethic and the spirit of capitalism*, London 1930

Webster, C., *The great instauration: science, medicine and reform, 1626–1660*, London 1975

Westerfield, R. B., *Middlemen in English business: particularly between 1660 and 1760*, New Haven 1915

White, J. G., *History of the three Royal Exchanges, the Gresham Lectures, and Gresham almshouses*, London 1896

Whyman, S. E., 'Land and trade revisited: the case of John Verney, London merchant and baronet, 1660–1720', *LJ* xxii (1997), 16–32

——— *Sociability and power in late-Stuart England: the cultural worlds of the Verneys, 1660–1720*, Oxford 1999

Wiles, R. M., *Freshest advices: early provincial newspapers in England*, [Columbus], Ohio 1965

Williams, J. E., 'Whitehaven in the eighteenth century', *EcHR* 2nd ser. viii (1955–6), 393–404

Wilson, C., *England's apprenticeship, 1603–1763*, 2nd edn, Harlow 1984

Wood, A. C., *A history of the Levant Company*, Oxford 1935

Worms, L., 'The book trade at the Royal Exchange', in Saunders, *Royal Exchange*, 209–26

Wright, L. B., 'Language helps for the Elizabethan tradesman', *Journal of English and Germanic Philology* xxx (1931), 335–47

——— *Middle-class culture in Elizabethan England*, Chapel Hill 1935

——— *Religion and empire: the alliance between piety and commerce in English expansion, 1558–1625*, New York 1965

Wrigley, E. A., 'A simple model of London's importance in changing English society and economy, 1650–1750', *P&P* xxxvii (1967), 44–70

Yamey, B. S., 'Scientific bookkeeping and the rise of capitalism', *EcHR* 2nd ser. i (1949), 99–113

———— 'Stephen Monteage: a seventeenth century accountant', *Accountancy* lxx (1959), 594–5

———— H. C. Edey and H. W. Thomson, *Accounting in England and Scotland: 1543–1800: double entry in exposition and practice*, London 1963

Yeo, G., 'A case without parallel: the bishop of London and the Anglican Church overseas, 1660–1748', *Journal of Ecclesiastical History* xliv (1993), 450–75

Zahedieh, N., 'London and the colonial consumer in the late seventeenth century', *EcHR* 2nd ser. xlvii (1994), 239–61

———— 'Credit, risk and reputation in late seventeenth-century colonial trade', *Research in Maritime History* xv (1998), 53–74

## Unpublished theses

Brooks, C., 'Taxation, finance and public opinion, 1688–1714', PhD thesis, Cambridge 1970

Crellin, V. H., 'The teaching of writing and the use of the copy book in schools: the influences of the writing schoolmaster, with special reference to the period c. 1700–1873', MPhil. thesis, London 1976

Harteker, L. M., 'Steward of the kingdom's stock: merchants, trade, and discourse in eighteenth-century England', PhD thesis, Chicago 1996

# Index